Architect's Pocket Book

This book is dedicated to the memory of
Charlotte Baden-Powell, for all her work, energy and
enthusiasm for creating this invaluable source for Architects.

Architect's Pocket Book

Third edition

Charlotte Baden-Powell

Third edition updated by Jonathan Hetreed and Ann Ross

ELSEVIER

Architectural
Press

AMSTERDAM • BOSTON • HEIDELBERG • LONDON • NEW YORK • OXFORD
PARIS • SAN DIEGO • SAN FRANCISCO • SINGAPORE • SYDNEY • TOKYO
Architectural Press is an imprint of Elsevier

Architectural Press is an imprint of Elsevier
The Boulevard, Langford Lane, Kidlington, Oxford OX5 1GB, UK
30 Corporate Drive, Suite 400, Burlington, MA 01803, USA

First edition 1997
Reprinted 1998, 1999
Second edition 2001
Reprinted with amendments 2002, 2003
Reprinted 2004, 2005, 2006
Third edition 2008
Reprinted 2009

Notice
No responsibility is assumed by the publisher for any injury and/or damage to persons
or property as a matter of products liability, negligence or otherwise, or from any use
or operation of any methods, products, instructions or ideas contained in the material
herein. Because of rapid advances in the medical sciences, in particular, independent
verification of diagnoses and drug dosages should be made

British Library Cataloguing in Publication Data
A catalogue record for this book is available from the British Library

Library of Congress Cataloging-in-Publication Data
A catalog record for this book is available from the Library of Congress

ISBN: 978-0-7506-8617-4

For information on all Architectural Press publications
visit our website at www.elsevierdirect.com

Printed and bound in *Hungary*

09 10 11 12   10 9 8 7 6 5 4 3 2

Working together to grow
libraries in developing countries

www.elsevier.com | www.bookaid.org | www.sabre.org

ELSEVIER   BOOK AID
           International   Sabre Foundation

Contents

Preface to the Third Edition

I first met Charlotte Baden-Powell to discuss the possibility of editing this edition in 2006, after an introduction from Peter Clegg. This remarkable book was clearly a very personal work for her and once I had enlisted Ann Ross's help, the three of us discussed how the spirit and modest simplicity of the book should be maintained while its contemporary coverage was enhanced. It was important to Charlotte that the book stayed small and retained its immediacy, and that we worked in a similar field of smaller scale architecture to her own.

As we have updated and revised sections, we have enlarged some and reduced others and thereby achieved the goal of a similar size; we hope in doing so that the really useful information in the book has been retained and supplemented while the losses have been only in depth or detail, for which more specific technical source material can be consulted.

The only instances in which we have included sections absent from the previous edition were those giving the briefest outlines of costs, law, insulation and computer-aided design for architects – all four subject to frequent detailed changes but we thought worth describing in general terms.

Just as Charlotte did, we welcome readers' responses, so that the book can continue to be improved.

Jonathan Hetreed

Preface to the Second Edition

'I *know* it's somewhere – but where?' . . .
. . . any architect, any time

The inspiration for this pocket book was the front section of the *Building Technician's Diaries* which were published in the 1960s and 70s. These small airmail paper pages were densely packed with useful information for the architect, surveyor and builder. Obviously concise, often rule-of-thumb but nevertheless marvellously useful. These diaries are no longer available and are of course wildly out of date. So it seemed to me that there is a need for a new small and more complete compendium which can sit beside the drawing board/computer and also be carried easily to site.

It is aimed primarily at the smaller practice and is particularly suitable for small works. The subjects range from general arithmetic and geometric data through building regulation requirements, the sizes of furniture, fittings, joists, materials, U-values, lighting data and much more.

The choice of what to include is necessarily subjective and is the result of running my own practice for 38 years. The subjects have been gleaned either from much more comprehensive works or the more imaginative and useful aspects of manufacturers' literature. I have deliberately not included anything about costs or legal matters as these change too frequently for the book to be of any lasting value. The choice of contents is inevitably subjective and I would be interested to hear from readers of any items which they would have liked to be included. The blank pages at the end of the book are provided for personal additions.

Every effort has been made to ensure that the information given is accurate at the time of publication. When compiling the book I found many things were incomplete, out-of-date or plainly wrong. The user should be aware that the information is concise, in order to suit the small size of a pocket book. Also that legislation is frequently changing and that the British Standards and Building Regulations are being constantly superseded. If in doubt, or further more detailed explanation is required, consult the source given at the bottom of the page, with the addresses and telephone numbers at the back of the book. Where no reference is given, this is because I have compiled the information from several sources.

This book is not a construction manual, it contains no typical detail drawings, but is instead a collection of information needed before such drawings are prepared.

The second edition contains 30 new pages of subjects ranging from Party Wall Awards and green issues to industrial processes. The new drawings include information about setting-up perspectives, wheelchairs, traditional doors and windows, colour spectrum, etc. Additions have also been made to the original text. Names and addresses have been updated and email and websites added.

The aim of the book is to include information from a wide range of sources. Facts which one knows are somewhere – but where? I like to think that this is the book I should have had to hand, both as a student and while running my private practice. I hope you do too.

Charlotte Baden-Powell

Acknowledgements to the Third Edition

We would like to thank the following for their help in checking our additions, revisions and updates:

Richard Dellar	Dellar Gregory Associates Construction & Claims Consultants for his help with costs and law
Peter Clegg	Architect for his help with sustainability environmental design
Nick Burgess	BSc, CEng, MIStructE, Associate and Senior Structural Engineer at Rexon Day Consulting for his complete revision of structures
Jonathan Reeves	Architect for his help with Computer-Aided Design
Brian Murphy	Environmental Consultant for his help with insulation

We would also thank:

Henry Fisher	Architectural Assistant for his help with revising and adding drawings
Jodi Cusack	at Architectural Press for her help in preparing the new edition.

All those who by their constructive comments on the second edition have helped us to make the third edition worth doing.

Jonathan Hetreed
Ann Ross

Acknowledgements to the Second Edition

I am greatly indebted to the following people for their help and advice:

Choice of contents	John Winter (architect)
	Bill Ungless (architect)
Geometric data	Francis Baden-Powell (architect)
Structural data	Howard Hufford (structural engineer)
	David Cook (geotechnical engineer)
Water byelaws	Graham Mays (Water Research Centre secretary)
Electrical wiring	Brian Fisher (electrical contractor)
Lighting	Martin Wilkinson (lighting consultant)
Joinery	James Toner (building contractor)
General reference data	Peter Gunning (quantity surveyor)
Typography	Peter Brawne (graphic designer)

I should also like to thank the many helpful technical representatives of the manufacturers listed at the back of the book.

My thanks are also due to:

Mari Owen, my secretary, for so patiently struggling with typing, re-typing and endlessly correcting a difficult text;

Neil Warnock-Smith, my publisher, for his support and enthusiasm for the original idea for the book;

Michael Brawne, Professor of Architecture and my husband, for his wise words, help and encouragement throughout.

Charlotte Baden-Powell

General Information

Climate maps

Wind – basic wind speeds in metres per second (m/s) and prevailing wind directions ➡

The figures show maximum gust speed likely to be exceeded on average only once in 50 years at 10 m above the ground in open country. To convert metres per second to miles per hour multiply by 2.24.

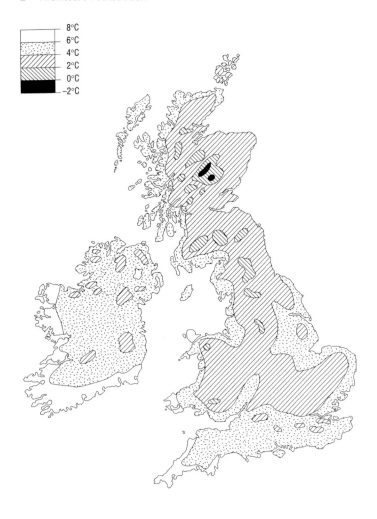

8°C
6°C
4°C
2°C
0°C
−2°C

Temperature – average for January

Temperature – average for July

Rain – annual average

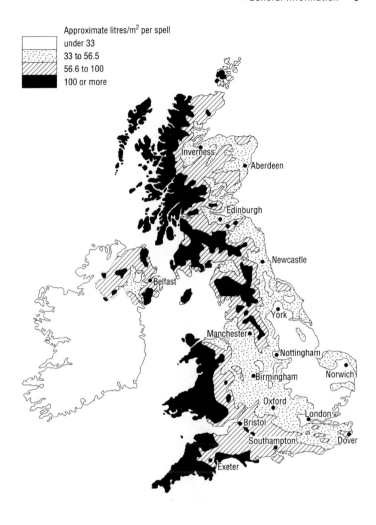

Approximate litres/m² per spell
under 33
33 to 56.5
56.6 to 100
100 or more

Rain – wind driven

Snow

Inland Areas
1 = Greater London
2 = S E England
3 = East Anglia
4 = Central S England
5 = E Midlands
6 = East England
7 = W Midlands
8 = Channel Islands
9 = SW England
10 = S Wales
11 = N Wales
12 = NW England
13 = Lake District
14 = Isle of Man
15 = Central N England
16 = N E England
17 = Borders
18 = Edinburgh & Dundee
19 = Aberdeen area
20 = SW Scotland
21 = Glasgow area
22 = Central Highlands
23 = Moray Firth area
24 = NE Scotland
25 = Argyll
26 = NW Scotland
27 = Orkney
28 = Shetland
29 = N Ireland

0 = Coastal stations
BL = Butt of Lewis
C = Channel light vessel
D = Dover
DS = Dowsing
J = Jersey
LE = Land's End
M = Malin Head
R = Ronaldsway
S = Sumburgh
SA = St Abb's Head
T = Tiree
V = Valencia

Sea areas, inland areas and coastal stations
used in weather forecasts by the Meteorological Office

Metric system

The **Système International d'Unités (SI)**, adopted in 1960, is an international and coherent system devised to meet all known needs for measurement in science and technology. It consists of seven base units and the derived units formed as products or quotients of various powers of the base units.

Note that base and derived units, when written as words, are always written with a lower case first letter, even if the word is derived from the name of a person.

SI Base units

metre	**m**	length
kilogram	**kg**	mass
second	**s**	time
ampere	**A**	electric current
kelvin	**K**	thermodynamic temperature
candela	**cd**	luminous intensity
mole	**mol**	amount of substance

SI Prefixes (showing the nine most common)

mega	**M**	× 1 000 000
kilo	**k**	× 1000
hecto	**h**	× 100
deca	**da**	× 10
deci	**d**	÷ 10
centi	**c**	÷ 100
milli	**m**	÷ 1000
micro	**μ**	÷ 1 000 000
nano	**n**	÷ 1 000 000 000

SI Derived units

celsius	**°C**	=	K	temperature
coulomb	**C**	=	As	electric charge
farad	**F**	=	C/V	electric capacitance
henry	**H**	=	W/A	inductance
hertz	**Hz**	=	c/s	frequency
joule	**J**	=	Ws	energy
lumen	**lm**	=	cd.sr	luminous flux
lux	**lx**	=	lm/m^2	illuminance
newton	**N**	=	$kg/m/s^2$	force
ohm	**Ω**	=	V/A	electric resistance
pascal	**Pa**	=	N/m^2	pressure
siemens	**S**	=	$1/\Omega$	electric conductance
tesla	**T**	=	Wb/m^2	magnetic flux density
volt	**V**	=	W/A	electric potential
watt	**W**	=	J/s	power
weber	**Wb**	=	Vs	magnetic flux

SI Supplementary units

radian	**rad**	=	unit of plane angle equal to an angle at the centre of a circle, the arc of which is equal in length to the radius
steradian	**sr**	=	unit of solid angle equal to an angle at the centre of a sphere subtended by a part of the surface equal in area to the square of the radius

Metric units

Length

kilometre	**km**	=	1000 metres
metre	**m**	=	length of path travelled by light in vacuum during a time interval of 1/299 792 458 of a second
decimetre	**dm**	=	1/10 metre
centimetre	**cm**	=	1/100 metre
millimetre	**mm**	=	1/1000 metre
micron	μ	=	1/100 000 metre

Area

hectare	**ha**	=	$10\,000\,m^2$
are	**a**	=	$100\,m^2$

Volume

cubic metre	$\mathbf{m^3}$	=	$m \times m \times m$
cubic millimetre	$\mathbf{mm^3}$	=	$1/1\,000\,000\,000\,m^3$

Capacity

hectolitre	**hl**	=	100 litres
litre	**l**	=	cubic decimetre
decilitre	**dl**	=	1/10 litre
centilitre	**cl**	=	1/100 litre
millilitre	**ml**	=	1/1000 litre

Mass or weight

tonne	**t**	=	1000 kilograms
kilogram	**kg**	=	1000 gram
gram	**g**	=	1/1000 kilogram
milligram	**mg**	=	1/1000 gram

Temperature

Kelvin (K)   The kelvin belongs to a group of seven SI base units used as a quantitive unit of thermodynamic temperature. It is named after Lord William Thompson Kelvin, a Scottish physicist (1824–1907). In 1848 he suggested a scale of temperature, now called *kelvin*, in which the zero point is *absolute zero* – the temperature at which the motions of particles cease and their energies become zero. The units of kelvin and degree celsius temperature intervals are identical (thus 1°C = 1 K), but the point of absolute zero in celsius is minus 273.15 K, thus 0°C = 273.15 K.

It is now customary for temperature and temperature intervals to be described in degrees celsius (°C) although colour temperature of light sources is measured in degrees kelvin (K).

Celsius (°C)   The celsius scale is a scale of temperature on which water freezes at 0° and boils at 100° under standard conditions. It was devised by Anders Celsius, a Swedish astronomer (1701–44). He originally designated zero as the boiling point of water and 100° as freezing point. The scale was later reversed.

Centigrade   A temperature scale using the freezing point of water as zero and the boiling point of water as 100°. The scale is now officially called *celsius* (see above) to avoid confusion in Europe where the word can mean a measure of plane angle and equals 1/10 000 part of a right angle.

Fahrenheit (°F)   A scale of temperature still used in the USA which gives the freezing point of water as 32° and boiling point as 212°. Named after Gabriel Daniel Fahrenheit, a Prussian physicist (1686–1736) who invented the mercurial barometer. The Fahrenheit scale is related to the Celsius scale by the following relationships:

temperature °F = (temperature °C $\times$ 1.8) + 32
temperature °C = (temperature °F − 32) $\div$ 1.8

Imperial units

Length
mile	=	1760 yards
furlong	=	220 yards
chain	=	22 yards
yard (yd)	=	3 feet
foot (ft)	=	12 inches
inch (in)	=	1/12 foot

Area
square mile	=	640 acres
acre	=	4840 square yards
rood	=	1210 square yards
square yard (sq yd)	=	9 square feet
square foot (sq ft)	=	144 square inches
square inch (sq in)	=	1/144 square foot

Volume
cubic yard	=	27 cubic feet
cubic foot	=	1/27 cubic yard
cubic inch	=	1/1728 cubic foot

Capacity
bushel	=	8 gallons
peck	=	2 gallons
gallon (gal)	=	4 quart
quart (qt)	=	2 pint
pint (pt)	=	1/2 quart
gill	=	1/4 pint
fluid ounce (fl oz)	=	1/20 pint

Weight

ton	=	2240 pounds
hundredweight (cwt)	=	112 pounds
cental	=	100 pounds
quarter	=	28 pounds
stone	=	14 pounds
pound (lb)	=	16 ounces
ounce (oz)	=	1/16 pound
dram (dr)	=	1/16 ounce
grain (gr)	=	1/7000 pound
pennyweight (dwt)	=	24 grains

Nautical measure

BS nautical mile	=	6080 feet
cable	=	600 feet
fathom	=	6 feet

Conversion factors

	Imperial to SI		**SI to Imperial**		
Length	1.609	mile	kilometre	km	0.6215
	0.9144	yard	metre	m	1.094
	0.3048	foot	metre	m	3.281
	25.4	inch	millimetre	mm	0.0394
Area	2.590	sq mile	sq kilometre	km^2	0.3861
	0.4047	acre	hectare	ha	2.471
	0.8361	sq yard	sq metre	m^2	1.196
	0.0929	sq foot	sq metre	m^2	10.7639
	645.16	sq inch	sq millimetre	mm^2	0.00155
Volume	0.7646	cubic yard	cubic metre	m^3	1.3079
	0.02832	cubic foot	cubic metre	m^3	35.31
	16.39	cubic inch	cubic millimetre	mm^3	0.000061
Capacity	28.32	cubic foot	litre	l	0.03531
	0.01639	cubic inch	litre	l	61.0128
	16.39	cubic inch	millilitre	ml	0.06102
	4.546	UK gallon	litre	l	0.21998
	28.4125	fluid ounce	millilitre	ml	0.0352
Mass	1.016	ton	tonne	t	0.98425
	0.4536	pound	kilogram	kg	2.20458
	453.6	pound	gram	g	0.002205
	28.35	ounce	gram	g	0.03527
Density	16.0185	$pound/ft^3$	$kilogram/m^3$	kg/m^3	0.06243
Force	4.4482	pound force	newton	N	0.22481
	14.59	pound f/foot	newton/metre	N/m	0.06854
Pressure, stress					
	4.882	$pound/ft^2$	$kilogram/m^2$	kg/m^2	0.2048
	107.252	$ton\ f/ft^2$	$kilonewton/m^2$	kN/m^2	0.009324
	47.8803	$pound\ f/ft^2$	$newton/m^2$	N/m^2	0.02088
	6894.76	$pound\ f/in^2$	$newton/m^2$	N/m^2	0.000145

	Imperial to SI		SI to Imperial		
Energy	3.6	kilowatt hour	megajoule	MJ	0.27777
Heat	1055.0	Btu	joule	J	0.000948
Heat flow	0.000293	Btu/h	kilowatt	kW	3415.0
Heat transfer	5.67826	Btu/ft^{2}h °F	watt/m^2 °C	W/m^2 °C	0.17611
Thermal conductivity	0.144228	Btu in/ft^{2}h °F	watt/m °C	W/m °C	6.93347
Cost	0.0929	£/sq foot	£/sq metre	£/m^2	10.7639

Approximate metric/Imperial equivalents

Length

1.5 mm	=	1/16″
3 mm	=	1/8″
6 mm	=	¼″
12.5 mm	=	½″
19 mm	=	¾″
25 mm	=	1″
100 mm	=	4″
600 mm	=	2′0″
2000 mm	=	6′8″
3000 mm	=	10′0″

Temperature

°C		°F	
100	=	212	boiling
37	=	98.6	blood heat
21	=	70	living room
19	=	66	bedroom
10	=	50	
0	=	32	freezing
−17.7	=	0	

Heat transfer

1 Btu/ft²h°F = 10 watt/m²°C

Lighting

10 lux	=	1 lumen/ft²

Area

1 hectare	= 2½ acres
0.4 hectare	= 1 acre

Weight

1 kilogram	= 2¼ lbs
28 grams	= 1 ounce
100 grams	= 3½ ounces
454 grams	= 1 lb

Capacity

1 litre	= 1¾ pints
9 litres	= 2 gallons

Pressure

1.5 kN/m²	= 30 lbs/ft²
2.5 kN/m²	= 50 lbs/ft²
3.5 kN/m²	= 70 bs/ft²
5.0 kN/m²	= 100 lbs/ft²

Glass thickness

2 mm	= 18 oz
3 mm	= 24 oz
4 mm	= 32 oz
6 mm	= ¼″

Greek alphabet

Capital	Lower case	Name	English transliteration
A	α	alpha	a
B	β	beta	b
Γ	γ	gamma	g
Δ	δ	delta	d
E	ε	epsilon	e
Z	ζ	zeta	z
H	η	eta	ē
Θ	θ	theta	th
I	ι	iota	i
K	κ	kappa	k
Λ	λ	lambda	l
M	μ	mu	m
N	ν	nu	n
Ξ	χ	xi	x
O	o	omicron	o
Π	π	pi	p
P	ρ	rho	r
Σ	σ (ς)*	sigma	s
T	τ	tau	t
γ	υ	upsilon	u
Φ	φ	phi	ph
X	χ	chi	ch, kh
Ψ	ψ	psi	ps
Ω	ω	omega	ō

*ς at end of word

Geometric data

Measurement of plane and solid figures

π (pi)   = 3.1416

Circumference
circle   = π × diameter
cone   = π × ½ major axis + ½ minor axis

Surface area
circle   = π × radius^2, or 0.7854 × diameter^2
cone   = ½ circumference × slant height
                         + area of base
cylinder   = circumference × length
                         + area of two ends
ellipse   = product of axes × 0.7854 (approx)
parabola   = base × 2/3 height
parallelogram   = base × height
pyramid   = ½ sum of base perimeters × slant height
                         + area of base
sector of circle   = (π × degrees arc × radius^2) ÷ 360
segment of circle   = area of sector minus triangle
sphere   = π × diameter^2
triangle   = ½ base × perpendicular height
triangle
(equilateral)   = (side)^2 × 0.433

Volume
cone   = area of base × 1/3 perpendicular height
cylinder   = π × radius^2 × height
pyramid   = area of base × 1/3 height
sphere   = diameter^3 × 0.5236
wedge   = area of base × ½ perpendicular height

Nine regular solids

Various types of polyhedra have exercised the minds of mathematicians throughout the ages, including Euclid, whose great work *The Elements* was intended not so much as a geometry text book but as an introduction to the five regular solids known to the ancient world. This work starts with the equilateral triangle and ends with the construction of the icosahedron.

The five so-called *Platonic* solids form the first and simplest group of polyhedra. They have regular faces, all of which touch one another, and the lines which make up any of the vertices form a regular polygon.

Further variations of the regular polyhedra, unknown in ancient times, are the *Kepler-Poinsot* star polyhedra. In all four cases the vertex figures spring from pentagrams. These polyhedra can be formed from the regular dodecahedron and icosahedron.

Kepler (1571–1630) found the two stellated dodecahedra, and Poinsot (1777–1859) discovered the great dodecahedra and the great icosahedron.

Five platonic solids

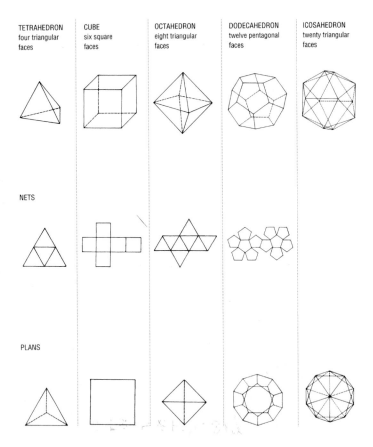

TETRAHEDRON
four triangular
faces

CUBE
six square
faces

OCTAHEDRON
eight triangular
faces

DODECAHEDRON
twelve pentagonal
faces

ICOSAHEDRON
twenty triangular
faces

NETS

PLANS

The Kepler–Poinsot star polyhedra

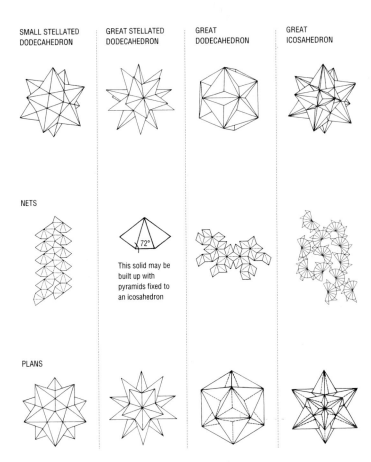

SMALL STELLATED
DODECAHEDRON

GREAT STELLATED
DODECAHEDRON

GREAT
DODECAHEDRON

GREAT
ICOSAHEDRON

NETS

72°

This solid may be
built up with
pyramids fixed to
an icosahedron

PLANS

Source: *Mathematical Models*

Golden section

The **golden section** or **golden mean** is an irrational proportion probably known to the ancient Greeks and thought to be divine by Renaissance theorists. It is defined as a line cut in such a way that the smaller section is to the greater as the greater is to the whole, thus:

AC : CB = CB : AB

The ratio of the two lengths is called *phi* Φ.

$$\Phi = \frac{\sqrt{5} + 1}{2} = 1.61803\ldots$$

For approximate purposes it is 1 : 1.6 or 5 : 8.
Φ is the ratio of line lengths in any pentagram.

The **golden rectangle** is one in which Φ is the ratio of one side to the other.

This is implicated in the mathematics of growth as demonstrated in the **Fibonacci series** 0, 1, 1, 2, 3, 5, 8, 13, 21, 34... where each number is the sum of the preceding two. This ratio of successive numbers increasingly approaches that of the golden rectangle.

The **Fibonacci spiral** is a curve
that increases constantly in
size without changing its
basic shape. This is
demonstrated by
using squares increasing
in the Fibonacci scale,
i.e. 1, 2, 3, 5, from the
diagram of which can be seen
three nearly golden rectangles.

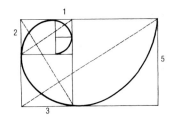

Leonardo Fibonacci (c.1170–1230) was an Italian mathematician who introduced arabic numerals to Christian Europe. He travelled extensively, particularly in North Africa where he learnt the decimal system and the use of zero. He published this system in Europe but mathematicians were slow to adopt it.

Le Corbusier used the Fibonacci series in his system of proportion 'Le Modulor'.

To draw a golden rectangle:

Draw a square ABCD.
Halve the base line at E.
From this point draw a line to
corner C and with radius EC
drop an arc to find point F.

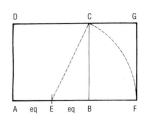

The golden rectangle is
AFGD as also is BFGC.

The angle between the diagonal and the long side of a golden rectangle is approximately 31.45°.

Paper sizes

International paper sizes

The basis of the international series is a rectangle having an area of one square metre (A0), the sides of which are in the proportion of $1:\sqrt{2}$. This is the proportion of the side and diagonal of any square. All the **A** series are of this proportion, enabling them to be doubled or halved and remain in the same proportion, which is useful for photographic enlargement or reduction. A0 is twice A1 which is twice A2 and so on. Where larger sizes than A0 are needed the A is preceded by a figure, thus 4A is four times A0.

The **B** series are sizes intermediate between any two A sizes. This series is used mostly for posters and charts. The **C** series are envelopes to suit the A sizes.

DL or long sizes are obtained by dividing the A and B series into three, four or eight equal parts parallel to the shorter side so that the proportion of $1:\sqrt{2}$ is not maintained. In practice, the long sizes should be produced from the A series only.

The dimensions of these series are of the *trimmed* or *finished* size.

	mm	inches		mm	inches
A0	841×1189	$33^{1}/_{8} \times 46\frac{3}{4}$	B0	1000×1414	$39^{3}/_{8} \times 55^{5}/_{8}$
A1	594×841	$23^{3}/_{8} \times 33^{1}/_{8}$	B1	707×1000	$27^{7}/_{8} \times 39^{3}/_{8}$
A2	420×594	$16\frac{1}{2} \times 23^{3}/_{8}$	B2	500×707	$19^{5}/_{8} \times 27^{7}/_{8}$
A3	297×420	$11\frac{3}{4} \times 16\frac{1}{2}$	B3	353×500	$13^{7}/_{8} \times 19^{5}/_{8}$
A4	210×297	$8\frac{1}{4} \times 11\frac{3}{4}$	B4	250×353	$9^{7}/_{8} \times 13^{7}/_{8}$
A5	148×210	$5^{7}/_{8} \times 8\frac{1}{4}$	B5	176×250	$6^{15}/_{16} \times 9^{7}/_{8}$
A6	105×148	$4^{1}/_{8} \times 5^{7}/_{8}$	B6	125×176	$4^{15}/_{16} \times 6^{15}/_{16}$
A7	74×105	$2^{7}/_{8} \times 4^{1}/_{8}$	B7	88×125	$3\frac{1}{2} \times 4^{15}/_{16}$
A8	52×74	$2^{1}/_{16} \times 2^{7}/_{8}$	B8	62×88	$2^{7}/_{16} \times 3\frac{1}{2}$
A9	37×52	$1^{7}/_{16} \times 2^{1}/_{16}$	B9	44×62	$1\frac{3}{4} \times 2^{7}/_{16}$
A10	26×37	$1^{1}/_{16} \times 1^{7}/_{16}$	B10	31×44	$1\frac{1}{4} \times 1\frac{3}{4}$

	mm	inches
C0	917 × 1297	$36^{1}/_{8}$ × $50^{3}/_{8}$
C1	648 × 917	$25^{1}/_{2}$ × $36^{1}/_{8}$
C2	458 × 648	18 × $25^{1}/_{2}$
C3	324 × 458	$12^{3}/_{4}$ × 18
C4	229 × 324	9 × $12^{3}/_{4}$
C5	162 × 229	$6^{3}/_{8}$ × 9
C6	114 × 162	$4^{1}/_{2}$ × $6^{3}/_{8}$
C7	81 × 114	$3^{3}/_{16}$ × $4^{1}/_{2}$
DL	110 × 220	$4^{3}/_{8}$ × $8^{5}/_{8}$

Source: *Whitaker's Almanack*

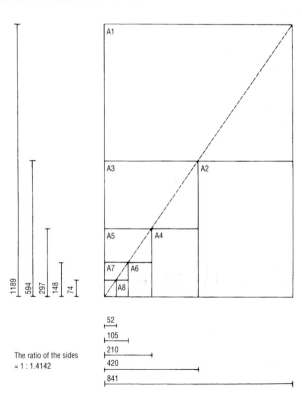

The ratio of the sides
= 1 : 1.4142

Paper sizes – **A** series

International A series paper and envelopes

Sizes most commonly used for correspondence:

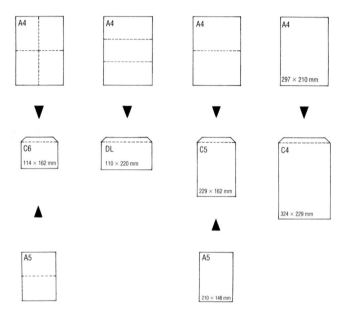

The second dimension of an envelope denotes the position of the opening flap.

Imperial paper sizes

Imperial sizes are still used for some printing and drawing papers, the most common of which are listed below:

	inches	mm
Quad Double Crown	60 × 40	1524 × 1016
Antiquarian	53 × 31	1346 × 787
Quad Crown	40 × 30	1016 × 762
Double Elephant	40 × 27	1016 × 686
Imperial	30 × 22	762 × 559
Double Crown	30 × 20	762 × 508
Double Foolscap	27 × 17	686 × 432
Cartridge	26 × 12	660 × 305
Royal	20 × 25	508 × 635
Crown	20 × 15	508 × 381
Post	19 × 15¼	483 × 387
Foolscap	17 × 13½	432 × 343

CAD

Most drawings are now produced on computers enabling instant transfer of information between architects, clients and consultants. There are many computer-aided design (CAD) systems available and the most commonly used programs are AutoCAD, AutoCAD LT, Microstation and Vectorworks, depending on the scale and complexity of projects. Drawings should be constructed in layers organising the project into different building elements, locations or materials.

Most architectural CAD software can also be used for 3D modelling, which can be useful in terms of design development and communication of ideas. These functions are often complemented by external applications such as Sketch Up, Cinema 4D, 3DS Studio Max and Artlantis, with further graphic enhancement provided by using image editing software like Photoshop.

Standard protocols apply for drawing methods and notation and many manufacturers now supply technical information in CAD format for downloading as dwg, dxf or PDF.

Drawing conventions

Demolition

removal of part

infilling opening

removal of area

making good after forming opening

Steps, ramps, slopes

direction of RISE ramp, stair or steps

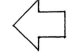

direction of FALL, natural drainage

direction of FALL, slope

dogleg staircase

ramp

FLOW direction of watercourse

Drawing conventions – continued

Landscape

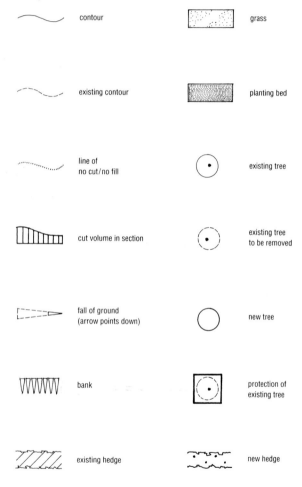

contour

grass

existing contour

planting bed

line of
no cut/no fill

existing tree

cut volume in section

existing tree
to be removed

fall of ground
(arrow points down)

new tree

bank

protection of
existing tree

existing hedge

new hedge

Masonry

brickwork

blockwork

stonework

Timber

any type sawn

softwood machined all round

hardwood machined all round

Site-formed materials

mulch

concrete

asphalt macadam

topsoil

granular fill

plaster render screed

subsoil

hard fill

Manufactured materials

board layer, membrane,
sheet – small scale

glass sheet

quilt – large scale

sheet, etc.– large scale

blockboard

insulation board

plywood

veneered blockboard

insulation quilt

Drawing conventions – continued

Doors   ## Windows

	hinged leaf		F	fixed light
	hinged leaf (alternative)			side hung (arrow points to hinge)
	hinged leaf normally closed			top hung
	hinged leaf normally open			bottom hung
	hinged leaf opening 180°			horizontal pivot
	hinged leaf opening both ways			vertical pivot
				vertical pivot reversible
	pair of hinged leaves			horizontal hinge projecting out (H window)
	sliding leaf			horizontal sliding
	revolving leaves			vertical sliding
	sliding/folding leaves end hung			slide and tilt
	sliding/folding leaves centre hung			tilt and turn

Source: BS 1192 : – 5 : 1998 *Construction drawing practice. Guide for structuring and exchange of CAD data*

Perspective drawing – method of setting up

1 Draw the plan to a scale and set it at the angle at which it is to be viewed.

2 Establish the position of the *Observer* on plan, preferably so that the building falls within a 30° cone. Any wider angled cone will produce a distorted perspective. The centreline of this cone is the *line of sight*.

3 Draw a horizontal line through the plan. This is called the *picture plane*, which is set at 90° to the line of sight. The further the picture plane is from the Observer, the larger the drawing will be.

4 Draw two lines parallel to the visible sides of the building – from the Observer to the picture plane – to determine the *vanishing points* (VP). As this building is orthogonal, these lines are at right angles to one another.

5 Draw the *horizon* where the perspective drawing will be. Draw vertical lines from the picture plane VPs to establish the VPs on the horizon.

6 Draw lines from the Observer to the three lower corners of the plan, cutting the picture plane.

7 Where these lines cut the picture plane at A, B and C, draw vertical lines up to find the three visible corners of the building.

8 Draw a vertical line from one of the two points where the picture plane cuts the plan to establish a *vertical scale line*. Mark this line to the same scale as the plan to determine the bottom and top edges of the building relative to the horizon. The horizon should be at about 1.6 m for normal eye level.

9 Connect these marks to the appropriate vanishing points to complete the outline of the building.

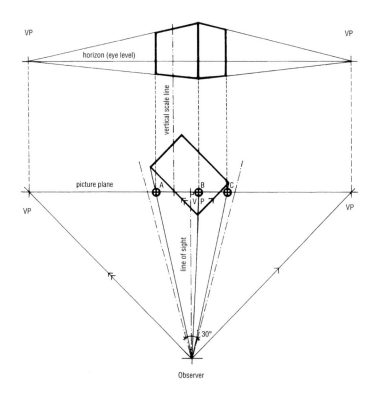

Perspective drawing – method of setting up

The classifications

- CI/SfB is the classification system most widely used by architectural specifiers. The system has been in operation for more than 30 years and is the industry standard.
- Uniclass is a UK classification system for structuring product literature and project information, incorporating both Common Arrangement of Work Sections (CAWS) and EPIC.
- EPIC is a European-wide classification system and should be included especially if technical literature is to be used on a pan-European basis.

CI/SfB Construction index

CI/SfB is a library system used by the building industry and is suitable for the smallest or largest office.

CI = Construction Index
SfB = Samarbetskommitten för Byggnadsfrägor
    – a Swedish system of the late 1940s.

CI/SfB notation has four divisions: | 0 | 1 | 2 & 3 | 4 |

Table 0   = Physical environment
Table 1   = Elements
Tables 2 and 3 = Constructions and Materials
Table 4   = Activities and Requirements

The current CI/SfB edition was issued in 1976 and, according to RIBA Information Services, is still widely used although the scheme is long overdue for revision.

CI/SfB Tables

Table 0 Physical environment

0   Planning areas
01   Extra terrestrial areas
02   International, national scale planning areas
03   Regional, sub-regional scale planning areas
04
05   Rural, urban planning areas
06   Land use planning areas
07
08   Other planning areas
09   Common areas relevant to planning

1   Utilities, civil engineering facilities
11   Rail transport
12   Road transport
13   Water transport
14   Air transport, other transport
15   Communications
16   Power supply, mineral supply
17   Water supply, waste disposal
18   Other

2   Industrial facilities
21–25
26   Agricultural
27   Manufacturing
28   Other

3   Administrative, commercial, proactive service facilities
31   Official administration, law courts
32   Offices
33   Commercial
34   Trading, shops
35–36
37   Protective services
38   Other

4   Health, welfare facilities
41   Hospitals
42   Other medical
43
44   Welfare, homes
46   Animal welfare
47
48   Other

5   Recreational facilities
51   Refreshment
52   Entertainment
53   Social recreation, clubs
54   Aquatic sports
55
56   Sports
57
58   Other

6   Religious facilities
61   Religious centres
62   Cathedrals
63   Churches, chapels
64   Mission halls, meeting houses
65   Temples, mosques, synagogues
66   Convents
67   Funerary, shrines
68   Other

7   Educational, scientific, information facilities
71   Schools
72   Universities, colleges
73   Scientific
74
75   Exhibition, display
76   Information, libraries
77
78   Other

8   Residential facilities
81 Housing
82 One-off housing units, houses
83
84 Special housing
85 Communal residential
86 Historical residential
87 Temporary, mobile residential
88 Other

9   Common facilities, other facilities
91 Circulation
92 Rest, work
93 Culinary
94 Sanitary, hygiene
95 Cleaning, maintenance
96 Storage
97 Processing, plant, control
98 Other, buildings other than by function
99 Parts of facilities, other aspects of the physical environment, architecture, landscape

Table 1   Elements

(--) Sites, projects, building systems

(1–) Ground, sub-structure
(10)
(11) Ground
(12)
(13) Floor beds
(14)–(15)
(16) Retaining walls, foundations
(17) Pile foundations
(18) Other substructure elements
(19) Parts of elements (11) to (18), cost summary

(2–) Primary elements, carcass
(20)
(21) Walls, external walls
(22) Internal walls, partitions
(23) Floors, galleries
(24) Stairs, ramps
(25)–(26)
(27) Roofs
(28) Building frames, other primary elements
(29) Parts of elements (21) to (28), cost summary

(3–) Secondary elements, completion if described separately from (2–)
(30)
(31) Secondary elements to external walls, external doors, windows
(32) Secondary elements to internal walls, internal doors
(33) Secondary elements to floors
(34) Secondary elements to stairs
(35) Suspended ceilings
(36)
(37) Secondary elements to roofs: rooflights etc
(38) Other secondary elements
(39) Parts of elements (31) to (38), cost summary

(4–) Finishes, if described separately

(40)
(41) Wall finishes, external
(42) Wall finishes, internal
(43) Floor finishes
(44) Stair finishes
(45) Ceiling finishes
(46)
(47) Roof finishes
(48) Other finishes to structure
(49) Parts of elements (41) to (48), cost summary

(5–) Services, mainly pipe and ducted

(50)–(51)
(52) Waste disposal, drainage
(53) Liquids supply
(54) Gases supply
(55) Space cooling
(56) Space heating
(57) Air conditioning, ventilation
(58) Other piped, ducted services
(59) Parts of elements (51) to (58), cost summary

(6–) Services, mainly electrical

(60)
(61) Electrical supply
(62) Power
(63) Lighting
(64) Communications
(65)
(66) Transport
(67)
(68) Security, control, other services
(69) Parts of elements (61) to (68), cost summary

(7–) Fittings

(70)
(71) Circulation fittings
(72) Rest, work fittings
(73) Culinary fittings
(74) Sanitary, hygiene fittings
(75) Cleaning, maintenance fittings
(76) Storage, screening fittings
(77) Special activity fittings
(78) Other fittings
(79) Parts of elements (71) to (78), cost summary

(8–) *Loose furniture, equipment

(80)
(81) Circulation loose equipment
(82) Rest, work loose equipment
(83) Culinary loose equipment
(84) Sanitary, hygiene loose equipment
(85) Cleaning, maintenance loose equipment
(86) Storage, screening loose equipment
(87) Special activity loose equipment
(88) Other
(89) Parts of elements (81) to (88), cost summary

(9–) External, other elements

(90) External works
(98) Other elements
(99) Parts of elements, cost summary

  *   Use only **(7–)** if preferred

Table 2   Constructions

A*	Constructions, forms	N	Rigid sheets for overlapping
B*		O	
C*		P	Thick coating work
D*		Q	
E	Cast in situ work	R	Rigid sheets
F	Blockwork, blocks	S	Rigid tiles
G	Large blocks, panels	T	Flexible sheets
H	Section work, sections	U	
I	Pipework, pipes	V	Film coating & impregnation
J	Wirework, meshes	W	Planting, plants, seeds
K	Quilt work, quilts	X	Components
L	Flexible sheets (proofing)	Y	Formless work, products
M	Malleable sheets	Z	Joints

*   Used for special purposes e.g.: resource scheduling by computer

Table 3   Materials

a*		p	Aggregates, loose fills
b*		q	Lime & cement binders, mortars, concretes
c*			
d*		r	Clay, gypsum, magnesia & plastic binders, mortars
e	Natural stone		
f	Precast with binder	s	Bituminous materials
g	Clay (dried, fired)	t	Fixing & jointing materials
h	Metal	u	Protective & process/property modifying materials
i	Wood		
j	Vegetable & animal materials	v	Paints
k		w	Ancillary materials
l		x	
m	Inorganic fibres	y	Composite materials
n	Rubbers, plastics etc	z	Substances
o	Glass		

*   Used for special purposes e.g.: resource scheduling by computer

Tables 2 and 3 are positioned in the third division of the label, either separately or together as required,

e.g. | | | | Ff | | | = precast blocks

Table 4   Activities, requirements

Activities, aids

(A)   Administration & management activities, aids
(Af) Administration, organization
(Ag) Communications
(Ah) Preparation of documentation
(Ai) Public relations, publicity
(Aj) Controls, procedures
(Ak) Organizations
(Am) Personnel roles
(An) Education
(Ao) Research, development
(Ap) Standardization, rationalization
(Aq) Testing, evaluating

(A1) Organizing offices, projects
(A2) Financing, accounting
(A3) Designing, physical planning
(A4) Cost planning, cost control, tenders, contracts
(A5) Production planning, progress control
(A6) Buying, delivery
(A7) Inspection, quality control
(A8) Handing over, feedback, appraisal
(A9) Other activities, arbitration, insurance

(B)   Construction plant, tools
(B1) Protection plant
(B2) Temporary (non-protective) works
(B3) Transport plant
(B4) Manufacture, screening, storage plant
(B5) Treatment plant
(B6) Placing, pavement, compaction plant
(B7) Hand tools
(B8) Ancillary plants
(B9) Other construction plant, tools

(C)   *Used for special purposes*

(D)   Construction operations
(D1) Protecting
(D2) Cleaning, preparing
(D3) Transport, lifting
(D4) Forming, cutting, shaping, fitting
(D5) Treatment, drilling, boring
(D6) Placing, laying & applying
(D7) Making good, repairing
(D8) Cleaning up
(D9) Other construction operations

Requirements, properties

(E)   Composition
(F)   Shape, size
(G)   Appearance
(H)   Context, environment
(J)   Mechanics
(K)   Fire, explosion
(L)   Matter
(M)   Heat, cold
(N)   Light, dark
(P)   Sound, quiet
(Q)   Electricity, magnetism, radiation
(R)   Energy, side effects, compatability, durability
(S)
(T)   Application
(U)   Users resources
(V)   Working factors
(W)   Operation, maintenance factors
(X)   Change, movement, stability factors
(Y)   Economic, commercial factors
(Z)   Peripheral subjects: presentation, time, space

Sources: RIBA Enterprises Ltd, NBS Services

Uniclass

CI/SfB is being superseded by a new system called **Uniclass** (Unified Classification for the Construction Industry). It was developed for the Construction Project Information Committee (CPIC) and the DoE Construction Sponsorship Directorate. The project was led by consultants from the National Building Specification (NBS) and is based on principles set out by the International Standards Organisation (ISO). The Construction Products Table is based on the work of Electronic Product Information Co-operation (EPIC).

It was designed for organizing information in libraries and projects, but can also be used for structuring files in databases. It is a faceted system which allows tables to be used independently or in combination with each other. It can be integrated with other information systems such as the Common Arrangement of Works Sections (CAWS), Civil Engineering Standard Method of Measurement (CESMM) and the Building Cost Information Service (BCIS) Standard Form of Cost Analysis.

Uniclass consists of 15 tables:

A	Form of information
B	Subject disciplines
C	Management
D	Facilities
E	Construction entities
F	Spaces
G	Elements for buildings
H	Elements for civil engineering works
J	Work sections for buildings
K	Work sections for civil engineering works
L	Construction products
M	Construction aids
N	Properties and characteristics
P	Materials
Q	Universal Decimal Classification

Source: RIBA Publishing

2
Planning

Planning and other permissions

Planning permission

Definitions

Original House:	The house as it was first built, or as it stood on 1 July 1948 if it was built before that date.
Highway:	All public roads, footpaths, bridleways and byways.
Special Area:	Conservation Area, National Park, Area of Outstanding Natural Beauty and the Norfolk and Suffolk Broads.
Volume:	Measured from external faces.

Summary of permissions
needed for work to dwellings and related property

1 Dividing off part of a house for use as a separate dwelling.
2 Use of a caravan in a garden as a home for someone else.
3 Dividing off part of a house for business or commercial work.
4 Providing a parking place for a commercial vehicle or taxi.
5 Building something that goes against the terms of any planning permission.
6 Work which might obstruct the view of road users.
7 Work which will involve a new or wider access to a trunk or classified road.
8 Additions or extensions to a flat or maisonette, including those converted from houses, excluding internal alterations which do not affect the external appearance.

House extensions

9   An addition which would be nearer to any highway than the nearest part of the original house unless there is at least 20 m between the extended house and the highway.

10 Covering more than half the area of land around the original house with additions or other separate buildings.

11 An extension to a terrace house or a house in a Special Area larger than 10 per cent, or up to 50 m^3, whichever is greater, of the volume of the original house.

12 An extension to any other kind of house larger than 15 per cent, or up to 70 m^3, whichever is greater, of the volume of the original house.

13 An extension which is larger than 115 m^3.

14 An extension which is higher than the highest part of the roof of the original house.

15 An extension where any part is more than 4 m high (except roof extensions) and is within 2 m of the property boundary.

16 Any roof extension, loft conversion or dormer window in a Special Area.

17 Any extension to a roof slope which faces a highway.

18 Roof extensions which would add more than 50 m^3 to the volume of the house or 40 m^3 to that of a terraced house. This allowance is not in addition to, but must be deducted from, any other allowances set out above.

Separate new buildings

on the land around the house

19 Any building (or structure) to be used other than for domestic purposes or which exceeds conditions set out in 9 and 10 above.

20 Any building more than 3 m high, or 4 m high if it has a ridged roof.

21 Any building in the grounds of a Listed Building or in a Special Area which would be more than 10 m^3.

22 A storage tank for heating oil larger than 3500 litres or more than 3 m above ground.

23 A tank to store liquefied petroleum gas (LPG).

Building a porch
24 With an area measured externally of more than $3\,m^3$.
25 Higher than $3\,m$ above ground.
26 Less than $2\,m$ from a road.

Erecting fences, walls and gates
27 If a house is a Listed Building.
28 If over $1\,m$ high where next to a road or over $2\,m$ elsewhere.

Planting hedges or trees
29 If a condition was attached to the planning permission of the property which restricts such planting or where the sight line might be blocked.

Erecting a satellite dish or antenna
Other than normal TV or radio aerials. There is a general permission to install antenna up to a specific size on property without the need for planning permission. This general permission depends on your house type and area.

New cladding
34 Cladding the outside of the house with stone, tiles, artificial stone, plastic or timber in a Special Area.

Driveways
35 If a new or wider access is made onto a major road. Approval of the highways department of the local council will also be needed if a new driveway crosses a pavement or verge.

Planning permission is not required for
Sheds, garages, greenhouses, domestic pet houses, summer houses, swimming pools, ponds, sauna cabins or tennis courts, unless they contravene the conditions described in 9, 10, 19, 20 and 21 above.

Patios, hard standings, paths and driveways unless used for parking a commercial vehicle or taxi.

Normal domestic TV and radio aerials – *but* see under Erecting a Satellite Dish or Antenna above.

Repairs, maintenance or minor improvements such as redecorating or replacing windows, insertion of windows, skylights or rooflights – *but* see the next section on Listed Buildings and Conservation Areas, where consents may be needed.

Other consents

Listed Buildings
A Listed Building includes the exterior and interior of the building and, with some exceptions, any object or structure within the curtilage of the building, including garden walls.

Listed Building Consent is needed to demolish a Listed Building, or part of one, or to alter or extend it in any way inside or out which would affect its architectural or historic character.

Certain minor works such as plumbing, electrical installations, and fitted furniture and appliances, as for kitchens and bathrooms, MAY be considered 'de minimis' and not require consent if the work is both non-destructive and reversible, but it is unwise to assume this. Check with the council first. It is a criminal offence to carry out any work without consent. No fees are required.

See also p. 56.

Conservation areas
Consent is needed to demolish any building in a Conservation Area with a volume of more than $115\,m^3$, or any part of such building. Consent may also be needed to demolish gates, walls, fences or railings. No fees are required.

National Parks, Areas of Outstanding Natural Beauty and the Broads (Special Areas)

Generally permissions to carry out building work in these areas are more limited, so check with the appropriate body first.

Trees and high hedges

Many trees have Tree Preservation Orders which mean consent is needed to prune or fell them. Trees are often protected in Conservation Areas. These normally exclude fruit trees or small decorative trees with trunks less than 100 mm in diameter. Six weeks' notice is needed before any work may be carried out.

Tall evergreen hedges over 2 m high may be subject to the Anti-Social Behaviour Act 2003 (Part 8).

Building Regulations approval

Almost all new building must comply with the Building Regulations except small, detached buildings without sanitary facilities such as sheds and garages. The Regulations are available in full on the internet.

Rights of way

If a proposed building would obstruct a public path then consult with the local authority at an early stage. If they agree to the proposal then an order will be made to divert or extinguish the right of way. No work should proceed until the order has been confirmed.

Advertising

Displaying an advertisement larger than $0.3 \, m^2$ outside a property may need consent. This can include house names, numbers or even 'Beware of the Dog'. Temporary notices up to $0.6 \, m^2$ relating to local events may be displayed for a short time. Estate Agents' boards, in general, should not be larger than $0.5 \, m^2$ on each side and may be banned in Conservation Areas.

Wildlife

If the proposed new building will involve disturbing roosts of bats or other protected species, then Natural England (NE), the Countryside Council for Wales (CCW) or Scottish Natural Heritage (SNH), whichever is appropriate, must be notified.

Source: *Planning – A Guide for Householders*
www.planningportal.gov.uk

Planning appeals

Considering an appeal

It is possible to appeal against a Local Planning Authority (LPA) which has refused Planning Permission, whether outline or full; or if they have given permission but with conditions which seem to the Appellant to be unreasonable; or if a decision has not been made within the time laid down, which is normally 8–13 weeks from registration. However, before lodging an appeal, the Appellant should consider modifying the scheme to suit the LPA. Generally if such a scheme is presented within 1 year of the refusal date, no extra planning fee is requested. Appeals should be a last resort. They take time and cost money. Most appeals are not successful. Proposals should fit in with the LPA's development plan for the area. Permission is unlikely to be given for development on greenbelt land or on good quality agricultural land, or for access to main roads. Inspectors judge appeals on their *planning merit*. They are unlikely to be swayed by personal considerations.

Making an appeal

Appeals must be lodged within 6 months of the date of the decision. The Secretary of State (SoS) can accept a late appeal, but will do so only in exceptional circumstances. Appeals are normally decided on the basis of *written representations* and a visit to the site by the planning inspector. However, where the Appellant or the LPA do not agree to this procedure, then the inspector can arrange for a *Hearing* or a *Local Inquiry*. Forms, whether for appealing against Planning Permission, Listed

Building Consent or Conservation Area Consent, should be obtained from the Planning Inspectorate in England and Wales, the Scottish Executive (SEIRU) in Scotland and the Planning Appeals Commission in Northern Ireland or on their websites.

Written representation

The appeal form, with documents and plans, should be sent to the Planning Inspector (PI) with copies of all papers also sent to the LPA. The LPA will send their report to the PI, copies of which will be sent to the Appellant, who is allowed to make comments. *Interested people* such as neighbours and environmental groups will be notified of the appeal and able to comment. When the Inspector is ready, a site visit is arranged. This may be an *unaccompanied* visit if the site can be viewed from public land or an *accompanied* visit when the site is on private land and where both the Appellant, or a representative, and the LPA must be present.

Hearings

Hearings are less formal and cheaper than a local inquiry and legal representatives are not normally used.

Local inquiry

This procedure is used if the LPA and the Appellant cannot decide on a written representation and the PI decides a hearing is unsuitable.

Written statements made by the LPA and the Applicant are sent to the PI with copies to one another.

Details of the inquiry must be posted on the site, and the LPA will inform local papers and anyone else likely to be interested.

Statements or representatives may be asked for from the Ministry of Agriculture, Fisheries and Food (MAFF) where the proposal involves agricultural land, or the Health and Safety Executive (HSE) where the proposal involves the storage of dangerous materials. All witnesses or representatives may be questioned or cross-examined. At the inquiry, anyone involved may use a lawyer or other professional to put their case. The Inspector will make visits to the site, alone, before the inquiry. As part of the inquiry, the Appellant and the LPA may ask for a visit with the Inspector to clarify any points raised about the site or surroundings.

Costs

The Appellant and the LPA will normally pay their own expenses, whichever procedure is used. However, if there is an inquiry or hearing, the Appellant can ask the LPA to pay some or all of the costs. The LPA may do likewise. The SoS will only agree to this if the party claiming can show that the other side behaved unreasonably and put them to unnecessary expense.

The decision

The Inspector sends the decision to the Appellant with copies to the LPA and anyone else entitled or who asked for a copy. In some cases the Inspector sends a report to the SoS with a recommendation as to whether or not the appeal should be allowed. The SoS does not have to accept the Inspector's recommendations. Where new evidence emerges before the decision is issued which may put new light on the subject, both parties will have a chance to comment before a decision is made and the inquiry may be re-opened.

The High Court

The only way an appeal can be made against the Inspector's decision is on legal grounds in the High Court. This challenge must be made within 6 weeks of the date of the decision. To succeed, it must be proved that the Inspectorate or the SoS have exceeded their powers or that proper procedures were not followed.

Source: *A Guide to Planning Appeals*

Party wall awards

The Party Wall etc Act 1996 has effect throughout England and Wales and involves the following proposed building work:

1 Work to an existing party wall, such as taking support for a new beam, inserting full-width DPCs, underpinning, raising, rebuilding or reducing the wall.
2 Building a new party wall on or astride a boundary line between two properties.
3 Constructing foundations for a new building within 3 m of a neighbouring building, where the work will go deeper than the neighbouring foundations.
4 Constructing foundations for a new building within 6 m of a neighbouring building where the work will cut a line drawn downwards at 45° from the bottom of the neighbour's foundations.

Notices must be served by the *building owner* to the *adjoining owner* or owners, which may include landlords as well as tenants, at least 2 months before the work starts or 1 month in advance for new work as described in 3 and 4 above. There is no set form for the Notice, but it should include: the owner's name and address; the address of the building (if different); full detailed drawings of the proposed work; and the starting date. It may also include any proposals to safeguard the fabric of the adjoining owner's property. The adjoining owner cannot stop someone exercising their rights given them by the Act, but can influence how and when the work is done. Anyone receiving a notice may give consent within 14 days, or give a counter-notice setting out modifications to the proposals. If the adjoining owner does not reply, a dispute is assumed to have arisen.

The Award

When consent is not received the two owners agree to appoint one surveyor to act for both sides, or two surveyors, one to act for each side. Surveyors appointed must take into account the interests of both owners. The surveyors draw up and supervise the *Award*, which is a statement laying down what work will be undertaken and how and when it will be done. It should include a *Schedule of Condition*, which describes in detail the state of the wall viewed from the adjoining owner's side. The Award will also specify who pays the construction costs and the surveyors' fees – usually the owner who initiates the work. The Award is served on all relevant owners, each of whom is bound by the Award unless appeals are made within 14 days to the county court.

Sources: *A Short Guide to the Party Wall Act 1996*
The Party Wall etc. Act 1996: Explanatory Booklet
Available online from www.communities.gov.uk

Listed buildings

English Heritage has the task of identifying and protecting historic buildings. This is done by recommending buildings of special architectural or historic interest to be included on statutory lists compiled by the Secretary of State, for National Heritage.

Buildings may be listed because of age, rarity, architectural merit, method of construction and occasionally because of an association with a famous person or historic event. Sometimes whole groups of buildings such as a model village or a complete square may be listed.

All buildings largely in their original condition before 1700 are likely to be listed, as are most between 1700 and 1840. Later on the criteria became tighter with time, so that post-1945 only exceptional buildings are listed.

Grades

Listed buildings are graded as follows:

Grade I   buildings of exceptional interest
Grade II*   important buildings of more than special interest
Grade II   buildings of special interest warranting every effort to preserve them

There are about 370 000 list entries, and of those over 92% are Grade II.

Listing applies to the entire building, including anything fixed to the building or in the grounds before 1 July 1948.

See p. 46 for permissions needed to add, alter or demolish a listed building.

Grade I and II* buildings may be eligible for grants from English Heritage, as may some Grade II buildings in conservation areas.

Residential listed buildings may be VAT zero-rated for approved alterations. See Notice 708 Buildings and Construction from H M Revenue and Customs.

For advice on how to get a building listed or other information, consult the Department of Culture, Media and Sport, and English Heritage, Heritage Protection Operations Team, 1 Waterhouse Square, 138–142 Holborn London EC1N 2ST. The responsibility for Consent for altering or extending a listed building lies with local planning authorities and ultimately with the Department of Communities and Local Government.

For listed buildings in Scotland, Northern Ireland and Wales, consult Historic Scotland, CADW, and Historic Buildings and Monuments Belfast respectively.

Sources: *Listing Buildings – The Work of English Heritage*
What Listing means – A Guide for Owners and Occupiers
The Right Hedge for You
Department for Culture Media and Sport – www.culture.gov.uk
Department of Communities and Local Government – www.communities.gov.uk
H M Revenue and Customs – www.hmrc.gov.uk

Building Regulations 2000

The approved documents

These documents are published as *practical guidance* to the Building Regulations, i.e. they are not the Building Regulations as such.

The mandatory **Requirement** is highlighted in green near the beginning of each document. The remaining text is for guidance only.

The Building Inspectorate accept that if this guidance is followed then the requirement is satisfied. There is no obligation to comply with these guidelines providing evidence is produced to show that the relevant requirement has been satisfied in some other way.

The purpose of the Building Regulation is to secure reasonable standards of health, safety, energy conservation and the convenience of disabled people.

A separate system of control applies in Scotland and Northern Ireland.

The regulations are published by the DCLG and are available from the Stationery Office and online.

Approved documents

Part A
Approved Document A – Structure (2004 edition)

Part B
Approved Document B (Fire safety) – Volume 1: Dwellinghouses (2006 Edition)

Approved Document B (Fire safety) – Volume 2: Buildings other than dwellinghouses (2006 Edition)

Part C
Approved Document C – Site preparation and resistance to contaminates and moisture (2004 edition)

Part D
Approved Document D – Toxic substances (1992 edition)

Part E
Approved Document E – Resistance to the passage of sound (2003 edition)

Part F
Approved Document F – Ventilation (2006 edition)

Part G
Approved Document G – Hygiene (1992 edition)

Part H
Approved Document H – drainage and waste disposal (2002 edition)

Part J
Approved Document J – Combustion appliances and fuel storage systems (2002 edition)

Part K
Approved Document K – Protection from falling collision and impact (1998 edition)

Part L – Dwellings
Approved Document L1A: Conservation of fuel and power (New dwellings) (2006 edition)
Approved Document L1B: Conservation of fuel and power (Existing dwellings) (2006 edition)

Part L – Buildings other than dwellings
Approved Document L2A: Conservation of fuel and power (New buildings other than dwellings) (2006 edition)
Approved Document L2B: Conservation of fuel and power (Existing buildings other than dwellings) (2006 edition)

Part M
Approved Document M – Access to and Use of Buildings (2004 edition)

Part N
Approved Document N – Glazing (1998 edition)

Part P
Approved Document P – Electrical safety - Dwellings (2006 edition)

Regulation 7
Approved Document for Regulation 7 (1992 edition)

Construction Design and Management Regulations

In the mid-1990s, fatal accidents in the construction industry were five to six times more frequent than in other areas of manufacture. Also, all construction workers could expect to be temporarily off work at least once in their working life as a result of injury. The Construction Design and Management Regulations (CDM) 1994, effective from 31 March 1995, were drafted to try and improve these statistics. The regulations were revised and clarified in 2007 and are explained in the Approved Code of Practice 'Managing health & safety in construction'.

'Designers are required to avoid foreseeable risks "so far as is reasonably practicable, taking due account of other relevant design considerations." The greater the risk, the greater the weight that must be given to eliminating or reducing it.'

The key aims of the CDM Regulations 2007 are to integrate health and safety into the management of the project and to encourage everyone involved to work together to:

- improve the planning and management of projects from the very start;
- identify hazards early on, so they can be eliminated or reduced at the design or planning stage and the remaining risks can be properly managed;
- target effort where it can do the most good in terms of health and safety; and
- discourage unnecessary bureaucracy.

Revisions to the regulations have been focussed on clarifying the client's responsibilities as the primary instigator of compliance with the regulations, and warning against inappropriate bureaucracy, which tends to obscure the real health and safety issues.

The Planning Supervisor has been renamed as the CDM Co-ordinator – a more accurate description of the role. To implement the regulations for any 'notifiable project', a CDM Co-ordinator (CC) must be appointed by the client. This can be anyone competent, and may be a member of the design team, contractors or even the client. For smaller projects, it simplifies procedures if the CC is also part of the design team, such as the architect or engineer.

The CC must advise and assist the client with their duties; notify the HSE of a 'notifiable project'; co-ordinate health and safety aspects of design work and co-operate with others involved with the project; facilitate good communication between client, designers and contractors; liaise with the principal contractor regarding ongoing design; identify, collect and pass on pre-construction information; prepare/update the Health & Safety file for the client on completion. They may also, if requested by a client, advise on the appointment of consultants and contractors as to their competence and resources in regard to CDM matters. If architects are to act as Planning Supervisors they must ensure that they receive certified HSE training, as failure to comply with the regulations could lead to criminal prosecution.

When CDM regulations are not applicable in full

Listed below are situations where the CDM regulations need not apply in full. However, the designer is still legally obliged to avoid foreseeable risks; give priority to protection for all; and include adequate H & S information in the design.

- Work carried out for domestic householders, on their own residences, used solely as a private dwelling (e.g. not as an office as well as a home).

- Work which is for 30 days or less duration and involves less than 500 person days on site and does not involve demolition or dismantling of a structure.

There are a number of construction-related activities that are listed as 'not construction' for the purposes of the regulations, including erecting and dismantling marquees, lightweight movable partitions as used for office screens, exhibition displays, etc; tree planting and general horticultural work; surveying including 'examining a structure for faults', and off-site manufacture of construction components, e.g. roof trusses, precast concrete and bathroom pods. CDM, therefore, does not apply to these works.

Source: *Managing Health and Safety in Construction*
HSE 2007

Standards – in the construction industry

Efforts are being made to harmonize standards throughout Europe so as to open up the single market for construction products. It is still something of a minefield, as harmonization at the beginning of the twenty-first century is not complete. Listed alphabetically below are the organizations and standards involved, which may help to clarify the current situation.

BBA – British Board of Agrément. This organization assesses and tests new construction products and systems which have not yet received a relevant BS or EN. It issues Agrément Certificates to those that meet their standards. The Certificate gives an independent opinion of fitness for purpose. Holders are subject to 3-yearly reviews to ensure standards are maintained. The BBA represents the UK in the UEAtc and is designated by the government to lead the issuing of ETAs.

BSI – British Standards Institution. This was the first national standards body in the world. It publishes British Standards (BS) which give recommended minimum standards for materials, products and processes. These are not mandatory, but some are quoted directly in the Building Regulations (see also EN below). All materials and components complying with a particular BS are marked with the BS kitemark together with the relevant BS number. BSI also publishes codes of practice (CP) which give recommendations for good practice in relation to design, manufacture, construction, installation and maintenance, with the main objectives being safety, quality, economy and fitness for purpose. Drafts for Development (DD) are issued when there is insufficient information for a BS or a CP. These are similar to ENVs.

CE mark – Communauté Européenne mark. This mark was introduced by the CPD, and is a symbol applied to products by their manufacturers to indicate their compliance with European member state regulations. It has nothing to do with quality or safety (unlike the BS kitemark). If the CE mark has a number attached, this signifies that the product has been independently tested.

CEN – Comité Européen de Nationalisation (also known as the European Committee for Standardisation). Its main aims are to harmonize national standards; promote implementation of the ISO; prepare ENs; co-operate with EFTA and other international governmental organizations and CENELEC (the electrotechnical counterpart of CEN). The BSI is a member of CEN.

CPD – Construction Products Directive. This is a directive produced by the European Commission introducing the CE mark.

EN – Euronorm (also known as European Standard). European Standards are published by the CEN for a wide range of materials. A full EN, known in the UK as a BS EN, is mandatory and overrules any conflicting previous BS, which must be withdrawn. Prospective standards where documentation is still in preparation are published as European prestandards (ENV). These are normally converted to full ENs after a 3-year experimental period.

EOTA – European Organization for Technical Approvals. Members of this organization issue ETAs. The UK is represented in EOTA by the BBA. EOTA polices organizations nominated by member states to make sure they all apply the same tests and level of expertise when preparing ETAs.

ETA – European Technical Approval. ETAs are issued by members of EOTA. They are available for products whose performance or characteristics fall outside the scope of a European Standard (EN) mandated by the EC, and are based upon assessment methods known as ETAGs (European Technical Approval Guidelines). Both ETAs and ENs enable products to which they refer to be placed in the single European market.

ISO – International Organization for Standardization. This organization prepares International Standards for the whole world. They are prefixed ISO and many are compatible and complement British Standards. In the UK, BSs and ENs that are approved by the ISO are prefixed BS ISO or BS EN ISO.

MOAT – Method of Assessment and Testing. These are the criteria and methods used by the BBA when testing products. Many MOATs have been developed in consultation with the European Agrément organizations under the aegis of the UEAtc.

QA – Quality Assurance. BS EN 9001 lays down procedures for various organizations to conform to a specification and thus acquire QA for a production or a service. RIBA Chartered Architects are required to adopt appropriate QA for their type and scale of work. BS EN 14001 2004 is the environmental equivalent standard that specifies requirements for an environmental management system for an organization to control and improve its environmental impacts and performance.

UEAtc – European Union of Agrément technical committee. A technical committee to which all European Agrément institutes belong, including the BBA for the UK. Its principal function is to facilitate trade in construction products between member states, primarily through its Confirmation process, whereby an Agrément Certificate issued by a UEAtc member in one country can be used to obtain a Certificate in another.

Costs and law

Costs and legal issues are described in principle and in outline only since both contract values and case law change too frequently for actual figures and legal detail to have lasting value.

Costs

The architect's role both as a cost advisor and as a certifier of contractors' valuations varies with the scale of projects. For most small projects and many of the simpler medium scale ones, the architect is both the client's cost advisor and responsible for checking as well as certifying payments to the contractor: awareness of current costs is therefore vital to architects working at this level with local experience usually the best guide, though several price books are available including those covering small works and refurbishment.

The simplest rule in estimating costs is that they decrease with scale and increase with complexity; time is also an issue but the most economic length of time for a construction project will vary for different contractors and circumstances; either forcing the pace for an earlier completion or slowing progress artificially may increase costs.

Project costs can be lower in the early stages of simpler less skilled work and cheaper materials and increase sharply towards completion as more skilled trades are required for services and finishing and more expensive components are fitted such as joinery, electrical and sanitary fittings.

Labour costs have grown steadily as a proportion of construction costs which is reflected in the growth of prefabrication and pre-finishing both of components such as windows, kitchens and bathroom pods, and of material elements such as wall, roof and floor panels; recently renewed enthusiasm for prefabrication has coined the term 'Modern Methods of Construction'.

Preliminary cost estimating for most projects is done on a pounds per square metre of internal floor area basis; the rates for different types and scales of buildings vary sharply, so that for example, a simple industrial shed may cost half as much per square metre as speculative housing which in turn may cost half as much per square metre as a hospital. Despite the decades since metrication, many in the commercial development world still work in square feet for both rents and build costs (10.67 sq ft = 1 sq metre).

For smaller projects, where the architect is often the client's only cost advisor, the work is typically tendered on the basis of drawings and a specification or schedule of works. The architect will agree the list of contractors with the client, issue the tenders, advise the client on the relative merits of the tenders received, negotiate any cost savings needed and arrange the contract between client and contractor; once the work starts, the architect will administer the contract on behalf of both parties, value the contractor's work – usually at monthly intervals – and prepare certificates for the client to pay, including where necessary any variations in the work covered by architects certificates. After completion the architect negotiates the final account with the contractor.

Larger projects – and especially those where the client wants detailed and explicit cost estimating, monitoring and control – usually include a Quantity Surveyor in the consultants team who may provide a series of estimates and carry out value engineering exercises during the briefing and design process, and then prepare a Bill of Quantities during the working drawings stage which describes the works in sufficient numeric detail so that tenderers can quote precisely against the Bill.

The QS advises the client on tenders received and prepares valuations during the contract as a basis for the architect's certificates, as well as dealing with the final account.

Whether or not a QS is involved, the architect is still responsible under most forms of contract payments and takes on the additional role of 'administering the contract'; in which role he is required to act fairly and impartially to both client and contractor in matters of cost, timing, quality, etc. It is important that architects make this clear to inexperienced clients at the outset.

One of the architect's most important duties relates to assessing extensions of time which can have substantial cost consequences – both in terms of contractors claims for loss and expense, and reductions of clients rights to liquidated damages.

Fees

There are no set fee scales for architects and the only advice that RIBA is allowed to give on fee levels is based on average fees charged, broad band graphs of which are included in their advice to clients.

For larger projects, fees are often charged on a percentage of final construction cost; smaller projects may be carried out on a time basis or against a lump sum quotation.

As for construction costs, fees tend to decrease with project scale and increase with complexity, so, for example, fees for a large new build warehouse on a greenfield site may be below 5% whereas the restoration and conversion of a small grade 1 listed building to a private home might involve fees as high as 20%.

RIBA's appointment documents advise what standard services are normally included within an architect's fee and what special services need to be separately negotiated.

Where several consultants work on a project, their fees will be individually negotiated with the client but it is important that each consultant's scope of work is clearly defined, so that there are neither gaps nor duplication in the service to the client.

For a project with an overall fee of 15%, the split between consultants might be: architect 7%; landscape architect 1.5%; structural engineer 2.5%; services engineer 1.5%;

quantity surveyor 2% and CDM coordinator 0.5% – though projects can involve very different relative demands for consultants skills.

Law

Architects' role in construction contracts is their main area of legal involvement but they may be asked by clients for legal advice in relation to Planning, Listed Buildings and Building Regulations, or in connection with health and safety under the CDM regulations (see p. 53), or boundary matters under the Party Wall Act (see p. 47), or a number of other relevant items of legislation such as Health & Safety at Work Act, Offices Shops & Railway Premises Act, etc. It is important that architects do not give clients advice beyond their expertise in legal matters and recommend their clients consult legal advisors when appropriate.

Legal disputes, particularly where litigation and arbitration are involved tend to be time consuming and costly; The Construction Act (Housing Grants, Regeneration and Construction Act Part II 1996) introduced adjudication as a simpler and swifter method of dispute resolution but it has its own rules and timetables of which architects need to be aware, particularly as timescales can be very tight. Architects should also remember that their own appointments with their clients are classed as construction contracts under the Construction Act, and they can, therefore, avail themselves of such remedies as the Act provides, such as: adjudication, suspension of services, right to staged payments, etc.

Disputes often arise between client and contractor over the architect's extension of time award.

Architects will need to consult their professional indemnity insurers or brokers when a dispute arises that might involve a claim against them. It may be more helpful to consult a professional contractual consultant in the first instance rather than a lawyer for advice on contractual disputes or claims.

Registered architects - and practising members of RIBA – are required to carry appropriate levels of professional indemnity insurance so that there is assurance of redress for clients – or others – who may suffer financially as a result of an architect's mistakes.

Contracts between the architect and their insurer involve the usual conditions and most critically that the architect informs their insurer as soon as possible of any 'circumstance likely to lead to a claim'. Since this condition is open to wide interpretation, it is helpful for architects to establish a positive advisory relationship with their broker or insurer.

Sustainability, energy saving and green issues

Matters which are considered relevant at the beginning of the twenty-first century.

Architects' responsibilities

Architects have responsibilities to their clients, their building users, the community and the wider world, as well as to their builders and consultants. Excessive resource – and especially energy – consumption and CO^2 generation are the most pressing problems facing the world: responsibility for resolving these problems lies most heavily on the industrialized world that has largely created them.

Around half the UK's CO^2 emissions are from building and buildings, two-thirds of which are from housing. It is stated government policy that by 2016 all new housing must be built to even higher carbon neutral standards or 'Level 6' in the Code for Sustainable Homes. This effectively means that the house is designed to need no space heating or cooling (the German passivhaus standard), and that residual energy use such as water heating, cooking, lighting and other appliances is balanced by at least as much ambient energy generated on site, for example by photovoltaic panels or wind turbines.

The three keys to successful design to meet the passivhaus standard are:

- Super-insulation of fabric and glazing – for example 400 mm of cellulose fibre or 200 mm of phenolic foam roof insulation.
- Design for effective control of internal and external heat gains – for example in passive solar design, heat reclaim ventilation, etc.
- Incorporation of available thermal mass – for example in dense floor and internal wall materials to absorb and even out heat gains.

New buildings are only a small fraction of the national stock: although designing new buildings to high standards is vital, the bulk of the problem lies with the poor standards of existing buildings.

The vast amount of alteration and refurbishment work represents the major opportunity that most people have to improve the environment and their own future.

Constraints on maximizing environmental improvements to some existing buildings include poor siting, overshadowing and historic building restrictions; the one advantage that many existing buildings have is substantial thermal mass, increasingly valuable in an age of global warming.

Land use planning and transport

New development should increase density and integrate uses to minimize transport (which accounts for over 30 per cent of UK CO_2); planning and facilities to encourage public transport, electric vehicles and cycle use should be included. Food and biomass production should ideally be allowed for locally. Site layouts should be solar oriented and minimize overshadowing.

Landscape design

- Direct enhancements of the environmental performance of buildings: shelter planting both for wind breaks and climbers attached to buildings; deciduous planting for seasonal shade (planted pergolas are more controllable than tree planting which may grow to shade solar panels and PVs); planted roofs for micro-climate, insulation and membrane protection; water conservation ponds for reuse and amenity; reed bed sewage treatment; biofuel cropping.

- Indirect enhancements in terms of the quality of life and the biosphere: planted roofs, permeable/informal pavings and sustainable drainage systems to minimize flooding; indigenous and site specific planting; allotments; composting provision; wildlife supportive planting to improve habitats and biodiversity.
- Process enhancements to minimize construction damage: thorough landscape surveys followed by enforceable wildlife and planting protection plans; pollution control during construction; high quality and motivated site management to prevent damage and promote landscape protection.

Environmental building design

Principal glazed elevations should be oriented south or between SW and SE to maximize useful solar gain passively and actively, without shading or obstruction of low angle winter sun but – and this is vital as the climate warms – with adequate secure ventilation and shading against high angle summer sun to prevent overheating; deciduous planting can provide seasonally adjusting shade at low cost. Northerly elevations for housing should have least glazing, though for some building types with high internal heat gains, such as offices, maximizing daylight via north lights may be a more effective energy saving measure.

New glazing should be to the best standards, for example triple soft-coat low-e glazing, gas-filled, thermal-spacers to centre pane U-values below 0.7 $Wm^2°C$.

Window location and design should allow for cross flow and high and low level ventilation including secure night ventilation to make best use of thermal mass.

Housing should be planned to provide principal spaces towards the south and 'buffer spaces' – usually service areas that can be heated to a lower temperature – to the north.

Super-insulated walling and roofing should be combined with dense internal linings, structure, floors and partitioning to provide appropriate thermal mass.

Conservatories can be used effectively as passive solar sunspaces but should not be substituted for basic space; they should be separated by insulated walling and glazing from other parts of the building. If they are heated at all, for frost protection of plants for example, they need to be separately thermostatically controlled so that lower temperatures are maintained; they need to be securely vented at high and low level to prevent overheating in summer and south facing sunspaces will need external shading or solar control glass in addition.

Building services

The objective should be to simplify and reduce building services to a minimum.

Complex services tend to increase both capital and maintenance costs and reduce user satisfaction through lack of understanding and control.

Where heating or cooling systems are necessary in existing buildings, radiant types such as underfloor water pipework tend to be most efficient for the majority of building types, especially high spaces. Local controls, such as thermostatic radiator valves, are important to allow for varying conditions and to avoid wasted heating; efficiency of existing systems can be improved by more specific control systems allowing for different temperatures in different zones and weather compensation.

Air conditioning should not be needed for normal occupation and should be excluded from new building designs.

Hot water services should be concentrated around heat sources and storage to minimize heat loss from pipework; wherever possible, hot water should be preheated by solar panels with high capacity super-insulated storage so as to avoid fuel use during summer.

Subject to site and planning restrictions, wind turbine installations should be considered with photovoltaics as a more costly, though more adaptable, alternative for providing site generated electricity which can also be grid connected.

Where substantial heating is required in larger existing buildings, combined heat and power (CHP) systems can provide heat and electrical generation simultaneously at high efficiency; biofuel boilers using wood pellets, wood chips, straw, logs, etc. are available to very high efficiencies and levels of automation, though local fuel availability and maintenance issues need to be resolved.

Ventilation systems are likely to be required because of the very high standards of airtightness required in new buildings; humidity-sensitive passive stack systems can be ideal domestically; powered heat reclaim vent systems are advisable for larger or more complex buildings.

Daylighting and artificial lighting should be considered together. High levels of daylight will reduce electrical consumption for lighting but glare may need to be controlled; use of horizontal blinds, light shelves, etc. can improve daylighting in deep plan spaces while reducing glare at the perimeter. Artificial lighting should be high efficiency, i.e. fluorescent or discharge lamps, and should be locally controlled or daylight/occupancy-sensor controlled in larger buildings. Both light fittings and window glazing need to be regularly cleaned to maintain efficiency.

Water consumption should be reduced by use of low water use appliances such as spray, percussive or electronic taps, low flush cisterns, fine spray showers, etc. Where site conditions permit, installation of below ground rainwater cisterns to collect roof drainage for use in WC flushing, external taps, etc., plus washing machine and bathing use if appropriately filtered, can be cost-effective due to savings on both water metering and sewerage charges. Grey water systems filter and recycle waste water from showers, baths and washing machines and need less tank space but require more maintenance than rainwater systems.

Materials

Environmental concerns should figure prominently alongside issues of function, aesthetics and cost in the selection of materials by architects. The environmental implications of particular materials specification are often complex and it may prove most practical to refer to the guides available such as 'BRE Green Guide to Specification'.

There are three main areas for environmental consideration:

- Embodied energy – the sum of all energy used in the extraction, processing, manufacture and delivery of a material. One of the best known high embodied energy materials is aluminium whose extraction and processing from bauxite requires very high energy input, though recycling and the use of 'green' hydro-electric power for smelting immediately complicate the picture.
- Toxicity – toxic pollution arising from extraction, processing and manufacture: toxins emitted in the installation and use of a material; toxins emitted in the decay, demolition and disposal of a material. PVC is probably the most notorious building material in this respect with both its manufacture and disposal at risk of being seriously toxic. Many materials including solvents (paints, preservatives, liquid tanking, etc.) and glues containing formaldehyde (as in chipboard, MDF, etc.) are best known for emitting toxic pollution in application and during occupation of buildings.
- Sourcing – the environmental implications of obtaining a material from a particular source or type of supplier. The best publicized issue in this respect is the one regarding

unsustainable forestry where the use of timber (generally an environmentally benign material), extracted in a non-environmental way, has led to widespread bans on its use without third party certification. The most respected certifier is the Forestry Stewardship Council (FSC) who have sustained independent probity over many years; the PEFC (Programme for Endorsement of Forest Certification) is also worthy of consideration.

In virtually all cases, there are more acceptable substitutes for environmentally damaging materials, though in some cases the substitutes may be less widely available or more costly. Some examples are given below:

Cement	Lime/cement reduction by PFA in mix
Chipboard and MDF	Timber/oriented strand board (OSB)/softwood plywood
Fibreglass/mineral wool	Cellulose fibre/sheep's wool
Lead sheet roofing	Tin-coated stainless steel
Oil-based insulation foams	Cork/foamed glass
PVC rainwater goods	Galvanized steel
PVC drainage goods	Clayware/polypropylene/ Polythene/Stainless steel
PVC roof membranes	EPDM, etc.
PVC-sheathed cables	Rubber-sheathed cables
Rainforest hardwoods	FSC Certified/temperate sourced hardwoods
Solvent-based paints, etc.	Waterbased/eco paints
Timber preservatives	No preservative/Boron preservatives
Vinyl flooring	Linoleum/natural rubber

In few cases are the substitutes either a perfect substitute or entirely free of adverse environmental consequences; the guides referred to above provide more details.

In some cases, there are serious practical disadvantages to the substitutes, for example there are no benign insulants to compare in performance for an equivalent thickness to the high performance petro-chemical foams such as phenolic foam and isocyanurate, which are nearly twice as effective as cellulose fibre or sheep's wool. Architects and their clients may decide that this is a more environmentally acceptable use of petroleum, rather than as petrol, and that the space saving is worth achieving.

Finishes

Reducing the use of finishes is generally environmentally beneficial: unfinished materials tend to be better quality, less processed, last longer and require less maintenance, thus reducing future environmental burdens; their higher capital cost is quickly offset once cycles of redecoration or renewal are considered. For example, a stone floor may cost more than a good quality carpet on a screeded floor but once the carpet requires replacement, the stone is quickly seen to have been the economic choice.

Unfinished materials are easier and more valuable to recycle or reuse since their lack of finishes makes them both easier to inspect and simpler to process.

Sources: *Green Guide to the Architect's Job Book*
BRE Green Guide to Housing Specification

Anthropometric data

Standing

Dimensions given are the average for British men and women. They include an allowance for clothing and shoes.

Sitting

Dimensions given are the average for British men and women. They include an allowance for clothing and shoes.

forward reach

| | men | 850 |
| | women | 780 |

MEN ┬ WOMEN

	MEN	WOMEN
top of head	+1340	+1280
eye level	+1220	+1170
shoulder height	+1040	+0985
u/s elbow	+0665	+0650
top of thigh	+0590	+0590
average seat height	+0440	+0440
floor	±0000	±0000

| from buttocks to back of calf | men | 480 |
| | women | 470 |

| from buttocks to front of knee | men | 615 |
| | women | 570 |

| extended leg | men | 1090 |
| | women | 965 |

Wheelchairs

	MEN	WOMEN
high reach	+1715	+1575
oblique reach	+1595	+1465
forward reach	+1410	+1295
head height	+1330	+1255
eye level	+1220	+1155
shoulder	+1035	+0990
elbow	+0690	+0690
thigh	+0605	+0605
seat	+0485	+0475
knuckle	+0380	+0420
foot height	+0145	+0165
floor	±0000	±0000

+ 0965 top of chair
+0710 top of arm rest
+0560 top of wheel
+0000 floor

reach over high table   men   600
                         women 550

1075
630
465

Turning circle ⌀ mm
large chair   1700
standard chair   1500
indoor chair   1400

Circulation

two self propelled wheelchairs
1800

two wheelchairs with attendants
1700

one self propelled wheelchair
900 (760 min)

one wheelchair with attendant
800

LIFT suitable for a wheelchair user
Car of at least 1100 wide × 1400 long internally
Clear landing area of 1500 × 1500
Clear door opening of 800
Lift controls set between +900 and +1200 h
and set at least 300 mm in from front wall inside car

1100
1400
300
800
1500
1500

100 min high kerb
to open sides
min width of ramp surface
1000 clear of obstructions
(900 clear for dwellings)

RAMPS

non-slip surface ↓

NB
Minimum dimensions of landings to be clear of door swings

1200
min length bottom landing

max 5 m long ramp for 1:12 slope which is max permitted slope

1500
min length intermediate landings

max 10 m long ramp for 1:15 slope

1200
min length top landing

Wheelchair access

Entrance lobbies & corridors – not in dwellings

min clear opening for entrance doors with min 300 clear space alongside leading edge of door

minimum width for entrance lobbies

minimum clear space between door swings

minimum clear space for manoeuvring chair into side doorways

minimum clear opening for internal doors

minimum unobstructed widths for corridors

Double doors to have at least one leaf with 800 mm clear opening

NB:

Minimum clear opening for doorways means clear of door thickness, doorstops and any full length pull handle.

In practice this requires a 1000 mm doorset to achieve a minimum 800 clear opening.

Principal entrance doors, doors in frequent use and doors across circulation routes should have glazed panels at least between heights of +0900 and +1500 but preferably with the u/s at +0450.

Means of Escape

See Approved Document B of the Building Regulations and BS 5588: Part 8: 1999

Audience & Spectator Seating

Six wheelchair spaces or 1/100th of spectator seating whichever is greater should be provided.

Each space to be 1400 × 900 with unobstructed view and adjacent to seated companions. The space may be created by readily removing seats for the occasion.

DWELLINGS

NOTE; Part M of the Building Regulations applies only to NEW DWELLINGS, not to existing dwellings nor extensions to existing dwellings.

ENTRANCE DOORS to have min clear opening 775 mm

DOORWAYS in relation to CORRIDORS as table below:

Doorway – clear opening mm	Corridor – minimum width mm
750 or wider	900 when approach head-on
750	1200 when approach not head-on
775	1050 when approach not head-on
800	900 when approach not head-on

A WC must be provided in the entrance storey of a dwelling – or the principal storey if there are no habitable rooms at the entrance level.

This WC compartment must be min. 900 wide with an opening-out door and a clear space 750 deep in front of the pan clear of any wash basin. This WC may be part of a bathroom.

NOTE

No frameless glass doors. No revolving doors unless very large as in airports. Door pulls and lever handles to be easy opening. Any door closers to be adjusted to open with minimum force and close slowly.

ACCESS to dwellings not steeper than 1:20 or ramps as shown on opposite page with dropped kerbs to any pavements.

ELECTRICAL SWITCHES & SOCKETS

Height of switches, socket outlets, bell pushes, telephone jacks, TV aerial sockets, etc. to be positioned between +0450 and +1200 above FFL.

Sources:

Approved Document M of the Building Regulations 2004

Metric Handbook

Designing for Accessibility

Furniture and fittings data

Living room

900

950

armchair

1500

two seater sofa

2100

three seater sofa

+1340

+0750 to 1200

+0440

±0000

700

750

750

750

coffee tables – 400 h

1000

500

400

+0750
+0600

+0000

1500

Home office desk and chair

1500

750

500

750

500

+1300

+700

±0000

upright piano

1500

650

900

350

+520

±0000

piano stool

1450 to 1500

1450 to 1800

grand piano 970 h

240

240

265

340

54% of books
will fit onto
shelves of
these clear
dimensions

25%
as above

18%
as above
(3% may
be larger)

155
180
255

bookshelves

Television

906

611

+1075

+0000

125

AUDIO-VISUAL AND MUSIC STORAGE
record sleeve   = 315 × 315 ×   3
video tape box   = 204 × 121 × 30
compact disc box = 142 × 125 × 12
DVD box   = 135 × 192 × 14
sheet music   = 340 × 250 max page size

+2250

±0000

550

250

longcase clock

Kitchen

standard worktop
600

300 to 350

top of tall cabinets	+2250 –
maximum reach	+2000 –
top of low wall cupboards	+1950 –
u/s cooker hood eye level	+1650 – / +1600 –
u/s wall cupboards	+1350 –
electric sockets	+1100 –
worktop top of appliances drawer line	+0900 – / +0850 – / +0740 –
plinth height	+0150 to – 0100
FFL	±0000 –

space for pipework ↗   cabinet depth

530   65   50

900

walking with tray

650

walking between wall and counter

450

squeezing between wall and counter

dishwasher   low level oven

700   1100

1150

800

SPACE needed in front of appliances under worktop

1200
minumum
space between
counters

KITCHEN TRIANGLE

To achieve a compact yet workable kitchen the triangle formed by lines linking sink to cooker and refrigerator should total between 3.6 m and 6.6 m long with a maximum of 7.0 m. Avoid circulation through the triangle – particularly between sink and cooker which should not be more than 1.8 m apart.

Allow a minimum 400 mm between hob and sink and any tall cupboards for elbow room.

Cooker should not be positioned near door or in front of window.

Keep electric sockets well away from sink area.

Provide lighting over worktops.

Install extractor fan over hob.

CABINETS width dimensions

600 tall cupboard/appliance housing 500 tall cupboard 300 tall cupboard 300 400 500 600 cupboard/appliance housing 800 cupboard/sink base 1000 cupboard/sink base/corner cupboard 1200 900 corner cupboard

wall cupboards

APPLIANCES

1000 1000 1200 600

500

+1650
+0900
+0150
+0000

600
ovens and oven ranges
1100

580
500
hob

600
850
under worktop single oven/dishwasher/larder fridge etc

600
900
built-in double oven

500
330
freestanding microwave

built in microwave

500
450

500
850
small refrigerator

600
1460
medium refrigerator

600
1750
fridge/freezer

908
1760
refrigerator

600
1800
built-in fridge/freezer

Dining room

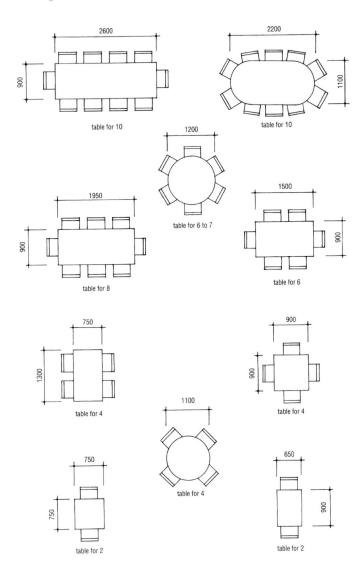

2600

900

table for 10

2200

1100

table for 10

1200

table for 6 to 7

1950

900

table for 8

1500

900

table for 6

750

1300

table for 4

900

900

table for 4

750

750

table for 2

1100

table for 4

650

900

table for 2

— + 1340 top of man's head

— + 1200 eye level

— + 1000 chair back

— + 0740 table top

— + 0440 seat

— ± 0000 FFL

| 550 | 450 |
| sitting space | foot space |

750
(650 wide per
minimum space needed   place setting)
to get up and sit down

1500

450

sideboard   900 mm h

350

740

bar stool

450

450

dining chair

Bedroom

1800
1500
1350

1900
2000

double beds

900

1900

single beds

750

550   minimum space
between beds with
room for small table

450   minimum space needed at sides
and ends for making bed –
ideally should be 700 mm

SPACE round beds   450

650

1250

cot – 1000 h

bedside table

450

450

600

— + 1400 head room

— + 1000 bedhead

— + 0550 top of mattress

— ± 0000 FFL

+1700
+1350

+0300
+0000

2000   1000

bunk beds

+1550
TO
+1100

+0000

2000

cabin bed

Short clothes hanging space

HANGING CLOTHES – average space requirements

Long clothes hanging space

a rail at this height will accommodate the longest garment while leaving space under shorter clothes for shoes

chest of drawers – 900 h

wardrobe – 1700 to 2100 h

BOOTS and SHOES	size overall per pair
men's wellington boots	$330 \times 240 \times 430\,h$
men's walking shoes	$330 \times 240 \times 120\,h$
women's high heeled shoes	$280 \times 180 \times 150\,h$
women's flat shoes	$280 \times 180 \times 90\,h$

Bathroom

long

standard

short

sitz

BATH

+2200 min. ceiling
+2100 top of shower rail
+1150 c/l mixer
+0530 top of bath
+0140 bottom of bath
±0000 FFL

DOUBLE ENDED

SHOWER-BATH

SHOWER

+2200 min. ceiling
+2100 top of shower rail
+1250 c/l mixer
+1050 grab rail
+0150 top of tray
±0000 FFL

BASIN

BIDET

bowl basin

corner wc

URINAL

WC

Miscellaneous data

Laundry and utility

washing machine and dryer

spin dryer

ironing board

Cleaning and refuse

broom

vacuum cleaner

dustbin

4 step ladder

140L wheeled bin
floor space required 680x750

240L wheeled bin
floor space required 780x940

1100L eurobin
floor space required 1575x1190

Hall and shed

1100

1000

1100

850   300

buggy/pushchair

1800

1070

560

bicycle

550

900

deckchair

1100

860

675

chest freezer

330   440

330

230

wine rack

Garden

240   450

550

meter box

1200

620

600

wheelbarrow

1300

950

360

lawnmower

560

1650

grass rake

1450

rake

1000

spade & fork

Domestic garages

2400
200 | 1600 | 600 ←minimum to get out of car
150
4300
average car size 4000 × 1600
150
2120
clear opening for 1981 (6'6") w door & frame
SINGLE GARAGE minimum size

2850
200 | 1700 | 950 ←allows for most doors to open fully
200
standard garage door heights are 1981 (6'6") and 2134 (7'0")
4900
family saloon 4500 × 1700
200
2275
clear opening for 2134 (7'0") w door & frame
SINGLE GARAGE for family saloon

3300
overhead beam for stirrup grip
5200
3000
800 min
SINGLE GARAGE for wheelchair user

4400
family saloon | mini
4900
4400
clear opening for 4267 (14'0") w door and frame

4700
family saloon | average sized car
4900
clear opening for

6050
workbench
6000
5020
clear opening for 4878 (16'0") w door and frame

Vehicle sizes and parking bay

VEHICLE	l	w*	h	radius
wheelchair – standard	1075	630	965	1500
bicycle	1800	560	1070	–
motor bicycle	2250	600	800	–
small car (Mini)	3050	1400	1350	4800
average sized car	4000	1600	1350	5250
family saloon	4500	1700	1460	5500
caravan – average touring	4500	2100	2500	–
Rolls Royce	5350	1900	1670	6350
hearse	5900	2000	1900	
skip lorry	7000	2500*	3350	8700
dustcart – medium capacity	7400	2290*	4000	7000
fire engine – medium size	8000	2290*	4000	7600
furniture van	11 000	2500*	4230	10 050

The standard parking bay is 2400 x 4800 which will accomodate most European cars.

2800 x 5800 will accommodate American and other large cars.

3300 x 5200 is the required minimum for a disabled parking bay.

*widths exclude wing mirrors which may add 600 to 800 mm to the body width

Radii should not necessarily be considered as turning circles. Turning circles depend upon the speed the vehicle is travelling, the hand of the driver (left hand differs from right), and overhang, particularly at front and back of vehicle. Allow 1.2 m clear space both sides of carriageway to accommodate overhang.

Bicycle parking

Up/down parking
with ramps for parking alternate cycles
at a higher level
90° parking @ minimum 310 mm centres
45° parking @ minimum 450 mm centres

Source: Autopa Ltd

Sanitary provision for public buildings

Summary of *minimum* facilities

There should be separate facilities for men and women.

Generally washbasins should be provided in equal numbers to WCs with one for every five urinals.

In most public buildings, a minimum of two WCs should be provided so that one may act as a reserve if the other is out of order.

Disabled toilets

Where there is space for only one toilet in a building, it should be a wheelchair accessible unisex toilet, wide enough to accommodate a standing height wash basin.

At least one wheelchair accessible WC should be provided at each location in a building where sanitary facilities are provided.

At least one WC cubicle should be provided in separate sex toilet accommodation for use by ambulant disabled people. In addition, where there are four or more WC cubicles in separate sex toilet accommodation, one of these should be an enlarged cubicle for use by people who need extra space.

Offices and shops

No. of persons	No. of WCs and basins
Up to 15	1
16–30	2
31–50	3
51–75	4
76–100	5
over 100	1 extra for each additional 25

There is no specific requirement for urinals, but if provided men's facilities may be reduced to:

No. of persons	No. of WCs and basins
Up to 20	1
21–45	2
46–75	3
76–100	4
over 100	1 extra for each additional 25

Factories

WCs	1 per 25 persons
Urinals	No specific requirement
Basins	1 per 20 persons for clean processes
	1 per 10 persons for dirty processes
	1 per 5 persons for injurious processes

Restaurants

	Men		Women	
WCs	Up to 400:	1 per 100	Up to 200:	2 per 100
	Over 400:	1 extra for each additional 250 or part thereof	Over 200:	1 extra for each additional 100 or part thereof

Urinals 1 per 25 persons

Basins 1 per WC and 1 per 5 urinals   1 per 2 WCs

Concert halls, theatres and similar buildings for public entertainment

	Men		Women	
WCs	Up to 250:	1	Up to 50:	2
	Over 250:	1 extra for each additional 500 or part thereof	50–100:	3
			Over 100:	1 extra for each additional 40 or part thereof

Urinals Up to 100: 2
Over 100:   1 extra for each
additional 80 or
part thereof

Cinemas

	Men		*Women*	
WCs	Up to 250: 1		Up to 75: 2	
	Over 250:	1 extra for each additional 500 or part thereof	76–100: 3	
			Over 100:	1 extra for each additional 80 or part thereof

Urinals Up to 200: 2
Over 200:   1 extra for each
additional 100 or
part thereof

WC compartments for disabled people

Wheelchair user

+1400 top vertical rail

+0800 bottom vertical rail
+0650 c/l horizontal rails

+0480 pan height

±0000 FFL

support rails to be 35 mm ø

lever handle →

pull rail →

↖ hinged support rail

single leaf doorset

mirror

mirror size 900 h × 400 w fixed with u/s at 900 above FFL

700 to 750

2200

These arrangements show the minimum provision that will comply with the Approved Document M of the Building Regulations 2004 edition

frontal transfer to WC

sideways transfer to WC

at the basin

Ambulant disabled user

– +1350 top vertical rail

– +0750 bottom vertical rail
– +0700 c/l horizontal rails
– +0480 pan height

– ±0000 FFL

SECTION

Note that this arrangement
presupposes a wash handbasin
elsewhere

400   500

800

1500
(1700)
(if door opening in)

PLAN

480

wc height

950

900

basin height

Trees for towns

Name	Ht m 25 yrs	Ht m mature	Location	Description
Acacia – false *Robinia pseudoacacia*	14	21	S	Open headed, rugged bark, thorny twigs. Ornamental and very drought and pollution tolerant
Ailanthus *Altissima* (tree of heaven)	18	21	S	Fast growing, imposing, with ash-like leaves. Female trees produce spectacular red fruit. Tolerant of industrial pollution
Almond *Prunus dulcis*	7	8	S	Pink or white flowers early spring, before dark green finely-toothed leaves and velvety green fruit
Birch – Himalayan *Betula utilis jaquemontii*	10	18	R	Vivid white bark, very strong upright stem. Forms a striking avenue. Casts only light shade
Catalpa *Bignonioides* (Indian bean)	10	12	P	Wide, domed crown, heart-shaped leaves, white flowers July, with beans in hot weather. Avoid cold/exposed sites. Good specimen tree
Cherry – gean* *Prunus avium* 'Plena'	12	15	S	One of the loveliest cherries, hardy, invariably producing masses of pure white drooping double flowers
Cherry – bird* *Prunus padus* 'Albertii'	7	14	S	Upright form of native 'bird cherry'. Racemes of white flowers in May, ideal for street planting
Chestnut – red *Aesculus × carnea* 'Briottii'	7	12	A	Slow growing, compact form with deep crimson flowers in June. Especially suitable for streets and avenues
Crab apple – *Malus floribunda*	5	9	S	Arching branches with early crimson flowers opening to white. Popular in streets and gardens. Scab and mildew-resistant
Crab apple *Malus tschonoskii*	6	12	S	Strong growing conical habit, good for narrow streets. Flowers tinged pink. Excellent autumn colour
Hawthorn (May) *Crataegus × lavellei*	6	8	S	Dense headed, with long glossy dark green leaves until December. Orange fruit persisting until January
Lime – silver *Tilia tomentosa*	10	18	R	Pyramidal dense habit, with large dark green leaves with white felted undersides. Aphid-free, so no drips – good for car-parking areas
Maidenhair *Ginko biloba*	7	30	P	Slow growing superb specimen tree, pale green, small, fan-shaped leaves turning yellow in autumn. Pollution-tolerant
Maple – field* *Acer campestre* 'Streetwise'	7	10	S	Neat form with dominant central leader and balanced crown. Brilliant autumn colour, very hardy

Trees for towns – continued

Name	Ht m 25 yrs	Ht m mature	Location	Description
Maple – silver *Acer saccarinum* 'Laciniatum'	15	25	R	Fast growing with pale green deeply cut leaves turning clear yellow in autumn. Good for wide roadsides. Not for windy sites
Mountain ash* *Sorbus aucuparia*	7	8	S	Strong growing with neat upright habit. Abundant bright orange berries in autumn. Good for street planting in grass verges
Oak – evergreen *Quercus ilex* (Holm oak)	7	28	P	Slow growing, broad-leaved evergreen specimen tree for parks. Good for coastal regions but not for coldest inland areas
Oak – scarlet *Quercus coccinea* 'Splendens'	15	18	P	Superb tree for large parks, with shiny dark green leaves. Spectacular crimson leaf colour in autumn. Requires lime-free soil
Plane – London *Platanus* × *hispanica*	12	28	S	Large, fast growing with boldly lobed leaves and flaking bark. Good street tree, tolerant of atmospheric pollution
Sycamore *Acer pseudoplatanus*	12	25	R	Fast growing. Wide-headed tree. Good for quick shelter in difficult situations and maritime sites. Tolerant of pollution
Tulip tree *Liriodendron tulipifera*	12	30	A	Fast growing, three-lobed leaves turning butter yellow. Good for avenues. Green/white July flowers on mature trees. Smoke-tolerant
Whitebeam* *Sorbus aria* 'Majestica'	7	12	S	Handsome round head, large bright green leaves with vivid white undersides. Very hardy and smoke-resistant

* = native tree
A = avenue
P = park
R = roadside
S = street

Trees listed above are recommended for various urban situations. Other varieties may be equally suitable, but check that they do not have invasive root runs, surface roots, brittle branches or cannot tolerate pollution.

All the trees listed, except the evergreen oak, are deciduous. Conifers are generally too large for most urban situations, and very few can cope with atmospheric pollution.

Sources: *The Hillier Designer's Guide to Landscape Plants Tree Planting Year 1973*

Hedges

Name	Leaves	Flowers	Growth	Prune	Site	Description
Beech* *Fagus silvatica*	D	–	fast	Aug	W, C	Pale green leaves in spring turning to rich copper, persisting through winter
Berberis *Berberis darwinii*	E	❀	fast	July	Sh	Shiny dark green prickly foliage, orange flowers in May followed by blue berries
Box – common* *Buxus sempervirens*	E	–	slow	Aug–Sep	Sh	Bushy shrub with glossy dark green leaves. Use the variety 'Suffruticosa' for dwarf edging
Cotoneaster *Cotoneaster sinosii*	SE	❀	medium	Feb–Aug	Sh	Leathery deep green leaves, small white flowers in June and persistent red berries in autumn
Eleagnus *Eleagnus pungens* 'Maculata'	E	–	fast	April	W, Sh	Leathery leaves with bright gold splash on slightly prickly twigs making dense hedge
Escallonia *Escallonia* 'C. F. Ball'	E	❀	medium	Oct	St, W	Glossy dark green leaves and crimson flowers June–Oct. Good for seaside. Not for cold areas.
Firethorn *Pyracantha* 'Watereri'	SE	❀	fast	May–July	Sh	Dense prickly stems, clusters of small white flowers in June and bright red fruits in autumn
Hawthorn (May)* *Crataegus monogyna*	D	❀	fast	July–Mar	W, Wet	Very thorny, white or pink blossom with small red haws in autumn
Holly* *Ilex aquifolium*	E	–	slow	Aug	Sh, W	Very dense prickly dark green leaves, bright red berries if both male and female plants adjacent
Hornbeam* *Carpinus betulus*	D	–	medium	Aug	Wet, Sh	Similar to beech, retaining coppery leaves in winter. Good for frost pockets and pleaching
Laurel *Prunus laurocerasus*	E	❀	medium	Aug	W, Sh	Large leathery glossy green leaves, long white flower spikes in April if buds not pruned
Photinia *P. × fraserii* 'Red Robin'	E	–	medium	Mar	–	Brilliant red new growth persisting until summer, reverting to dark green in winter
Privet *Ligustrum ovalifolium*	SE	–	fast	as nec.	Sh	Dense hedge with medium–sized green leaves, clusters of creamy white flowers in July
Yew* *Taxus baccata*	E	–	slow	Aug	W, C, Sh	Very hardy, dense dark green needles with bright red fruits attractive to birds

* = native species; E = evergreen; D = deciduous; SE = semi–evergreen; W = wind resistant;
C = will grow on chalk; Sh = will tolerate shade; St = will tolerate salt–laden winds.

Sources: Buckingham Nurseries Hedging catalogue
The Right Hedge for You

3
Structures

Design of structural elements can be carried out by permissible stress or ultimate limit state (ULS). Permissible stress limits the loading to a predetermined safe working stress, commonly known as elastic design as deformation of the element is recoverable (elastic). ULS factors the loads (partial safety factors) to be carried and the design is related to the potential ultimate failure of the structural element. Deflection of the structural element is limited to the elastic deformation of the material and the effect on what is being carried. There are different deflection limits for different materials.

Steel, concrete and masonry are generally designed to ULS; timber to permissible stress. For isolated steel beams and columns, permissible stress is generally more appropriate for steelwork design.

Examples given are using the less complicated permissible stress design.

Increasing complexity of wind loading codes and ULS design codes (including EuroCodes) are more suited for computer applications.

Information given is for guidance only and should give an indication of the size of structural members required to assist with developing a scheme. All structural elements should be checked by a qualified Chartered Structural Engineer for Building Regulation and construction purposes. Consultation with a Chartered Structural Engineer is advised at an early design stage to ensure structural feasibility of the proposals.

Weights of materials (for further information, see BS 648)

Material	Description	Quantity of unit	kg/m²	kg/m³
aluminium	cast			2770
aluminium roofing	longstrip	0.8 mm	3.70	
asphalt roofing	with vapour barrier	20 mm	47.00	
ballast	loose, graded			1600
bituminous felt roofing	3 layers + vapour barrier		11.10	
blockboard	sheet	18 mm	10.50	
blockwork	high strength	100 mm	220.00	
	aerated	100 mm	64.00	
	lightweight	100 mm	58.00	
	foundation	255 mm	197.00	
brass	cast			8425
brickwork	blue	115 mm	276.60	2405
	engineering	115 mm	250.00	2165
	sand/cement	115 mm	240.00	2085
	London stock	115 mm	212.00	1845
	fletton			1795
calcium silicate board	sheet	6 mm	5.80	
cement				1440
chalk				2125
chipboard	flooring grade C4	18 mm	13.25	
	furniture grade C1A	18 mm	11.75	
chippings	flat roof finish	1 layer	4.75	
clay	undisturbed			1925
concrete	reinforced 2% steel			2400
	plain			2300
copper	cast			8730
copper roofing	longstrip	0.6 mm	5.70	
cork	granulated			80
cork flooring	tiles	3.2 mm	3.00	
cork insulation	board	50 mm	6.50	
felt	roofing underlay		1.30	
glass	clear float	4 mm	10.00	
	clear float	6 mm	15.00	
	clear float	10 mm	25.00	
glass wool	quilt	100 mm	1.02	
gravel	loose			1600
hardboard	medium	6.4 mm	3.70	
hardboard	standard	3.2 mm	2.35	

Material	Description	Quantity of unit	kg/m²	kg/m³
hardwood	greenheart			1040
	oak			720
	iroko, teak			660
	mahogany			530
hardwood flooring	boards	23 mm	16.10	
iron	cast			7205
lead	cast			11 322
	sheet	code 4	20.40	
	sheet	code 7	35.72	
lime	lump			705
	quick			880
linoleum	sheet	3.2 mm	4.50	
MDF	sheet	18 mm	13.80	
mortar	lime			1680
parquet	flooring	15 mm	7.00	
partitions	plastered brick	115 + 25 mm	250.00	
	plastered block	100 + 25 mm	190.00	
	p/b & skim on timber studs	100 + 25 mm	120.00	
patent glazing	alum. bars @ 600 mm c/c	single	19.00	
	alum. bars @ 600 mm c/c	double	35.00	
paving	concrete	50 mm	122.00	
perspex	corrugated sheets		4.90	
plaster	lightweight – 2 coat	13 mm	10.20	
	hardwall – 2 coat	13 mm	11.60	
	lath and plaster		29.30	
plasterboard	gyproc wallboard	9.5 mm	9.00	
	plaster skimcoat	3 mm	2.20	
plywood	sheet	6 mm	4.10	
polystyrene	expanded, sheet	50 mm	0.75	
PVC roofing	single ply membrane	2 mm	2.50	
quarry tiles	laid in mortar	12.5 mm	32.00	
roofing tiles	clay – plain	100 mm gauge	77.00	
	clay – single pantile	315 mm gauge	42.00	
	concrete – double roman	343 mm gauge	45.00	
	concrete – flat slate	355 mm gauge	51.00	
rubber stud flooring	tiles	4 mm	5.90	

Weights of materials –   continued

Material	Description	Quantity of unit	kg/m²	kg/m³
sand	dry			1600
sarking	felt		1.30	
screed	cement/sand	50 mm	108.00	
shingle	coarse, graded, dry			1842
shingles	roof, untreated	95 mm gauge	8.09	
	tantalized	95 mm gauge	16.19	
slate	slab	25 mm	70.80	
slate roofing	best	4 mm	31.00	
	medium strong	5 mm	35.00	
	heavies	6 mm	40.00	
snow	fresh			96
	wet, compact			320
softboard	sheet	12.5 mm	14.45	
softwood	pitch pine, yew			670
	spruce			450
	western red cedar			390
softwood flooring	boards	22 mm	12.20	
soil	compact			2080
	loose			1440
stainless steel roofing	longstrip	0.4 mm	4.00	
steel	mild			7848
	sheet	1.3 mm	10.20	
stone	Bath			2100
	granite			2660
	marble			2720
	slate			2840
	York			2400
stone chippings				1760
tarmac		25 mm	53.70	
terrazzo	paving	16 mm	34.20	
thatch	including battens	300 mm	41.50	
timber	see hardwood softwood			
vinyl flooring	tiles	2 mm	4.00	
water				1000
weatherboarding	softwood	19 mm	7.30	
		25 mm	8.55	
woodwool	slabs	50 mm	36.60	
zinc	cast			6838
zinc roofing	longstrip	0.8 mm	5.70	

Newtons

The unit of force, the *newton*, is derived from the unit of mass through the relationship that force is equal to mass times the gravitational pull of 9.81 metres *per second per second* (9.81 m/s^2), in the direction of the force, e.g. 1 kilogram f = 9.81 newtons.

For approximate purposes 100 kgf = 1 kN.

Alternatively one newton is that force which, if applied to a mass of one kilogram, gives that mass an acceleration of one metre *per second per second* (1 m/s^2) in the direction of the force, so 1 N = 1 kg × 1 m/s^2.

When calculating the weight of materials for structures, the kilograms must be multiplied by 9.81 to get the equivalent figure in newtons (or 9.81 ÷ 1000 for kN).

As a general rule, the following expressions are used:

superimposed loads	kN/m^2
mass loads	kg/m^2 or kg/m^3
stress	N/mm^2
bending moment	kNm
shear	kN

1 N/mm	=	1 kN/m
1 N/mm^2	=	1 × 10^3 kN/m^2
1 kNm	=	1 × 10^6 Nmm

Imposed loads

Imposed floor loads (for further information, see BS 6399 Part 1)

Floor type	Distributed load kN/m^2*	Concentrated load kN*
Houses and blocks of flats not more than three storeys, no more than four self-contained units per floor	1.5	1.4
Bedrooms and dormitories except for those in single family dwelling units and in hotels and motels	1.5	1.8
Hotels bedrooms, hospital wards, toilet areas	2.0	1.8
Public, institutional and communal dining rooms, lounges, cafes and restaurants, billiard rooms	2.0	2.7
Operating theatres, X-ray rooms, utility rooms, reading rooms with no book storage	2.0	4.5
Offices for general use	2.5	2.7
Garages for vehicles under 2500 kg	2.5	9.0
Classrooms, chapels, banking halls	3.0	2.7
Hotel kitchens and laundries, laboratories	3.0	4.5
Offices with fixed computing equipment	3.5	4.5
Assembly buildings with fixed seating	4.0	3.6
Shop floors for retailing	4.0	3.6
Hotel bars	5.0	3.6
Assembly buildings without fixed seating, gymnasia, dance halls	5.0	3.6
Factories, workshops and similar buildings	5.0	4.5
Garages, parking and workshops for vehicles exceeding 2500 kg	To be determined for specific use	
Boiler rooms, plant rooms including weight of machinery	7.5	4.5
Bookstores, warehouses (per metre of storage height)	2.4	7.0
Stationery stores (per metre of storage height)	4.0	9.0

Floor type		Distributed load kN/m²*	Concentrated load kN*
Corridors, hallways and aisles, etc. in institutional-type buildings (not subjected to crowds or wheeled vehicles), hostels, guest houses, residential clubs and communal areas in flats over three storeys. Foot traffic only		3.0	4.5
Stairs and landings as above		3.0	4.0
Corridors, hallways and aisles, etc. in all other buildings including hotels, motels and institutional buildings. Foot traffic only		4.0	4.5
Stairs and landings as above		4.0	4.0
Corridors, hallways and aisles, etc. in all other buildings including hotels, motels and institutional buildings. Foot traffic only		5.0	4.5
Balconies	Single family dwelling units and communal areas in blocks of flats with limited use (no greater than three storeys)	1.5	1.4
	Guest houses, residential clubs and communal areas in blocks of flats over three storeys	Same as rooms to which they have access, but with a minimum of 3.0	1.5/m run concentrated at the outer edge
	All others	Same as rooms to which they have access, but with a minimum of 4.0	1.5/m run concentrated at the outer edge

* Whichever produces the greater stress or deflection

Reduction in total distributed imposed floor load

	1	2	3	4	5–10	10+
Number of floors including roof carried by member	1	2	3	4	5–10	10+
Percentage reduction in total distributed load on all floors carried by member	0	10	20	30	40	50 max
Area supported m^2	40	80	120	160	200	250
Percentage reduction in total distributed imposed load	0	5	10	15	20	25 max

Imposed roof loads (for further information, see BS 6399 Part 3)

Roof type	Comments	Distributed load kN/m^2*		Concentrated load kN*
All roofs	Where access is needed in addition to that needed for cleaning and repair	1.5	or	1.8
Flat roofs and sloping roofs up to 30°	Where no access is needed except for cleaning and repair	0.6	or	0.9
Roof slopes between 30° and 60° (α°) measured on plan	Where no access is needed except for cleaning and repair	$0.6 (60 - \alpha)/30$	or	0.9
Roof slopes 60° or more	0	0		0.9

* Whichever produces the greater stress.

Where access is needed for cleaning and repair, these loads assume spreader boards will be used during work on fragile roofs.

For buildings in areas of high snowfall, snow loading should be taken into consideration. The snow loading is a function of location, altitude and roof pitch. For buildings with parapets, valleys or changes in roof level, there can be local accumulation of snow from drifting. See BS 6399 Part 3 for further guidance.

Fire resistance

Minimum periods for elements of structure (minutes)

Building type		Basement storey		Ground and upper storeys			
		more than 10m deep	less than 10m deep	less than 5m high	less than 20m high	less than 30m high	more than 30m high
Flats and maisonettes		90	60	30[a]	60[c]	90[b]	120[b]
Houses		n/a	30[a]	30[a]	60[g]	n/a	n/a
Institutional[d], residential		90	60	30[a]	60	90	120[e]
Offices	without sprinklers	90	60	30[a]	60	90	X
	with sprinklers	60	60	30[a]	30[a]	60	120[e]
Shops & Commercial	without sprinklers	90	60	60	60	90	X
	with sprinklers	60	60	30[a]	60	60	120[e]
Assembly & Recreational	without sprinklers	90	60	60	60	90	X
	with sprinklers	60	60	30[a]	60	60	120[e]
Industrial	without sprinklers	120	90	60	90	120	X
	with sprinklers	90	60	30[a]	60	90	120[e]
Storage & other non-residential	without sprinklers	120	90	60	90	120	X
	with sprinklers	90	60	30[a]	60	90	120[e]
Car parks for light vehicles	open sided park	n/a	n/a	15[f]	15[f]	15[f]	60
	any other park	90	60	30[a]	60	90	120[e]

X = not permitted
a   Increased to 60 minutes for compartment walls separating buildings.
b   Reduced to 30 minutes for any floor within a maisonette, but not if that floor contributes to the support of the building.
c   As b above and, in the case of existing houses, of no more than three storeys being converted into flats. This may be reduced to 30 minutes providing the means of escape conform to section 2 of requirement B1.
d   Multi-storey hospitals should have a minimum 60 minutes standard.
e   Reduced to 90 minutes for elements not forming part of the structural frame.
f   As 'a' above and increased to 30 minutes for elements protecting the means of escape.
g   30 mins for 3 storey dwellings; 60 mins for compartment walls.

Source: *Building Regulations Approved Document B vol 2 –* Table A2.

Bending moments and beam formulae

Bending moments and deflection formulae

Type of beam	Loading diagram	Maximum bending moment	Maximum shear	Maximum deflection d
Freely supported with central load		$\dfrac{WL}{4}$	$\dfrac{WL}{2}$	$dc = \dfrac{WL^3}{48EI}$
Freely supported with distributed load		$\dfrac{WL}{8}$	$\dfrac{W}{2}$	$dc = \dfrac{5WL^3}{384EI}$
Freely supported with triangular load		$\dfrac{WL}{6}$	$\dfrac{W}{2}$	$dc = \dfrac{WL^3}{60EI}$
Fixed both ends with central load		$\dfrac{WL}{8}$	$\dfrac{W}{2}$	$dc = \dfrac{WL^3}{192EI}$
Fixed both ends with distributed load		$\dfrac{WL}{12}$	$\dfrac{W}{2}$	$dc = \dfrac{WL^3}{384EI}$
One end fixed, the other end freely supported		$\dfrac{WL}{8}$	$SA = \dfrac{5W}{8}$ $SB = \dfrac{3W}{8}$	$d = \dfrac{WL^3}{185EI}$ at x = 0.42 L
Cantilever with end load		WL	W	$dB = \dfrac{WL^3}{3EI}$
Cantilever with distributed load		$\dfrac{WL}{12}$	W	$dB = \dfrac{WL^3}{8EI}$

W = total load   ↓ = point load
w = kN/m   ▥ = distributed load
L = length   ↑ = free support
E = modulus of elasticity
I = moment of inertia   = fixed support
S = shear

Safe loads on subsoils (BS 8004: 1986)

Presumed allowable bearing values under static loading

Subsoil	Type	Bearing kN/m^2
Rocks	Strong igneous and gneissic rocks in sound condition	10 000
	Strong limestones and sandstones	4000
	Schists and slates	3000
	Strong shales, mudstones and siltstones	2000
Non-cohesive soils	Dense gravel, dense sand and gravel	>600
	Medium dense gravel, medium dense sand and gravel	<200 to 600
	Loose gravel, loose sand and gravel	<200
	Compact sand	>300
	Medium dense sand	100 to 200
	Loose sand	<100
Cohesive soils	Very stiff boulder clays, hard clays	300 to 600
	Stiff clays	150 to 300
	Firm clays	75 to 150
	Soft clays and silts	<75

Notes:
1 These values are for preliminary design only. Foundations always require site investigation first.
2 No values are given for very soft clays and silts; peat and organic soils; made-up or filled ground as presumably these would be thought unsuitable for any building.
3 Values for **Rocks** assume that foundations are carried down to unweathered rock.
4 Widths of foundations for **Non-cohesive soils** to be not less than one metre.
5 **Cohesive soils** are susceptible to long-term settlement.
6 Generally foundations should not be less than 1.0 to 1.3 m depth to allow for soil swell or shrink, frost and vegetation attack.

Timber (BS 5268: Part 2: 1996)

Grade stress and moduli of elasticity for various strength classes

Strength Class	Bending parallel to grain N/mm²	Tension parallel to grain N/mm²	Compression parallel to grain N/mm²	Compression* perpendicular to grain N/mm²		Shear parallel to grain N/mm²	Modulus of elasticity		Density average Kg/m³
							Mean N/mm²	minimum N/mm²	
C14	4.1	2.5	5.2	2.1	1.6	0.60	6800	4600	350
C16	5.3	3.2	6.8	2.2	1.7	0.67	8800	5800	370
C18	5.8	3.5	7.1	2.2	1.7	0.67	9100	6000	380
C22	6.8	4.1	7.5	2.3	1.7	0.71	9700	6500	410
C24	7.5	4.5	7.9	2.4	1.9	0.71	10800	7200	420
TR26	10.0	6.0	8.2	2.5	2.0	1.10	11000	7400	450
C27	10.0	6.0	8.2	2.5	2.0	1.10	12300	8200	450
C30	11.0	6.6	8.6	2.7	2.2	1.20	12300	8200	460
C35	12.0	7.2	8.7	2.9	2.4	1.30	13400	9000	480
C40	13.0	7.8	8.7	3.0	2.6	1.40	14500	10000	500
D30	9.0	5.4	8.1	2.8	2.2	1.40	9500	6000	640
D35	11.0	6.6	8.6	3.4	2.6	1.70	10000	6500	670
D40	12.5	7.5	12.6	3.9	3.0	2.00	10800	7500	700
D50	16.0	9.6	15.2	4.5	3.5	2.20	15000	12600	780
D60	18.0	10.8	18.0	5.2	4.0	2.40	18500	15600	840
D70	23.0	13.8	23.0	6.0	4.6	2.60	21000	18000	1080

Notes:

C14–C40 are for softwoods

C16 is considered to be sufficient for general use (former classification = SC3)

C24 is a good general quality timber (former classification = SC4)

TR26 is for manufactured softwood trusses

D30–40 are for hardwoods

* Where the specification prohibits wane at bearing areas, use the higher value

Rectangular timber beam formula (uniformly distributed load)

1 Obtain the total imposed and dead loading for the beam (W) in kN.
2 Select a strength class of timber to define bending stress (σ) in N/mm^2 and modulus of elasticity (E) in N/mm^2.
3 Choose breadth of beam (b) in mm.
4 Calculate the maximum bending moment (M) in kNm.

Check stress (σ):

$$M = \frac{WL}{8}$$

$$M = \sigma Z, \text{ and } Z = \frac{bd^2}{6}$$

$$\therefore \quad M = \sigma \frac{bd^2}{6} \text{ or } db^2 = \frac{6M}{\sigma}$$

$$\text{hence } d = \sqrt{\frac{WL \times 6 \times 10^6}{8 \times b \times \sigma}}$$

Check deflection (δ):

For spans up to 4.67 m, maximum deflection allowable is span $\times$ 0.003. Above 4.67 m deflection is limited to 14 mm for domestic floors.

For a single member, use E_{min}

$$\delta = L \times 0.003 = \frac{5WL^3}{384EI}, \text{ and } I = \frac{bd^3}{6}$$

$$\text{hence } d = \sqrt[3]{\frac{WL^2 \times 52.08 \times 10^3}{E \times b}}$$

The depth of the section to use will be the greater of those calculated for stress or deflection.

Where:

b = breadth of beam, mm; d = depth of beam, mm; f = flexural stress, N/mm^2; L = clear span, m; M = bending moment, kNm; W = total load, kN; Z = section modulus, mm^3; I = second moment of area, mm^4; E = modulus of elasticity, N/mm^2

Timber floor joists

(For further information see TRADA Span tables for solid timber members in floors, ceiling and roofs (excluding trussed rafter roofs) for dwellings).

Maximum clear spans for C16 grade softwood (m)

Dead load (kN/m^2)	<0.25		0.25 to 0.50		0.50 to 1.25	
Joist centres (mm)	400	600	400	600	400	600
Joist size (b × d) (mm)	**Maximum Clear Span (m)**					
47 × 97	2.03	1.59	1.93	1.47	1.67	1.23
47 × 120	2.63	2.26	2.52	2.05	2.22	1.66
47 × 145	3.17	2.77	3.04	2.59	2.70	2.15
47 × 170	3.71	3.21	3.55	3.00	3.14	2.56
47 × 195	4.25	3.64	4.07	3.41	3.56	2.91
47 × 220	4.75	4.08	4.58	3.82	3.99	3.26
75 × 120	3.07	2.69	2.94	2.57	2.65	2.29
75 × 145	3.70	3.24	3.54	3.10	3.19	2.78
75 × 170	4.32	3.79	4.14	3.63	3.73	3.23
75 × 195	4.87	4.34	4.72	4.15	4.27	3.67
75 × 220	5.32	4.82	5.15	4.67	4.77	4.11

Dead loads exclude the self-weight of the joist.
The table allows for an imposed load of not more than 1.5 kN/m^2 and a concentrated load of 1.4 kN, but not for concentrated loads from trimmers, partitions etc.
All joists beneath a bath should be doubled.

Floor decking (See NHBC Standards 6.4 –D14)

Joist centres (mm)	400	450	600
	Thickness of decking (mm)		
T & G softwood boarding	16	16	19
Chipboard	18	18	22
Plywood	12	12	16
Oriented strand board	15	15	18/19

Note: Oriented strand board should be laid with the stronger axis at right angles to the support.

Timber ceiling joists

(For further information see TRADA Span tables for solid timber members in floors, ceiling and roofs (excluding trussed rafter roofs) for dwellings.)

Maximum clear spans for C16 grade softwood (m)

Dead load (kN/m^2)	<0.25		0.25 to 0.50	
Joist centres (mm)	400	600	400	600
Joist sizes (b × d) (mm)	**Maximum Clear Span (m)**			
38 × 72	1.15	1.11	1.11	1.06
38 × 97	1.74	1.67	1.67	1.58
38 × 120	2.33	2.21	2.21	2.08
38 × 145	2.98	2.82	2.82	2.62
38 × 170	3.66	3.43	3.43	3.18
38 × 195	4.34	4.05	4.05	3.74
38 × 220	5.03	4.68	4.68	4.30
47 × 72	1.27	1.23	1.23	1.18
47 × 97	1.93	1.84	1.84	1.74
47 × 120	2.56	2.43	2.43	2.27
47 × 145	3.27	3.08	3.08	2.87
47 × 170	4.00	3.74	3.74	3.46
47 × 195	4.73	4.41	4.41	4.07
47 × 220	5.47	5.08	5.08	4.67

The table allows for an imposed load of not more than 0.25 kN/m^2 and a concentrated load of 0.9 kN.
No account has been taken for other loads such as water tanks or trimming around chimneys, hatches, etc.
Minimum bearing for ceiling joists should be 35 mm.

Engineered Joists and Beams

Engineered timber joists (TJI joists) allow for increased spans and reduced shrinkage in timber floor structures as well as more efficient use of material. Their higher cost means they compete with sawn timber only on larger spans and larger projects; typical savings in cross-section of section for a given joist depth as compared to sawn C24 softwood would be 20 to 30 per cent.

Parallam Beams (parallel strand lumber) have a vastly improved permissible stress and modulus of elasticity allowing of the order of 50 per cent increase in span on equivalent section of C24 softwood.

Brickwork and blockwork (BS 5628: Part 1: 1992)

Slenderness ratio of load bearing brickwork and blockwork walls

The slenderness ratio involves the thickness and height and the conditions of support to the top and bottom of a wall, pier or column. It is defined as effective height ÷ effective thickness.

Effective height of walls
When the floor or roof spans at right angles to the wall with sufficient bearing and anchorage:
effective height = ¾ of actual height between centres of supports
For concrete floors having a bearing on walls, irrespective of the direction of span:
effective height = ¾ of actual height
For floors or roof spanning parallel with wall without bearing (but wall restrained to floor/roof plane with lateral restraint straps):
effective height = actual height
For walls with no lateral support at top:
effective height = 1½ times actual height

Effective thickness of walls
For solid walls:
effective thickness = actual thickness
For cavity walls:
effective thickness = 2/3 × (thickness of one leaf + thickness of the other) or thickness of outer or inner leaf, whichever is greatest.

The slenderness ratio should never exceed 27, except in cases of walls less than 90 mm thick where it should not exceed 20.

For more information see Building Regulation Approved Document A.

Concrete (BS 8500-1: 2002)

The grade of concrete required depends on several factors such as exposure, chemical attack and whether the concrete is reinforced. The cover to the reinforcement depends on the grade of concrete, exposure and potential chemical attack (from de-icing salts and ground water).

The following information is extracted from Table A.7 of BS 8500-1: 2002 (Guidance on the selection of designated and standardized prescribed concrete in housing and other applications). For concrete subjected to sulphates and hydrostatic head of ground water, refer to a Chartered Structural Engineer.

Application (concrete containing embedded metal should be treated as reinforced)	Designated concrete	Standardized prescribed concrete
Foundations		
Blinding and mass concrete fill	GEN1	ST2
Strip footings	GEN1	ST2
Mass concrete footings	GEN1	ST2
Trench fill foundations	GEN1	ST2
Fully buried reinforced foundations	RC30	N/A
General applications		
Kerb bedding and backing	GEN0	ST1
Drainage works to give immediate support	GEN1	ST2
Other drainage works	GEN1	ST2
Oversite below suspended slabs	GEN1	ST2
Floors		
House floors with no embedment metal		
– Permanent finish to be added, e.g. screed of floating floor	GEN1	ST2
– No permanent finish to be added e.g. carpeted	GEN2	ST3
Garage floors with no embedded metal	GEN3	ST4
Wearing surface: light foot and trolley traffic	RC30	ST4
Wearing surface: general industrial	RC40	N/A
Wearing surface: heavy industrial	RC50	N/A
Paving		
House drives and domestic parking	PAV1	N/A
Heavy-duty external paving with rubber tyre vehicles	PAV2	N/A

Steelwork

Universal beams –
Safe distributed loads (kN)
for grade 43 steel

Beam serial size* mm	Mass kg/m	Spans (m)										Lc
		2.0	2.5	3.0	3.5	4.0	4.5	5.0	5.5	6.0	7.0	m
		Deflection co-efficients										
		112.0	71.68	49.78	36.57	28.00	22.12	17.92	14.81	12.44	9.143	
406 × 140	46	**513**	**411**	**342**	**293**	**257**	228	205	187	171	147	2.58
	39	**414**	**331**	**276**	**236**	**207**	184	165	150	138	118	2.41
356 × 171	67	**662**	**567**	**472**	405	354	315	283	258	236	202	3.72
	57	**574**	**473**	**394**	338	296	263	237	215	197	169	3.50
	51	**519**	**420**	**350**	300	263	234	210	191	175	150	3.38
	45	**453**	**363**	**302**	259	227	201	181	165	151	130	3.23
356 × 127	39	**377**	**302**	**252**	216	189	168	151	137	126	108	2.33
	33	**311**	**248**	**207**	177	155	138	124	113	104	89	2.18
305 × 165	54	**479**	**398**	**331**	284	249	221	199	181	166	142	3.69
	46	**412**	**342**	**285**	**244**	214	190	171	155	143	122	3.53
	40	**370**	**296**	**247**	**212**	185	165	148	135	123	106	3.38
305 × 127	48	**404**	323	269	231	202	180	162	147	135	115	2.59
	42	**351**	280	234	200	175	156	140	127	117	100	2.45
	37	**311**	249	207	178	156	138	124	113	104	89	2.37
305 × 102	33	**274**	219	183	156	137	122	110	100	91	78	1.90
	28	**232**	185	154	132	116	103	93	84	77	66	1.79
	25	**190**	152	127	109	95	84	76	69	63	54	1.64
254 × 146	43	**333**	**267**	222	191	167	148	133	121	111	95	3.41
	37	**286**	**229**	191	164	143	127	115	104	95	82	3.22
	31	**233**	186	155	133	117	104	93	85	78	67	2.96
254 × 102	28	203	163	135	116	102	90	81	74	68	58	2.01
	25	175	140	117	100	88	78	70	64	58	50	1.87
	22	149	119	99	85	74	66	60	54	50	43	1.75
203 × 133	30	**184**	147	123	105	92	82	74	67	61	53	3.03
	25	153	122	102	87	77	68	61	56	51		2.80
203 × 102	23	136	109	90.6	77.7	68.0						2.22
178 × 102	19	101	80.8	67.3	57.7	50.5						2.21
152 × 89	16	72.6	58.1	48.4	41.5	36.3						2.01
127 × 76	13	49.6	39.6	33.0	28.3	24.8						1.82

* Note that serial size is NOT actual size. Manufacture of beams of different weights of a given serial size involves moving the rollers in or out. The depth between the inside faces of the flanges remains constant, so the flange thickness and overall height vary.

Notes: See p. 120

Steel joists (RSJ) – Safe distributed loads (kN) for grade 43 steel

(Please note that these sections are not frequently rolled – check for availability.)

Joist nominal size mm	Mass kg/m	Spans (m)										Lc
		1.50	1.75	2.0	2.25	2.50	2.75	3.0	3.25	3.5	4.0	
		Deflection co-efficients										m
		199	146	112	88.5	71.7	59.2	49.8	42.4	36.6	28.0	
254 × 203	82				**518**	**500**	**454**	**416**	**304**	*357*	*312*	5.80
203 × 152	52	**362**	**356**	**311**	**277**	*249*	*226*	*207*	*191*	178	156	4.47
152 × 127	37	*210*	*180*	*158*	*140*	*126*	115	105	97	90	79	3.79
127 × 114	30	*136*	*116*	*102*	90	81	74	68	63	58	51	3.55
127 × 114	27	*131*	*112*	*98*	87	79	71	65	60	56	49	3.61
102 × 102	23	*84*	72	63	56	51	46	42	39	36	32	3.48
89 × 89	19	*61*	52	46	41	36	33	30	28	26	23	3.33
76 × 76	13	37	31	27	24	22	20	18	17	16	14	2.95

Notes:
These safe loads are designed in accordance with BS 449 (permissible stresses) and assume that the compression flange of the beam is laterally restrained if the span of the beam exceeds Lc. Sufficient lateral restraint can be achieved by positive mechanical fixing of floor joists to the flange (i.e. using cleats or straps). Skew nailing to timber plates or blocking into the web is generally not acceptable.
Loads printed in **bold** type may cause overloading of the unstiffened web, the capacity of which should be checked.
Loads printed in *italic* type do not cause overloading of the unstiffened web, and do not cause deflection exceeding span / 360.
Loads printed in ordinary type should be checked for deflection.

Source: British Constructional Steelwork Association Ltd

Steel hollow sections

Hot formed structural hollow sections (SHS) are manufactured to BS 4360: 1990 and BS 4848 Part 2: 1991.

The square and rectangular sections have tight corner radii which have higher geometric properties and therefore a higher load carrying capacity in compression than cold formed sections.

Cold formed hollow sections (CFHS) are manufactured to BS 6363: 1989.

The square and rectangular sections have larger corner radii which give lower geometric properties than hot formed sections of the same size and thickness. Cold formed hollow sections must NOT be substituted in a direct size-for-size basis for hot formed hollow sections without checking the design. Where structural properties are not critical, CFHS provide a cheaper solution.

SHS = structural hollow section
CHS = circular hollow section
RHS = rectangular hollow sections including square sections
CFHS = cold formed hollow section

Structural steel hollow sections
External sizes in mm

Hot formed			Cold formed		
circular	square	rectangular	circular	square	rectangular
○	▢	▯	○	▢	▯
26.9	40 × 40	50 × 30	26.9	25 × 25	50 × 25
42.4	50 × 50	60 × 40	33.7	30 × 30	50 × 30
48.3	60 × 60	80 × 40	42.4	40 × 40	60 × 30
60.3	70 × 70	90 × 50	48.3	50 × 50	60 × 40
76.1	80 × 80	100 × 50	60.3	60 × 60	70 × 40
88.9	90 × 90	100 × 60	76.1	70 × 70	70 × 50
114.3	100 × 100	120 × 60	88.9	80 × 80	80 × 40
139.7	120 × 120	120 × 80	114.3	90 × 90	80 × 60
168.3	140 × 140	150 × 100	139.7	100 × 100	90 × 50
193.7	150 × 150	160 × 80	168.3	120 × 120	100 × 40
219.1	160 × 160	200 × 100	193.7	140 × 140	100 × 50
244.5	180 × 180	200 × 120	219.1	150 × 150	100 × 60
273.0	200 × 200	200 × 150	244.5	160 × 160	100 × 80
323.9	250 × 250	250 × 100	273.0	180 × 180	120 × 40
406.4	300 × 300	250 × 150	323.9	200 × 200	120 × 60
457.0	350 × 350	300 × 100	355.6	250 × 250	120 × 80
508.0	400 × 400	300 × 200	406.4	300 × 300	140 × 80
		400 × 200	457.0		150 × 100
		450 × 250	508.0		160 × 80
		500 × 300			180 × 80
					180 × 100
					200 × 100
					200 × 120
					200 × 150
					250 × 150
					300 × 100
					300 × 200
					400 × 200

Seamless Hot formed hollow sections also available with thicker walls 457 to 771 mm Ø
Jumbo Hot formed square hollow and rectangular sections also available with thicker walls 350 to 750 mm square

Source: Corus: tubes and pipes

Lintels

There are many suppliers of lintels, both precast concrete and pressed metal. Precast lintels can be either composite or non-composite. Composite lintels rely on brickwork being built on top of the 65 deep lintels. Particularly for longer spans, this allows safer handling on site of lighter lintels. Such lintels MUST be propped until the brickwork over has cured. Similarly, all long span lintels should be propped until masonry over has cured.

Lintels are rarely, if ever, cast on site.

Lintel selector guides are available on the websites of the various manufacturers. You will need to know the thickness of the inner and outer leaves, the width of the cavity, clear span and loads to be carried.

The following is just a small example of what is available on the web.

Precast concrete lintels

Stowell Concrete Limited
(www.stowellconcrete.co.uk)

COMPOSITE lintel maximum uniformly distributed load for clear span kg/m (including self-weight of lintel)

Section w × h	No. of courses	0.60 m	0.75 m	0.90 m	1.05 m	1.20 m	1.35 m	1.50 m	1.65 m	1.80 m	1.95 m	2.10 m	2.25 m	2.40 m	2.55 m	2.70 m	2.85 m
100 × 65 mm	2	2033	1407	1029	785	617	497	408	340	288	246	212	185	162	143	127	133
	5	2743	1900	1392	1062	836	674	554	463	392	336	291	254	223	197	175	156
	8	4166	2889	2118	1618	1275	1030	849	711	603	516	449	393	347	308	274	246
150 × 65 mm	2	2168	1498	1094	833	653	524	430	357	301	257	221	191	166	146	129	–
	5	4002	2773	2030	1550	1219	983	809	676	572	490	424	370	325	288	245	–
	8	5837	4046	2967	2266	1785	1442	1188	994	844	725	628	549	484	429	383	–
220 × 65 mm	2	2377	1639	1193	904	706	565	459	380	317	269	228	196	169	147	127	–
	5	5940	4115	3015	2300	1811	1460	1201	1004	851	729	631	560	484	428	381	–
	8	8195	5679	4161	3177	2501	2019	1661	1389	1178	1010	875	764	672	596	530	–

NON-COMPOSITE lintel maximum uniformly distributed load for clear span kg/m (including self-weight of lintel)

Section w × h	0.75 m	0.90 m	1.05 m	1.20 m	1.35 m	1.50 m	1.65 m	1.80 m	1.95 m	2.10 m	2.25 m	2.40 m	2.55 m	2.70 m	2.85 m	3.00 m	3.15 m	3.30 m	3.75 m	4.05 m
150 × 100 mm	2381	1937	1282	1006	808	662	551	464	395	340	295	257	226	199	176	157	140	125	–	–
100 × 150 mm	3590	2628	1880	1480	1191	976	816	691	638	511	458	390	344	302	272	244	219	198	–	–
140 × 150 mm	–	–	3564	2806	2263	1862	1557	1319	1131	979	855	751	665	592	529	476	429	389	–	–
100 × 215 mm	–	–	–	–	–	2952	2694	2413	2140	1882	1624	1402	1202	1122	1004	856	723	664	517	423

Naylor precast concrete lintels
(www.naylorlintels.co.uk/lintelsselector.asp)

Hi-Spec Range Lintel: R6	⊡
Section Properties	
Height	145 mm
Width	100 mm
M_S	5.564 kNm
M_U	9.609 kNm
$M_{U/1.5}$	6.406 kNm
Limiting M_R	5.564 kNm
Effective depth	95 mm
Self-weight	35 Kg/m

Load Table

Clear Span (mm)	Overall Length (mm)	Effective Span (mm)	Allowable Load (kN/m)			
			M_R	S_{R100}	S_{R150}	Limiting
700	900	795	70.07	50.74		50.74
900	1100	995	44.61	40.47		40.47
1000	1200	1095	36.77	36.74		36.74
1200	1500	1295	26.19		32.88	26.19
1500	1800	1595	17.14			17.14
1800	2100	1895	12.04			12.04
2100	2400	2195	8.89			8.89
2400	2700	2495	6.80			6.80
2700	3000	2795	5.34			5.34
3000	3300	3095	4.29			4.29
3200	3600	3295	3.75			3.75

Naylor precast concrete lintels – continued

Hi-Spec Range Lintel: R8	
Section Properties	
Height	215 mm
Width	140 mm
M_S	14.259 kNm
M_U	25.710 kNm
$M_{U/1.5}$	17.140 kNm
Limiting M_R	14.259 kNm
Effective depth	141.67 mm
Self-weight	72 Kg/m

Load Table

Clear Span (mm)	Overall Length (mm)	Effective Span (mm)	Allowable Load (kN/m)			
			M_R	S_{R100}	S_{R150}	Limiting
700	900	800	177.51	100.57		100.57
900	1100	1000	113.35	80.31		80.31
1000	1200	1100	93.55	72.95		72.95
1200	1500	1341	62.64		62.22	62.22
1500	1800	1641	41.60		50.72	41.60
1800	2100	1941	29.53			29.53
2100	2400	2241	21.97			21.97
2400	2700	2541	16.93			16.93
2700	3000	2841	13.40			13.40
3000	3300	3141	10.83			10.83
3200	3600	3341	9.49			9.49

Steel lintels for cavity walls

Lintels are made from galvanized steel with polyester powder corrosion-resisting coating. Single lintels are available with the steel bent into a 'top hat' shape using the cavity to give height to the lintel, but these form a thermal bridge across the cavity and may cause local condensation, so separate lintels for each leaf are advisable. To support masonry to the outer leaf, angle lintels are used, typically in conjunction with a separate box lintel to the inner leaf.

Bases of internal leaf lintels are slotted for plaster key.

Other profiles

Rebated combined lintels – for window/door frames set back in reveals.

Lintels for closed eaves – for windows tight under sloping roofs.

Lintels for walls with masonry outer skin and timber frame inside.

Lintels for masonry outer skin where inner skin is carried by concrete lintel.

Lintels for internal partitions and load bearing walls.

Special profiles for various styles of arches and cantilevered masonry corners.

I G Lintels
(www.igltd.co.uk/)

70–95mm cavity – wide inner leaf

L1/S WIL 75

For 70–95 mm cavity wall with wide inner
block/brick construction.
Standard duty loading condition.

* A continuous bottom plate
added

Note: maximum block dimensions 150 mm (70 mm cavity)
Load ratio 1 – applies to loads with an inner to outer leaf ratio of
between 1 : 1 and 3 : 1.
This ratio is normally applicable to lintels that support: a. masonry
b. masonry and timber floors
Load ratio 2 – applies to loads with an inner to outer leaf ratio of
between 4 : 1 and 19 : 1.
This ratio is normally applicable to lintels supporting: a. constructions with concrete floors b. eaves applications

Manufactured length 150 mm increments	0600 1350	1500 1650	1800	1950 2100	2250 2400	2550 3000	*3150 3600	*3750 4200
Height 'h'	93	90	110	134	158	167	192	192
Thickness 't'	2	2	2	2	2	2.6	3.2	3.2
Total UDL(kN) Load ratio (1)	12	13	20	19	24	27	30	27
Total UDL(kN) Load ratio (2)	10	11	17	17	20	21	26	25

L1/HD WIL 75

For 70–95 mm cavity wall with wide inner
block/brick construction.
Heavy duty loading condition.

* A continuous bottom plate added

Note: maximum block dimensions 150 mm (70 mm cavity)
Load ratio 1 – applies to loads with an inner to outer leaf ratio of between 1 : 1 and 3 : 1.
This ratio is normally applicable to lintels that support: a. masonry b. masonry and timber floors
Load ratio 2 – applies to loads with an inner to outer leaf ratio of between 4 : 1 and 19 : 1.
This ratio is normally applicable to lintels supporting: a. constructions with concrete floors b. eaves applications

Manufactured length 150 mm increments	0600 1200	*1300 1500	*1650 1800	*1950 2100	*2250 2700
Height 'h'	93	107	157	157	192
Thickness 't'	3.2	3.2	3.2	3.2	3.2
Total UDL(kN) Load ratio (1)	20	25	35	30	36
Total UDL(kN) Load ratio (2)	17	22	27	25	32

L1/XHD WIL 75

For 70–95 mm cavity wall with wide inner block/brick construction.
Extra heavy duty loading condition.

'h' nominal

95   68   125

* A continuous bottom plate added

Note: maximum block dimensions 150 mm (70 mm cavity)
Load ratio 1 – applies to loads with an inner to outer leaf ratio of between 1 : 1 and 3 : 1.
This ratio is normally applicable to lintels that support: a. masonry b. masonry and timber floors
Load ratio 2 – applies to loads with an inner to outer leaf ratio of between 4 : 1 and 19 : 1.
This ratio is normally applicable to lintels supporting: a. constructions with concrete floors b. eaves applications

Manufactured length 150 mm increments	*0600 1500	*1650 1800	*1950 2100
Height 'h'	157	192	192
Thickness 't'	3.2	3.2	3.2
Total UDL(kN) Load ratio (1)	45	45	50
Total UDL(kN) Load ratio (2)	40	40	40

If thermal bridging is an issue, each leaf could be supported on a box lintel. If the external leaf is facing brick, then an angle would be required.

Box 100

For internal openings, eaves or 100 block
and tile hanging.

Manufactured length 150 mm increments	0600 1500	1650 1800	1950 2400	2550 2700	2850 3600	3750 4200	4350 4800
Height 'h'	75	150	150	150	215	215	215
Thickness 't'	2	1.6	2	2	2.5	2.5	2.5
Total allowable UDL (kN)	18	18	25	20	30	25	20

Box 140

For internal openings, eaves or 140/150 block
and tile hanging.

Manufactured length 150 mm increments	0600 1500	1650 1800	2250 2400	2550 2700	2850 3600	3750 4200	4350 4800
Height 'h'	145	145	145	145	220	220	220
Thickness 't'	1.6	2	2	2	2.5	2.5	2.5
Total allowable UDL (kN)	15	30	25	20	34	30	25

L10

For use with single 102 mm brickwork wall construction. Light duty loading condition.

'h' nominal

95

Note: This lintel must be propped during construction.
To achieve loading figures indicated, lintel must be built-in with brickwork/blockwork as shown. In addition, it must be suitably restrained during construction. Heavier duty variants available.

Heavy duty and wider masonry variants available.

Manufactured length 150 mm increments	0600 1200	1350 1800	1950 2700	
Height 'h'	60	110	210	
Thickness 't'	3.0	3.0	28	
Total allowable UDL (kN)	14	8	10	

L11

For use with single leaf face brick or block wall.

150   225   95   95

Note: This lintel must be propped during construction.
To achieve loading figures indicated, lintel must be built-in with brickwork/blockwork as shown. In addition, it must be suitably restrained during construction. Heavier duty variants available.

Heavy duty and wider masonry variants available.

Manufactured length 150 mm increments	0600 1800	1950 2400	2550 3000	
Height 'h'	150	225	225	
Thickness 't'	2.5	2.5	3.0	
Total allowable UDL (kN)	16	20	22	

Wind loads – simple calculation

BS 6262: 1982 CP describes a simple method of obtaining wind loads. This can be used for buildings less than 10 metres above ground level and where the design wind speed is less than 52 metres per second (m/s). This method should not be used for cliff-top buildings.

Find the basic wind speed from the map on p. 1. Multiply by a correction in Table 1 to get the design wind speed (m/s). Find the appropriate maximum wind loading from Table 2.

This should only be used for wind loads applied to glazing units and not the whole building. For more detailed wind calculations, refer to BS 6399: Part 2.

Table 1: Correction factors for ground roughness and height above ground

Height above ground	Category 1	Category 2	Category 3	Category 4
3 m or less	0.83	0.72	0.64	0.56
5 m	0.88	0.79	0.70	0.60
10 m	1.00	0.93	0.78	0.67

Category 1   Open country with no obstructions. All coastal areas.
Category 2   Open country with scattered wind breaks.
Category 3   Country with many wind breaks, e.g. small towns, city outskirts.
Category 4   Surfaces with large and frequent obstructions, e.g. city centres.

Table 2: Wind loading – probable maximum

Design wind speed m/s	Wind loading N/m^2	Design wind speed m/s	Wind loading N/m^2
28	670	42	1510
30	770	44	1660
32	880	46	1820
34	990	48	1920
36	1110	50	2150
38	1240	52	2320
40	1370		

Precast concrete floors

Precast concrete floors are used for ground floors over sloping or made-up ground where in-situ slabs may not be economic, and for upper floors where fire-resisting and sound insulating construction is needed, between flats for example. They can be used in a fully precast, 'dry' construction with a floating floor finish, or in a composite way with an in-situ structural topping or screed, which can improve structural performance and acoustic insulation. Crane handling of the beams is normally required so they are less used on smaller projects.

There are two main types of precast concrete floor: wideslab (sometimes known as hollowcore) and beam and block.

Bearing required is generally 75 mm onto steelwork and 100 mm onto masonry. Where shared bearing is required on a masonry wall, the wall should be 215 mm thick (except for short span beam and block floors where staggered bearing might be possible).

Wideslab floors are precast slabs 1200 mm wide with hollow cores (150 thick slab minimum). The depth of unit can vary from 100 mm–450 mm, depending on span and loading.

Beam and block floors are inverted T sections, 150–225 deep, with concrete blocks spanning between units. The blocks can span short or long direction (or alternate), depending on span and loading. All beams are sometimes required under partitions.

There are many manufacturers of precast concrete floors who provide a design and supply service. The following information is a small example of what is available on the internet.

Milbank Floors
(www.milbank-floors.co.uk)

The load/span tables show the maximum clear span for both domestic and other loading conditions, such as nursing homes, hotels and commercial developments. These tables are provided as a guide only. Please contact Milbank Floors for specific information.

Wideslab/Hollowcore

SECTION

Prestressed Hollowcore Plank Load Span Table			Maximum span in metres. Spans below allow for characteristic service (live) loads + self weight + 1.5 kN/m² finishes and 1.5 kN/m² partitions							
Unit reference	Unit depth (mm)	Self weight (kN/m²)	Imposed live load kN/mm²							
			0.75	1.5	2.0	2.5	3.0	4.0	5.0	7.5
PS-250	250	3.46	10.0	9.53	9.25	8.96	8.74	8.30	7.93	7.14
PS-200	200	2.97	8.87	8.41	8.14	7.89	7.67	7.27	6.92	6.24
PS-150H	150	2.95	7.05	6.68	6.47	6.27	6.09	5.77	5.90	4.95
PS-150L	150	2.48	7.42	7.00	6.76	6.54	6.34	5.99	5.69	5.11
PS-100s	100	2.35	5.18	4.89	4.71	4.56	4.41	4.17	3.95	3.54

Beam and Block

150 mm deep T beam (based on 1/2 hour fire resistance) Medium density infill blocks 1350 kg/m² − 65 mm screed finish			Spans below allow for characteristic service (live) load + self weight + 1.5 kN/m² finishes + 1.5 kN/m² partitions Imposed live load kN/mm²							
Beam centres*	** Type of block spacing	Self weight (kN/m²)	0.75	1.5	2.0	2.5	3.0	4.0	5.0	7.5
			Maximum span in metres							
	W	1.76	4.07	3.82	3.67	3.54	3.42	3.21	3.04	2.54
	A	1.88	4.56	4.20	4.12	3.97	3.84	3.61	3.42	3.04
	N	2.09	5.27	4.95	4.77	4.61	4.46	4.20	3.98	3.55
	W	2.10	5.02	4.74	4.57	4.41	4.27	4.02	3.81	3.40
	A	2.27	5.46	5.16	4.98	4.81	4.66	4.39	4.17	3.73
	N	2.52	6.02	5.71	5.51	5.33	5.17	4.89	4.64	4.16
	N	2.76	6.37	6.05	5.85	5.66	5.50	5.20	4.95	4.44

** W=Wide (440 mm) A=Alternate (440 + 215 mm) N=Narrow (215 mm)

225 mm deep D Beam (based on 1 hour fire resistance) Medium density infill blocks 1350 kg/m^2 − 65 mm screed finish			Spans below allow for characteristic service (live) load + self weight + 1.5 kN/m^2 finishes + 1.5 kN/m^2 partitions. Imposed live load kN/mm^2							
	* Type of block spacing	Self weight (kN/m^2)	0.75	1.5	2.0	2.5	3.0	4.0	5.0	7.5
Beam centres			**Maximum span in metres**							
	W	2.36	6.31	5.94	5.73	5.54	5.37	5.07	4.81	4.30
	A	2.62	6.95	6.57	6.34	6.14	5.96	5.63	5.35	4.80
	N	3.08	7.84	7.39	7.20	6.98	6.78	6.43	6.12	5.52
	W	3.03	7.49	7.09	6.86	6.66	6.46	6.13	5.84	5.26
	A	3.35	8.00	7.60	7.36	7.15	9.95	6.60	6.29	5.68
	N	3.84	8.63	8.22	7.98	7.76	7.55	7.19	6.87	6.23
	N	4.22	8.95	8.54	8.30	8.08	7.88	7.51	7.19	6.54

** W = Wide (440 mm) A = Alternate (440 + 215 mm) N = Narrow (215 mm)

4
Services

Drainage

Foul drains recommended minimum gradients

Peak flow l/s	Pipe size mm	Minimum gradient	Maximum capacity l/s
<1	75	1 : 40	4.1
<1	100	1 : 40	9.2
>1	75	1 : 80	2.8
>1	100	1 : 80*	6.3
>1	150	1 : 150†	15.0

* Minimum of 1 WC   † Minimum of 5 WCs

Land drains in normal soils – minimum gradients

Pipe Ø	Gradient	Pipe Ø	Gradient
50	1 : 500	150	1 : 2160
75	1 : 860	175	1 : 2680
100	1 : 1260	200	1 : 3200
125	1 : 1680	225	1 : 3720

Traps minimum sizes and seal depths

Appliance	Ø trap mm	Seal depth mm		Ø trap mm	Seal depth mm
washbasin	32	75	waste disposer	40	75
bidet	32	75	urinal	40	75
bath*	40	50	sink	40	75
shower*	40	50	washing machine*	40	75
syphonic WC	75	50	dishwasher*	40	75

*Where these fittings discharge directly into a gully the seal depth may be reduced to a minimum of 38 mm.

Hepworth waste valves used in lieu of traps avoid the risk of suction emptying the traps on long pipe runs.

Sources: *Building Regulations–Approved Document H*
Hepworth Building Products

Inspection chamber covers
Typical dimensions

Covers are manufactured in steel plate, galvanized steel and cast iron – overall sizes for cast iron will be larger. Covers may have single or double seals, plain or recessed tops, and be multiple leaf or continuous for ducting. Alternative features include chambered keyholes, handlift recesses and locking screws.

Most covers are available in the load classes shown below.

Typical clear opening mm	Overall frame mm
300 × 300	370 × 370
450 × 450	520 × 520
600 × 450	670 × 520
600 × 600	670 × 670
750 × 600	820 × 670
750 × 750	820 × 820
900 × 600	970 × 670
900 × 900	970 × 970
1000 × 1000	1070 × 1070

Load classes for inspection chamber covers

Class	Wheel load (slow moving traffic)	Typical application
A	5 kN	Pedestrian, cycle tracks
AA	15 kN	Private drives, car parking areas
AAA	25 kN	Restricted access roads
B	50 kN	Commercial delivery, refuse collection
C	65 kN	All roads but positioned within 0.5 m of kerb
D	108 kN	All roads restricted only by wheel loading

Source: St Gobain Pipelines

Single stack drainage system

Soil vent pipe should be terminated with a cage or perforated cover. It should finish at least 900 mm above any opening within 3 m of stack.

The stack may terminate within a building if fitted with an approved air admittance valve providing the drain is ventilated to outside elsewhere.

In buildings of not more than two storeys the ventilating stack, above the highest branch, may be reduced to 75 mm ø

1.7 m max for 32 mm ø pipe 3 m max for 40 mm ø pipe. Slope for 32 mm ø waste pipes to be between 20 mm/m for 1.7 m pipes and 120 mm/m for 0.6 m long pipes *

3 m max for 40 mm ø pipe 4 m max for 50 mm ø pipe Slope between 18 to 90 mm/m

To avoid cross flow small similar sized connections should be offset at least 110 mm on 100 mm ø stack

sink

basin

110 min offset (250 min for 150 ø stack)

bath

wc

200 min offset

angled connection or 50 mm ø parallel junction where a waste branch directly opposite a WC would enter the stack within 200 mm below the WC branch connection centre line

Junction between WC branch & stack made with 50 mm min radius or at 45°

TRAPS
Where larger size of waste branches are used, the trap size is not increaed but the tail of the trap should be lengthened by 5 mm. See p. 137 for minimum trap sizes and seal depths

3 m max for 40 mm ø pipe 4 m max for 50 mm ø pipe Slope between 18 and 90 mm/m

6 m max for single WC Slope 18 mm/m mın

Stack to be 100 mm ø May be 75 mm if serving not more than one siphonic WC with 75 mm outlet

450 mm min between lowest branch and drain invert in single dwellings of up to 3 storeys

200 min

1.5 m max

a ground floor WC may connect directly to drain providing the drop is less than 1.5 m between crown of trap and drain invert

NOTE
Separate ventilating pipes will be needed if the figures for branch length and slope are exceeded (Unless Hepworth waste valves are used in lieu of traps)

large radius bend at bottom of stack at least 200 mm

* 'Waste pipe lengths are not limited if Hepworth waste valves are used in lieu of traps'

Sources: *Building Regulations Approved Document H*
Hepworth Building Products

Rainwater disposal
Calculation of gutter and downpipe sizes

In the UK, the maximum rainfall intensity is generally taken as 75 mm per hour or 0.0208 litres per second (l/s). Note that this does not necessarily mean only high rainfall areas such as West Wales and Scotland but, in surprisingly odd pockets like Norfolk and Oxford, heavy downpours can exceed this figure.

To calculate the size of rainwater goods it is necessary to determine the *effective roof area* which, in the case of pitched roofs, is as follows:

Effective
roof area = (H ÷ 2 + W) × L = m²
Where H = vertical rise between
eaves and ridge
W = plan width of slope
L = length of roof

To determine the maximum flow multiply the effective area by 0.0208.

Typical maximum flow capacities

Gutter mm	Downpipe mm	Outlet at one end of roof				Outlet at centre of roof			
		Level gutter m²	l/s	Gutter to fall m²	l/s	Level gutter m²	l/s	Gutter to fall m²	l/s
75 half round	51 Ø	15	0.33	19	0.40	25	0.54	30	0.64
110 half round	69 Ø	46	0.96	61	1.27	92	1.91	122	2.54
116 square	62 sq	53	1.10	72	1.50	113	2.36	149	3.11t

Refer to manufacturers' catalogues for actual flow capacities, as profiles of gutters can vary.

Rule of thumb

100–112 mm gutter with 68 mm Ø downpipe placed at centre of gutter will drain 110 m² effective roof area; placed at end of gutter will drain 55 m² effective roof area. Gutter will drain more if laid to slight (1: 60) fall.

Water supply regulations

The Water Supply (Water Fittings) Regulations 1999 super-sede the Water Supply Byelaws. Their aim is to prevent: waste, misuse, undue consumption, contamination or false measurement of water supplied by a *Water Undertaker* (WU). The regulations should be read in conjunction with the WRAS Guide, which includes detailed information of sizes, flow rates, valves, etc. Below is a VERY BROAD and BRIEF interpretation of the regulations.

Application of the regulations

The regulations apply only to fittings supplied with water by a WU. They do not apply to water fittings for non-domestic or non-food production purposes providing the water is metered; the supply is for less than 1 month (3 months with written consent) and no water can return through a meter to a mains pipe. They do not apply to fittings installed before 1 July 99.

Notification

Water undertakers must be notified of the following:

Erecting any building, except a pond or swimming pool of less than 10 000 litres capacity

Altering any water system in non-residential premises

Changing the use of a property

Building over or within 2 m of a public sewer. A CCTV survey may be necessary

Installing:

- A bath with a capacity greater than 330 litres
- A bidet with ascending spray or flexible hose
- A single shower unit with multi-head arrangement
- A pump or booster drawing more than 12 litres/min
- A water softener with a waste or needing water for regeneration or cleaning
- A reduced pressure zone valve or any mechanical device which presents serious health risks
- A garden watering system other than hand-held hose
- External pipes higher than 730 mm or lower than 1350 mm
- An automatically filled pond or swimming pool with a capacity of more than 10 000 litres

Contractor's certificate

Contractors approved by the WU must issue certificates to clients stating that the work complies with the regulations. For items of *Notification* (see above) copies of these certificates must be sent to the WU. Contravention of the regulations may incur a fine not exceeding £1000 (in 2000 AD).

Fluid categories

Water is described in five fluid categories ranging from 'wholesome' water supplied by a WU to water representing serious health hazards. These categories are used, amongst other things, to define which type of *backflow prevention* (see below) is required.

Contamination and corrosion

Water for domestic use or food purposes must not be contaminated by materials such as lead and bitumen. Water fittings must not be installed in contaminated environments such as sewers and cesspits.

Quality and testing

Water fittings should comply with British Standards ·or European equivalent and must withstand an operating pressure of not less than 1.5 times the maximum operating pressure. All water systems must be tested, flushed and, if necessary, disinfected before use.

Location

Water fittings must not be installed in cavity walls, embedded in walls or solid floors, or below suspended or solid ground floors unless encased in an accessible duct. External pipes underground must not be joined by adhesives nor laid less than 750 mm deep or more than 1350 mm deep unless written consent is obtained.

Protection against freezing

All water fittings outside buildings or located within buildings but outside the thermal envelope should be insulated against freezing. In very cold conditions, in unheated premises, water should be drained down before the onset of freezing or alternative devices installed to activate heating systems.

Backflow protection

Except where expanded water from hot water systems is permitted to flow backwards, water installations must have adequate devices for preventing backflow as follows:

- To prevent backflow between separate premises
- Connection of grey or rainwater to a 'wholesome' water pipe
- Bidets with flexible hoses, spray handsets, under-rim water inlets or ascending sprays
- WC cisterns with pressure flushing valves
- WCs adapted as bidets
- Baths with submerged inlets (e.g. jacuzzis)
- Non-domestic washing machines and dishwashers
- Sprinkler systems, fire hose reels and fire hydrants
- Garden hoses and watering systems

Cold water services

Every dwelling, including those in multi-storey dwellings should have separate *stop valves* for mains entry pipes inside each premises.

Drain taps must be provided to completely drain water from all pipes within a building.

All domestic premises must have at least one tap for *drinking water* supplied directly from the mains.

Cold water cisterns

Cold water cisterns for dwellings are no longer mandatory providing there is adequate *water flow rate* and *mains pressure in the street.* Check this with the WU before designing new installation.

Cisterns must be fitted with *float valves* and *servicing valves.* *Overflow/warning* pipes, with vermin and insect-proof screens must be fitted to discharge conspicuously to outside. Where cisterns are joined together, care must be taken to avoid one cistern overflowing into another and that water is fully circulated between cisterns and not short-circuited. Cisterns should be *insulated* and be fitted with light and insect-proof *lids.* 330 mm minimum unobstructed space must be provided above the cistern for inspection and maintenance.

Hot water services

Temperature control devices and *relief valves* must be fitted to unvented water heaters. *Expansion valves* must be fitted to unvented hot water systems larger than 5 litres. Primary circuit vent pipes should not discharge over domestic cisterns nor to a secondary system. Secondary circuit vent pipes should not discharge over feed and expansion cisterns connected to a primary circuit. Ideally, hot water should be stored at 60°C and discharged at 50°C (43°C for shower mixers). Long lengths of hot water pipes should be *insulated* to conserve energy.

Garden water supplies

Double check valves (DCVs) must be fitted to hose union taps in new houses. Hose union taps in existing houses should be replaced with hose union taps which incorporate DCVs. Watering systems must be fitted with DCVs as well as *pipe interrupters with atmosphere vent and moving element* at the hose connecting point or a minimum of 300 mm above the highest point of delivering outlet.

Pools and fountains filled with water supplied by a WU must have an *impervious lining.*

WCs and Urinals

Single flush cisterns to WCs should not exceed 6 litres capacity. Manual *pressure flushing* valves to WC cisterns must receive at least 1.2 litres/second flow at the appliance. WC cisterns installed before July 99 must be replaced with the same size cistern. Existing single flush cisterns may not be replaced by dual-flush cisterns.

Automatic *urinal flushing cisterns* should not exceed 10 litres capacity for a single urinal and 7.5 litres/hour per bowl, stall or 700 mm width of slab.

Urinal pressure valves should deliver no more than 1.5 litres per flush.

Low water consumption WC pans and cisterns are available down to 4 litres. Passive Infra-red (PIR) flush controls are available to minimise wastage in urinals. Waterless urinals are available but require a careful cleaning regime.

Sources: Water Supply (Water Fittings) Regulations 1999 The WRAS Water Regulations Guide

Water storage
Plastic cold water cisterns
Rectangular

Litres	galls	size l × w × h mm	weight kg*
18	4	442 × 296 × 305	0.9
68	15	630 × 448 × 420	3.2
91	20	665 × 490 × 510	4.2
114	25	700 × 540 × 532	5.0
182	40	940 × 610 × 590	7.3
227	50	1155 × 635 × 600	9.0

Circular

Litres	galls	size Ø @ top × h mm	weight kg*
114	25	695 × 510	3.5
182	40	795 × 590	4.4
227	50	860 × 620	4.8
273	60	940 × 620	5.8
455	100	1060 × 750	10.4
591	130	1060 × 920	14.5

* Empty weight – one litre of water weighs one kilogram so full weight of cistern equals litre capacity in kilograms plus empty weight.

Source: Titan Environmental Ltd

Water hardness

 soft to moderately soft
hard to moderately soft
hard to very hard

Hard water supplies lead to lime-scale formation in and around appliances; this leads to substantial reductions in efficiency, particularly in boilers and hot water cylinders. Scale formation can be reduced by fitting scale reducers to incoming cold mains. These work by magnetism, electronic charge or chemical treatment to reduce the amount of hard scale formed and clear scale deposits, retaining the calcium carbonate in suspension; they are low in cost and appear to have no health effects.

Water softeners remove the calcium carbonate from the water, rendering it 'soft'; they should be fitted near drinking water taps – typically at kitchen sinks. They require recharging with salt at regular intervals and are substantially more expensive to install and maintain than conditioners.

In hard water areas, it is advisable to fit conditioners or softeners to all buildings with hot water systems.

Hot water usage

Typical average consumption – litres

bath	60 per bath
shower	2.5 per minute
power shower	10–40 per minute
handwashing	2 per person
hairdressing	10 per shampoo
cleaning	10 per dwelling per day
kitchen sink	5 per meal

Cold water fill appliances

dishwasher	13 per cycle
washing machine	45–70 per cycle

Hot water storage

Typical storage requirements @ 65°C – litres per person

house or flat	30
office	5
factory	5
day school	5

boarding school	25
hospital	30
sports centre	35
luxury hotel	45

Domestic indirect copper hot water cylinders

BS ref.	Unlagged Height A mm	Unlagged Diameter B mm	Capacity litres	Heat Surface m^2
0	1600	300	96	0.42
1	900	350	80	0.31
–	600	400	62	0.26
2	900	400	96	0.42
3	1050	400	114	0.50
4	675	450	84	0.37
5	750	450	95	0.48
6	825	450	106	0.53
7	900	450	117	0.61
8	1050	450	140	0.70
9	1200	450	162	0.79
9E	1500	450	206	0.96
10	1200	500	190	0.88
11	1500	500	245	1.10
12	1200	600	280	1.18
13	1500	600	360	1.57
14	1800	600	440	1.97

50 mm or 100 mm CFC free urethane foam lagging insulation will be added to increase the diameter of the cylinder.

Building Regulations require hot water cylinders to have factory applied insulation designed to restrict heat losses to 1 watt per litre or less.

In soft water areas, copper cylinders should be specified with an aluminium protector rod which is fixed inside the dome by the manufacturers. This encourages the formation of a protective film on the copper and will lengthen the life of the cylinder which may otherwise be subject to pitting.

Source: Range Cylinders Ltd

Unvented mains pressure cylinders

Mains pressure cylinders

For buildings with good mains pressure and appropriately sized water main pipework, mains pressure hot water supply offers significant advantages including equal pressure hot and cold supplies, adequate pressure at all locations for showers, location of the cylinder anywhere and elimination of cold water storage tanks; existing systems of pipework need to be checked for mains pressure.

Appropriate mains pressure cylinders are widely available in stainless steel and enamelled mild steel, pre-insulated, with single or double coils for boiler and solar applications, though in fewer sizes than copper tank-fed cylinders.

Cylinders for solar water heating

Hot water cylinders installed with solar water systems should be as large as practicable so as to maximise the efficiency of the system; although the solar coil in the base of the cylinder will heat the whole cylinder, the boiler coil in the upper part will heat only the upper part, so, when there is no further preheating from the solar system, at night for example, once the solar hot water is used, the boiler can heat only half the cylinder capacity.

U-values

To understand the use of U-values it is necessary to distinguish between the thermal measurement expressions below:

Thermal conductivity (K-value)
The heat (W) transmitted through unit area (m^2) of a material of unit thickness (m) for unit temperature difference (K) between inside and outside environments, expressed as W/mK (or W/m °C).

Thermal resistivity (R-value)
The reciprocal of thermal conductivity, i.e. mK/W (or m °C/W). It measures how well a material resists the flow of heat by conduction.

Thermal resistance (R-value)
This means how well a *particular thickness* of material resists the passage of heat by conduction, calculated from the R-value in units of m^2K/W (or m^2 °C/W).

Thermal transmittance (U-value)
The reciprocal of thermal resistance, i.e. W/m^2K (or W/m^2 °C). This measures the amount of heat transmitted per unit area of a particular thickness per unit temperature difference between inside and outside environments.

U-value calculation formula:

$$U = \frac{1}{R_{SI} + R_{SO} + R_A + R_1 + R_2 + R_3 \ldots}$$

where R_{SI} = thermal resistance of internal surface
R_{SO} = thermal resistance of external surface
R_A = thermal resistance of air spaces within construction
R_1, R_2, R_3, etc. = thermal resistance of successive components

$$R = \frac{1}{\text{K-value}} \times \frac{\text{thickness of material mm}}{1000}$$

R-values

Surface resistance R-values normal exposure		m²K/W	Air space R-values 25 mm exposure	m²K/W R$_A$
	R$_{SI}$ inside surface	R$_{SO}$ outside surface	in cavity wall	0.18
			loft space under sarking	0.18
			between metal cladding & lining	0.16
roof/ceiling	0.10	0.04	in cold flat roof	0.16
Wall	0.12	0.06	loft space under metal cladding	0.14
			between roofing tiles & felt	0.12
floor	0.14	0.04	behind tile hanging	0.12

K-values

Thermal conductivity of typical building materials

Material		kg/m³	W/mK	Material		kg/m³	W/mK
asphalt	19 mm	1700	0.50	phenolic foam	board	30	0.020
blocks	lightweight	1200	0.38	plaster	gypsum	1280	0.46
	med. weight	1400	0.51		sand/cement	1570	0.53
	heavyweight	2300	1.63		vermiculite	640	0.19
bricks	exposed	1700	0.84	plasterboard	gypsum	950	0.16
	protected	1700	0.62	polystyrene	expanded	25	0.032
calcium silicate	board	875	0.17				−0.040
chipboard		800	0.15	polyurethane	board	30	0.025
concrete	aerated slab	500	0.16				−0.028
	lightweight	1200	0.38	rendering	external	1300	0.50
	dense	2100	1.40	roofing tiles	clay	1900	0.85
felt/bitumen	3 layers	960	0.50		concrete	2100	1.10
fibreboard		300	0.06	screed		1200	0.41
fibreglass	quilt	25	0.033	stone	reconstructed	1750	1.30
			−0.04		sandstone	2000	1.30
glass	sheet	2500	1.05		limestone	2180	1.50
hardboard	standard	900	0.13		granite	2600	2.30
mineral wool	quilt	12	0.033	stone chippings		1800	0.96
			−0.04	timber	softwood	650	0.14
	slab	25	0.035	vermiculite	loose	100	0.063
mortar	normal	1750	0.80	woodwool	slabs	600	0.11

Conservation of fuel and power

The *requirement* of Building Regulations part L 2006 is that reasonable provision shall be made for the conservation of heat and power by limiting heat gains and losses through the building fabric and services, and by providing energy efficient services and controls, and by providing the building's owner with sufficient information for efficient operation.

The regulations are split into L1 A for new dwellings, L1B for existing dwellings and L2A & B for new and existing non-dwellings.

For new buildings, compliance has to be demonstrated by SAP calculations comparing CO_2 emission rates of the building as designed with a Target Emission Rate, along with a demonstration of air-tightness by pressure testing on site. Limited trade-offs are permitted within maximum and average U-values so that for example use of a limited life renewable energy system should not be used as a basis for a poorly insulated building.

For works to existing buildings, compliance can be demonstrated in several ways including the elemental method where it is desired to minimise calculations. The requirement will be met if the U-values of the elements do not exceed those listed below *and*, in the case of dwellings, providing the area of windows, doors and roof lights does not exceed 25 per cent of the total floor area.

In addition, the efficiency of the boiler in a dwelling must equal or exceed the SEDBUK (Seasonal Efficiency of a Domestic Boiler in the UK) ratings set out below. Note that the elemental method cannot be used for buildings with direct electric heating.

Standard U-values for construction elements (where two figures given, first is for extensions and second for existing buildings)

Exposed element	W/m^2 K
Pitched roof (between 11°–70°) with insulation between rafters	0.20
Pitched roof with insulation between joists	0.16
Flat roof (0°–10°) or roof with integral insulation	0.20/0.25
Walls, including basement walls	0.30/0.35
Floors, including ground floors and basement floors	0.22/0.25
Metal framed windows, roof windows, rooflights (area weighted average for the whole building)	2.20

Standard U-values for construction elements – continued

Wooden or PVC framed windows, roof windows, rooflights, doors (area weighted average for the whole building)	1.8/2.00
Vehicle access and similar large doors	1.5

Type of condensing boiler	Minimum SEDBUK% rating
mains natural gas	88
LPG	88
Oil (combination boiler only)	82
Oil	85

Summary of U-values:
Elemental method of calculation (where 2 figures given, the first is for extensions and the second for existing buildings)

For a material change of use, i.e. a conversion, a 'reasonable upgrade' is required that is technically, functionally and economically feasible with an example of this being an upgrade whose simple payback is no more than 15 years.

Table 5 gives acceptable upgrades in U values as:

Cavity walls from	0.70	to	0.55
Other walls from	0.70	to	0.35
Floors from	0.70	to	0.25
Pitched roofs, ceiling insul	0.35	to	0.16
Pitched roofs, rafter insul	0.35	to	0.20
Flat roofs/integral insul	0.35	to	0.25

Source: Building Regulations Approved Documents L1 & L2 2006

Heat losses

As a rough guide, building heat losses will be between 20 to 50 W/m^3.

For normal conditions and temperatures 30 W/m^3 is average. Higher figures for tall, single storey buildings or large areas of glazing, lower figures for well-insulated buildings with minimal exposure, e.g. a building with 400 m^3 of heated space may require between 8 and 20 kW depending on conditions.

Recommended indoor temperatures	**°C**
Warehousing; factory – heavy work	13
General stores	15
Factory – light work; circulation space	16
Bedroom; classroom; shop; church	18
Assembly hall; hospital ward	18
Offices; factory – sedentary work	19
Dining room; canteen; museum; art gallery	20
Laboratory; library; law court	20
Living room; bed-sitting room;	21
Sports changing room; operating theatre	21
Bathroom; swimming pool changing room	22
Hotel bedroom	22
Indoor swimming pool	26

Source: *Series A Design data CIBSE*

Heat loss calculation

The heat loss from a room is the addition of all the individual *surface heat losses* of the doors, windows, walls, floor and ceilings, plus any *ventilation loss.*

Surface heat loss from any of these elements is calculated as:

element area m^2 × (inside °C – outside °C) × U-value of fabric = watts lost

For inside temperatures see list of *Recommended Indoor Temperatures* on p. 153. For outside temperature – 1°C is the figure normally used in the UK.

Ventilation loss is the heat lost through cracks and gaps in doors and windows.

With an average level of draught-proofing the following air changes per hour are assumed:

living rooms, bed-sitting rooms = 1
bedrooms = ½
kitchens and bathrooms = 2
halls and stairways = 1½
rooms with chimneys **add** = +1

Ventilation loss is then calculated as:

no. air changes/hour × room volume m^3 × (inside °C – outside °C) × 0.33 = watts lost

When assessing the size of a radiator for a room it is usual to add between 10 per cent and 15 per cent to allow for imprecision of heat loss calculations and for faster warm-up times.

Source: *The Which? Book of Plumbing and Central Heating*

Central heating and hot water systems

CONVENTIONAL CENTRAL HEATING and HOT WATER INSTALLATION
This system uses storage cisterns, usally located in the roof space to provide pressure for the hot water storage system, which consists of an indirect cylinder being fed from the boiler. Cold water may also be distributed around the house from the main storage cistern. Solar water heating can be added straightforwardly to this system by substituting a larger twin coil hot water cylinder and a solar thermal collector.

INDIRECT UNVENTED STORAGE SYSTEM with SEALED PRIMARY
This system stores hot water at mains pressure and provides space heating and water cyclinder may be located anywhere. Solar hot water can be simply added by substituting a larger twin coil mains pressure cyclinder and a solar thermal collector.

● = Service main   Ⓐ = Motorised valve   B = Boiler   C = Controls

◄► = Stopcock   ⊥ = Pump   R = Radiator   T = Thermosat

Sp = solar panel   TCC = Twin coil alternative cyclinder for solar

UNVENTED SYTEM with INSTANTANEOUS COMBINATION BOILER
This system is most suitable for small houses and flats where space is at a premium. As there is no hot water storage cylinder, the flow of hot water will be somewhat reduced but this is usually only noticed when running a bath or simultaneously using several taps. Some combination boilers are designed to suit preheated water, but many are not; space will be required for a solar preheat cylinder.

PRIMARY HEAT STORE with DIRECT VENTED PRIMARY
Here the hot water is stored at low pressure in a tank which is fed by a small feed tank over it. Mains water is fed into a high capacity coil where it is heated at mains pressure and blended with cold to stabilize the temperature. The system may be heated by a boiler or an immersion heater. With a boiler the recovery time is very fast. The flow rate is slightly less than an unvented storage system. Combining solar water heating with a thermal store simply requires an additional coil in the base of the store.

Source: Ideal Standard Ltd (revised for solar)

Radiators typical sizes and outputs

Panel radiators – steel

Heights: 300, 450, 600, 700 mm
Lengths: 400 to 3000 in 100 mm increments

Type	Thickness	Approx Output*
Single panel without convector	47 mm	1500 W/m²
Single panel with convector	47 mm	2200 W/m²
Double panel with convector	77 mm	3300 W/m²
Double panel with double convector	100 mm	4100 W/m²

* m² measured on elevation

Multicolumn radiators – steel

Heights: 185, 260, 300, 350, 400, 450, 500, 550, 600, 750, 900, 1000, 1100, 1200, 1500, 1800, 2000, 2200, 2500, 2,800, 3000 mm

Type	Thickness	Approx Output*
Two columns wide	62 mm	2150 W/m²
Three columns wide	100 mm	3000 W/m²
Four columns wide	136 mm	3700 W/m²
Five columns wide	173 mm	4600 W/m²
Six columns wide	210 mm	5400 W/m²

* m² measured on elevation
Sources: Caradon Ideal Ltd, Zehnder Ltd

Underfloor heating is the most widely used large-scale radiant heating system which has the efficiency benefit of promoting a temperature gradient to match human comfort, i.e. 'warm feet and cool head'. The mostly radiant aspect – most 'radiators' actually work largely by convection – avoids the build-up of hot air at ceiling level, particularly in high spaces. With comfort achievable at lower temperatures, fuel savings of 20 percent or more as compared to a radiator system, are common.

Floors are typically heated by oxygen-barriered polythene hot water pipes embedded in screed or set into insulation below timber floors. With pipes at 150 mm centres, heat outputs of around 120 W per sqm of a tiled or similar floor finish can be expected from a water temperature of 45°C. The low water temperature allows for the most efficient use of condensing boilers or alternative heat sources such as ground source heat pumps.

Electric underfloor heating has similar design advantages but typically high running costs and the environmental disadvantages of high primary energy use as with any electrical heating.

Ventilation

Means of ventilation

Required by the Building Regulations for rooms without full mechanical ventilation

	Rapid ventilation (e.g. opening window)	Background ventilation	Minimum fan extract rates or PSV*
Domestic buildings			
Habitable room	1/20th floor area	8000 mm²	no requirement
Kitchen	opening window (unsized) **or** fan with 15 mins overrun timer	4000 mm²	30 l/s (108 m³/h) adjacent to hob **or** 60 l/s (216 m³/h) elsewhere **or** PSV
Utility room	opening window (unsized) **or** fan with 15 mins overrun timer	4000 mm²	30 l/s (108 m³/h) **or** PSV
Bathroom (with or without WC)	opening window (unsized) **or** fan with 15 mins overrun timer	4000 mm²	15 l/s (54 m³/h) **or** PSV
Sanitary accommodation (separate from bathroom)	1/20th floor area **or** fan @ 6 l/s (21.6 m³/h)	4000 mm²	no requirement (but see rapid ventilation)
Non-domestic buildings			
Occupiable room	1/20th floor area	<10 m² = 4000 mm² >10 m² = 4000 mm² + 400 mm² per m² of extra floor area	no requirement

Means of ventilation – continued

	Rapid ventilation (e.g. opening window)	Background ventilation	Minimum fan extract rates or PSV*
Non-domestic buildings continued			
Kitchen (domestic type i.e. not a commercial kitchen)	opening window (unsized)	4000 mm^2	30 l/s (108 m^3/h) adjacent to hob **or** 60 l/s (216 m^3/h) elsewhere
Bathrooms (including shower rooms)	opening window (unsized)	4000 mm^2 per bath/ shower	15 l/s (54 m^3/h) per bath/shower
Sanitary accommodation (and/or washing facilities)	1/20th floor area **or** fan @ 6 l/s (21.6 m^3/h) per WC **or** 3 air changes/h	4000 mm^2 per WC	no requirement (but see rapid ventilation
Common spaces (where large numbers of people gather)	1/50th floor area **or** fan 1 l/s (3.6 m^3/h) per m^2	no requirement	no requirement (but see rapid ventilation
Rest rooms (where smoking permitted)	1/20th floor area	<10 m^2 = 4000 mm^2 >10 m^2 = 4000 mm^2 + 400 mm^2 per m^2 of extra floor area	16 l/s (57.6 m^3/h) per person

* PSV = passive stack ventilation
See notes on next page

Means of ventilation
Notes to tables on pages 157 and 158

Rapid ventilation openings should have some part at least 1.75 m above floor level. Methods of **background ventilation** are typically adjustable trickle ventilators or airbricks with hit-and-miss louvres located at least 1.75 m above floor level.

PSV means passive stack ventilation operated manually and/or automatically by sensor or controller in accordance with BRE Information Paper 13/94 or a BBA Certificate.

Passive stack systems are usually adequate for domestic-sized WCs, bathrooms and kitchens; since they have no fans or motors they consume no energy and require no maintenance apart from cleaning. Duct sizes are typically 125 mm diameter or equivalent rectangular section. They need to rise vertically at least 2 m and preferably 3 m above inlets and can include only limited bends; they need to discharge via special terminals at or near roof ridges.

An **open flued appliance** may be considered to provide ventilation if it has a free flue area of at least 125 mm diameter and is permanently open, i.e. no damper.

However if an open flued appliance is within the same room as an extract fan this may cause spillage of flue gases so:

Where a **gas appliance** and a fan are located in a kitchen the *maximum* extract rate should be 20 l/s (72 m³/h).

An extract fan should *not* be provided in the same room as a **solid fuel appliance**.

Kitchens, utility rooms, bathrooms and WCs which do not have openable windows should be provided with an *air inlet*, e.g. a 10 mm gap under the door.

Kitchen extract ventilation 'adjacent to hob' means within 300 mm of centreline of hob and should be either a cooker hood or a fan with a humidistat.

Utility rooms which are accessible only from outside the building need not conform with the ventilation requirements of the Building Regulations.

Adjacent rooms may be considered as one room if there is a permanent opening(s) of at least 1/20th of the combined floor areas, in the dividing wall.

Where a non-habitable space such as a **conservatory** adjoins a habitable room, the habitable room may be ventilated with opening(s) of at least 1/20th of the combined floor areas in both the dividing wall and the wall to the outside, both openings to have at least 8000 mm^2 background ventilation. The opening(s) to the dividing wall may be closable.

Source: *Building Regulations Approved Document F1 2006*

Heat reclaim vent systems

HRV systems can be particularly appropriate for new, low energy, 'airtight' buildings and those with multiple extract needs or where passive systems are not feasible.

Typically, multiple bathrooms, WCs, kitchens etc. within a single occupancy have linked extracts powered by a single low speed (boostable) fan through a heat exchanger to preheat incoming replacement air that is delivered to circulation areas or main spaces, achieving heat reclaim efficencies around 70%. In summer, airflow is diverted away from the heat exchanger. For a small house or flat, the central fan unit is typically the size of a small kitchen wall cupboard; flat or round section ducts can be located in floor, loft or partition voids.

For very low energy buildings without space heating systems, heating coils fed from a water heating appliance can be incorporated in HRV systems to give a warm air back-up.

Extractor fans

Sizing of fans

The size of a fan should take into account the size of the room and not necessarily be the minimum required by the Building Regulations.

It therefore makes sense to calculate the size of fan needed by using the desired number of air changes per hour and relating them to the room size.

Suggested air changes per hour for typical situations

Domestic		Non-domestic	
Living rooms	3–6	Cafés and restaurants	10–12
Bedrooms	2–4	Cinemas and theatres	6–10
Bathrooms	6–8	Dance halls	12–15
WCs	6–8	Factories and workshops	6–10
Kitchens	10–15	Commercial kitchens	20–30
Utility rooms	10–15	Offices	4–6
Halls and passages	3–5	Public toilets	6–8

To calculate the extract performance needed for a fan, multiply the volume of a room (m^3) by the number of air changes per hour required (ACH):

e.g. Domestic kitchen $4\,m \times 5\,m \times 2.5\,m = 50\,m^3$
air changes required $= 12$
$50 \times 12 = \mathbf{600\,m^3/h}$

one m^3/h	$= 0.777\,l/s$
one l/s	$= 3.6\,m^3/h$

Siting of fans

- Site fans as far away as practicable from the main source of air replacement which is usually the room door.
- Site fans where there is reasonable access for cleaning and maintenance.
- Fans in bathrooms must be sited out of reach of a person using a fixed bath or shower and must be kept well away from all sources of spray.
- Insulate ducts passing through unheated roof spaces to minimize condensation.
- Slope horizontal ducts slightly away from fan.
- Vertical ducts, and ducts in roof spaces, should be fitted with a condensate trap with a small drainpipe to outside.
- See pp. 157–159 for Building Regulation requirements and siting of extractor fans.

Types of fans

Axial fans are designed to move air over short distances, as through walls or windows.

Centrifugal fans are designed to move air over long distances and perform well against resistance built up over long lengths of ducts.

Sources: Vent-Axia Ltd and Xpelair Ltd

Electrical installation

Electricity

Electricity is sold by the *unit*.
One unit is consumed at the rate of one kilowatt for one hour (kWh)

Comparative costs of domestic appliances

Appliance	Time per unit
3 kW radiant heater	20 minutes
2 kW convector heater	30 minutes
iron	2 hours
vacuum cleaner	2 hours
colour TV	6 hours
100 watt lamp	10 hours
60 watt lamp	16 hours
20 watt mini fluorescent	50 hours
Tall larder refrigerator	63 hours

Typical usage of larger appliances		kWh
chest freezer	per week	5–8
dishwasher	one full load	1
cooker	per week for family of four	23
hot water cylinder	per week for family of four	85

Fuses – rating for 230 volt AC appliances

Rating	Colour	Appliance wattage
2 amp	black	250 to 450
3 amp	red	460 to 750
5 amp	black	760 to 1250
13 amp	brown	1260 to 3000

To find the correct amp rating of a socket for an appliance, divide the watts of the appliance by the volts i.e. watts ÷ 230 = amps.

Electrical installation graphic symbols

SUPPLY and DISTRIBUTION

electricity meter	
transformer	
distribution board	
isolator	
terminal to earth	
fuse	
circuit breaker	
lightning protection	
cable / conduit on diagrams	
cable / conduit on plans	

POWER

socket outlet	
switched socket outlet	
twin socket outlet	
socket outlet with pilot lamp	
connection unit	
switched connection unit	
connection unit with cable outlet	
connection unit with pilot lamp	
connection unit, four gang	
shaver socket	
cooker control unit with two pole switch	

COMMUNICATIONS SOCKETS

FM radio	
television	
private service television	
closed circuit television	
telephone	
telex	
modem	
fax	

SWITCHES

one pole switch	
one pole switch, two gang	
two, three, four pole switches	
two way switch	
intermediate switch	
switch with pilot lamp	
pull cord switch	
switch, time operated	
switch, period operated	
switch, temperature operated	
dimmer switch	
push button switch	
push switch, illuminated	
push on/push off switch	

LUMINAIRES

luminaire	
enclosed luminaire	
reflector	
spotlight open, enclosed	
flood open, enclosed	
linear open, enclosed	
emergency/safety open, enclosed	
emergency/safety self contained	
linear emergency/safety open, enclosed	
luminaire on wall open, enclosed	
luminaire on pole open, enclosed	
luminaire on suspension cable	
luminaire with built-in pull cord	

Source: BS 1192: Part 5: 1998

Electric circuits in the home

socket for TV amplifier

lighting circuit

ring circuit

fan

bathroom light

connection unit for bathroom heater

triple pole switch for servicing fan

shaver socket

water heater

2-way switches from ground to first floor

←lighting circuit

dimmer switch

light switch

2-gang light switch

connection units for appliances

security light

ring circuit

junction box

double pole switch to Greenhouse supply

30 20 30 30 30 30   5 5

main switch

split load consumer unit with RCD protection to the power circuit breakers

double pole switch to garage supply

meter

Electricity Company cut-out
PME protective multiple earth terminal

mains supply live and neutral

Greenhouse

low voltage transformer

Garage

freezer

armoured underground cable to 2-way consumer unit in greenhouse

garden fountain and lighting

armoured underground cable to 2-way consumer unit in garage

Lighting

As buildings are made more energy efficient, artificial lighting has become a more significant part of the energy balance. Building Regulations Part L require the use of a proportion of low energy fittings in new housing.

The use of fluorescent fittings instead of tungsten lamps typically saves 80 per cent of the electricity used and in non-domestic buildings where lamp changing is a significant cost, the typically 5 to 8 times longer lamp life increases the cost advantage to over 100 per cent despite the higher purchase costs.

Quality of light remains a disadvantage of fluorescent lamps for some applications, especially display, though LED (light emitting diode) fittings offer a useful alternative at similarly low energy use.

Poor design, lowest cost fittings and inadequate maintenance of fluorescent lighting has contributed (along with air-conditioning and indoor pollution) to 'sick building syndrome' in commercial buildings; use of electronic gear avoids the unpleasant flicker of start up and of older lamps, as well as allowing dimming linked to daylight levels to reduce energy consumption.

Particularly in offices, the general use of IT and VDU screens has shifted lighting demand away from general high light levels to glare-free lighting, often at lower levels generally combined with personally controlled task lighting.

Lighting glossary

candela (cd)   The SI unit of *luminous intensity* which is either light flux per solid angle – explained as quantities, or lumen per steradian – defined in terms of units.

CIE   Commission Internationale de l'Eclairage, who devised the *Colour Rendering Index*.

colour rendering   The ability of a light source to render colours naturally without distorting the hues seen under a full radiator (similar to daylight) in which all the wavelengths of the visible spectrum are present.

Colour Rendering Index (CRI)   An index based on eight standard test colours where the unit is *Ra*. Ra100 is the maximum value. Ra85 and above is considered appropriate for everyday comfort. The index can also be arranged in values of 1 to 4 according to DIN 3035.

Colour temperature   The absolute temperature of a black radiator (reference light source) which emits the same colour irradiation as a given light source measured in degrees Kelvin (K).

Compact flourescent   Small scale flourescent lamps, often with integral gear, for long life low energy use in small fittings.

Correlated Colour Temperature (CCT)   The colour appearance determined from its colour temperature given in degrees Kelvin. The lower the figure the warmer the light. Less than 3300 K is warm (red); 3300–5300 K intermediate and more than 5300 K cold (blue). The human eye cannot differentiate between individual spectral colours of a light source, it can only perceive a mixture of colours.

crown silvered lamp   A GLS lamp with part of the bowl silvered to project light backwards to avoid glare. Normally used with parabolic reflectors to give a narrow beam forwards.

dichroic mirror lamp   A small lamp with a built-in spiral, often faceted mirror reflector. This may be specifically made with honeycomb facets for medium–wide distribution and trapezoid facets for narrow beams. The mirror is made to reflect only certain colours of light and transmit heat radiation so as to produce a cool beam of light. The facets help to reduce striations in the beam, producing softer focusing with blurred edges to the beam.

discharge lamp   A light source from an electrical discharge passing through a glass containing vapour or gas.

efficacy   The ratio of initial lumens divided by lamp watts (lm/W). Typical efficacy for a GLS lamp is 8–18 rising to 100–180 for a low pressure sodium lamp.

Elliptical (E)   The shape of some discharge lamps.

Emergency lighting   Low output battery-powered lighting for escape purposes when mains power fails.

Flood (F)   A lamp designed with a wide beam.

fluorescent tube   A discharge tubular lamp, generally fitted with argon and low pressure mercury vapour. It has a phosphor coating on the inside giving off light (fluorescing) when excited by an electric arc through the vapour.

GLS   General Lighting Service: standard *tungsten filament* pear shaped lamps.

halogen lamp   An incandescent lamp filled with low pressure vapour of iodine or bromine. Sometimes referred to as *tungsten-halogen*.

HID   High Intensity Discharge lamps, i.e. *metal-halide, mercury* and *sodium* lamps.

HP   High Pressure, descriptive of some *mercury* and *sodium* lamps.

ILCOS   *International Lamp Coding System* produced by the International Electrotechnical Commission in 1993.

illuminance   The amount of light falling on a surface. The unit is *lux* which is one lumen per square metre (lm/m^2).

incandescent lamp   A tungsten filament enclosed in a glass envelope either under vacuum or filled with inert gas so that it can be electrically heated without burning out. Incandescent means luminous or glowing with heat; as a result can be an inefficient light source emphasizing reds, yellows and greens while subduing blues.

initial lumens   The light output of a lamp measured after one hour for incandescent lamps and 100 hours for fluorescent and discharge lamps. Lumens quoted in manufacturers' catalogues are 'initial' lumens.

IS   Internally Silvered. Used to describe the internal lining of a reflector lamp.

LED   LEDs are 'solid state' emitters of coloured light made from similar materials (semiconductors) to those used to manufacture electronic integrated circuits. They produce light by a very different method to incandescent, fluorescent or discharge lamps and do not require heat or high voltages to operate. An LED 'die' which typically measures just 0.25 × 0.25 mm, is encapsulated into a solid resin to produce an individual LED component with connecting leads.

LIF   Lighting Industry Federation (UK).

Light-Loss Factor (LLF)   The loss in light output from a luminaire due to dirt on the lamp or fitting. Now more normally referred to as *maintenance factor*.

Light Output Ratio (LOR)   The ratio of the total light emitted by a luminaire to the total output of the lamp(s) it contains – which is always less than unity.

lumen (lm)   The unit of *luminous flux* used to measure the amount of light given off by a light source.

lumen maintenance   The speed of decline of the initial amount of light.

luminaire   A light fitting.

luminance   The brightness of a surface in a given direction, measured in *candelas* per square metre (cd/m^2).

luminous flux   The flow of light energy from a source, or reflected from a surface, standardized for the human eye and measured in *lumens*. It is used to calculate *illuminance*.

luminous intensity   The amount of energy in a cone of light from a source. Units expressed in *candelas* (lumen/steradian).

lux   The unit of *illuminance* measured in lumens per square metre (lm/m^2). Bright sunlight is 100 000 lux; full moon is 1 lux.

maintained illuminance   The minimum light level over an area immediately prior to cleaning/re-lamping.

maintenance factor   The proportion of initial light output from an installation after some specified time.

mercury lamps   *Discharge lamps* filled with mercury vapour with moderate *colour rendering*, emphasizing yellows and blues which shift towards violet while subduing reds.

metal halide lamps   High pressure mercury discharge lamps with additives which can vary the light appearance from warm to cool.

opal   Describes an internal white silica coating to a lamp which diffuses the light and conceals the filament more positively than *pearl*.

PAR   Parabolic Aluminised Reflector (lamp). The number following PAR is the number of eighths of an inch of the lamp diameter, e.g. PAR38 = 4¾"Ø.

pearl   The acid etched internal finish to a lamp to mask and diffuse the glare from the filament. Less positive than *opal or satin*.

Rated Average Life (RAL)   The time by which 50 per cent of lamps installed can be expected to have failed.

reflector lamp (R)   A lamp with an *internally silvered* lining.

satin A lamp finish similar to *opal*.

sodium lamp (SON)   A highly efficient lamp with a warm yellow light, used mainly for street and flood lighting. It has poor colour rendering, with the low pressure (SOX) types making all colours except yellow appear brown or black.

spot (S)   A lamp producing a narrow beam of light as opposed to the medium/wide beam of a *flood*.

switchstart   A fluorescent lamp circuit incorporating a starter switch.

tri-phosphor lamp   A *fluorescent* lamp with good colour rendering.

tungsten-filament lamp   An *incandescent* lamp.

tungsten-halogen lamp   A *halogen* lamp.

Lighting: levels and colours

Comparative light levels	lux
Bright sunlight	100 000
Worktop near window	3 000
Precision task lighting	1 000*
Drawing boards	750*
Kitchen preparation areas	500*
General reading	300*
Entrance halls	150*
Corridors, storage	100*
Full moon on clear night	1

*Recommended minimum light levels

Colour temperatures	K
Blue sky	10 000
Uniform overcast sky	7 000
Average natural daylight	6 500
HP mercury cool white lamp	4 000
Fluorescent warm white lamp	3 000
Halogen filament lamp	3 000
GLS tungsten filament	2 700
HP sodium lamp	2 050

CIE Colour Rendering Index

Ra		Group
100	Where accurate colour matching is required, e.g. printing inspection	1A
90	Where good colour rendering is required, e.g. shops	1B
80	Where moderate colour rendering is acceptable	2
60	Where colour rendering is of little significance but marked distortion unacceptable	3
40	Where colour rendering is of no importance	4
20		

Lamps

Listed on the following pages is a survey of the main types of lamps available.

Excluded are the many variations of certain types and those which may be used for more specialized situations such as infra-red, UV stop, horticultural, black light, etc. Also excluded are the high output low sodium lights used mainly for road lighting. The list is therefore not comprehensive and manufacturers' catalogues should be consulted for more information.

Lumens quoted are for *Initial lumens*. The lowest values have been given, which are for pearl or opal versions of a lamp or the 'warmer' colour temperature fluorescent tubes.

Sources: G.E. Lighting Ltd, Osram Ltd, Philips Lighting Ltd, Concord Sylvania

Lamp bases

B22d B22d–3 B15d P40s P28s BA20d

E40s E27s E14s E12

GX38q PG22 BHP30s GX9.5 G17q / G17t G38 G6.35

G4 GY7–9 GY16 R7s G22 GY9.5 EMEP GX5.3 GZ4

Incandescent lamps

ILCOS code	Description	Watts	Size l × Ø	Lumens	Peak cd	Colour K	Life h
IAA	**GLS**	25	103 × 60	225	–	2700	1000
	standard bulb,	40	103 × 60	410	–	2700	1000
	pearl and clear	60	103 × 60	700	–	2700	1000
		75	103 × 60	930	–	2700	1000
		100	103 × 60	1350	–	2700	1000
		150	129 × 68	2100	–	2700	1000
		200	160 × 80	3000	–	2700	1000
		300	110 × 88	4550	–	2700	1000
		500	110 × 88	8200	–	2700	1000
IAA	**GLS Rough**	40	103 × 60	240	–	2700	1000
	Service	60	103 × 60	485	–	2700	1000
	RS, shock resistant and dustproof	100	103 × 60	850	–	2700	1000
I	**GLS mushroom**	40	88 × 50	385	–	2700	1000
	pearl, smaller than	60	88 × 50	660	–	2700	1000
	standard GLS	100	94 × 60	1250	–	2700	1000
I	**GLS double**	40	103 × 60	370	–	2700	2000
	life	60	103 × 60	630	–	2700	2000
	some also rated	100	103 × 60	1200	–	2700	2000
	3 000 hours	150	129 × 68	1900	–	2700	2000
IAA	**GLS colour**	15	103 × 60	–	–	2700	1000
	red, blue, green,	25	103 × 60	–	–	2700	1000
	yellow, orange &	40	103 × 60	–	–	2700	1000
	pink	60	103 × 60	–	–	2700	1000
IBP	**Golf Ball**	25	75 × 45	185	–	2700	1000
	small round, clear	40	75 × 45	350	–	2700	1000
	and opal	60	75 × 45	580	–	2700	1000
IAG	**Globe**	40	138 × 95	260	–	2700	1500
	large round,	60	138 × 95	470	–	2700	1500
	clear & opal	100	138 × 95	1020	–	2700	1500
IBB	**Candle**	25	97 × 35	185	–	2700	1000
	clear, opal,	40	97 × 35	350	–	2700	1000
	plain & twisted	60	97 × 35	580	–	2700	1000
IRA	**Crown silvered**	60	104 × 60	485	–	2700	1000
	clear lamp with	100	128 × 68	970	–	2700	1000
	silvered bowl to avoid glare						
IBS	**Pygmy**	15	57 × 28	105	–	2700	1000
	clear, compact,	25	63 × 28	175	–	2700	1000
	also coloured, RS, heat resistant						

Incandescent lamps – continued

ILCOS code	Description	Watts	Size l × Ø	Lumens	Peak cd	Colour K	Life h
IBT	**Striplight**	30	221 × 25	190	–	2700	1000
	two lengths,	30	284 × 25	190	–	2700	1000
	clear & opal	60	221 × 25	420	–	2700	1000
		60	284 × 25	420	–	2700	1000
IRR	**Reflector**	25	85 × 50	–	180	2700	1000
	pearl crown with	40	85 × 50	–	400	2700	1000
	integrated	60	103 × 64	–	750	2700	1000
	aluminium	75	115 × 80	–	1000	2700	1000
	reflector,	100	115 × 80	–	1400	2700	1000
	variants include	150	180 × 125	–	2500	2700	1000
	coloured R,B,G,						
	A & horticultural						
IRR	**Infra-red**	150	180 × 125	–	–	2700	6000
	Reflector	250	180 × 125	–	–	2700	6000
	heater lamp with	275	180 × 125	–	–	2700	6000
	clear or red front						
IPAR	**PAR 38**						
	with 15°	60	136 × 124	–	2600	2700	2000
	parabolic 30°	60	136 × 124	–	1100	2700	2000
	reflector, 15°	80	136 × 124	–	4000	2700	2000
	also coloured 30°	80	136 × 124	–	1750	2700	2000
	R, B, G, Y, A 15°	120	136 × 124	–	7000	2700	2000
	30°	120	136 × 124	–	3000	2700	2000
IPAR	**PAR 56**						
	narrow spot	300	127 × 178	–	70000	2700	2000
	medium flood	300	127 × 178	–	30000	2700	2000
	wide flood	300	127 × 178	–	10000	2700	2000

Incandescent lamps

GLS

crown silvered

PAR 38

mushroom

pygmy

reflector

golf ball

striplight

candle

globe

PAR 56

Data not given for standard incandescent lamps since soon redundant for energy reasons.

Halogen: low voltage

ILCOS code	Description		Watts	Size l × Ø	Lumens	Peak cd	Colour K	Life h
HRG	**35 mm Ø**	7°	12	41 × 35	–	6400	2900	2000
	Dichroic 12 V	10°	20	41 × 35	–	5500	2900	3500
	open and	30°	20	41 × 35	–	600	2900	3500
	closed	8°	35	41 × 35	–	9000	2900	3500
	versions	30°	35	41 × 35	–	1300	2900	3500
HRG	**50 mm Ø**	36°	20	49 × 51	–	500	3050	3500
	Dichroic 12 V	18°	35	49 × 51	–	3600	3050	3500
	open and	38°	35	49 × 51	–	970	3050	3500
	closed	10°	50	49 × 51	–	12000	3050	3500
	versions	38°	50	49 × 51	–	1550	3050	3500
HMG	**100 mm Ø**	3°	35	65 × 100	–	53000	3000	3500
	Metal	4°	50	65 × 100	–	55000	3000	3500
	Reflector	21°	50	65 × 100	–	3300	3000	3500
	12 V	18°	75	65 × 100	–	6750	3000	3500
HSG	**Capsule –**		10	33 × 9	140	–	3000	3000
	single ended		20	33 × 9	350	–	3000	3000
	12 V		35	33 × 9	650	–	3000	3000
			50	44 × 12	1000	–	3000	3000
			75	44 × 12	1600	–	3000	3000
			100	44 × 12	2300	–	3000	3000

Halogen lamps

dichroic 35 mm & 50 mm

PAR 30

PAR 38

metal reflector

linear halogen

BTT halogen

single ended capsule

globe halogen

tubular halogen

Halogen: mains voltage

ILCOS code	Description		Watts	Size l × Ø	Lumens	Peak cd	Colour K	Life h
HEGPAR PAR 30		10°	75	91 × 97	–	6900	2900	2500
	halogen	30°	75	91 × 97	–	2200	2900	2500
	reflector	10°	100	91 × 97	–	10000	2900	2500
		30°	100	91 × 97	–	3500	2900	2500
HEPAR PAR 38		11°	75	136 × 124	–	10500	3050	3000
	halogen	30°	75	136 × 124	–	2800	3050	3000
	infra-red	11°	100	136 × 124	–	15500	3050	3000
	reflector	30°	100	136 × 124	–	4200	3050	3000
HDF	**Linear–halogen**		200	79 × 10	3100	–	2900	2000
	double ended		300	118 × 8	4800	–	2900	2000
	also 100,150,250 &		500	118 × 10	9500	–	2900	2000
	1500 watts and		750	190 × 10	15000	–	3000	2000
	225,375 & 1000		1000	190 × 10	21000	–	3000	2000
	watt infra–red		2000	331 × 10	44000	–	3000	2000
	coated							
HDF	**Globe–halogen**		60	139 × 95	700	–	2900	2000
	white and clear		100	139 × 95	1300	–	2900	2000
			150	139 × 95	2000	–	2900	2000
HEGBT BTT–halogen			60	115 × 47	700	–	2900	2000
	clear & opal		100	115 × 47	1100	–	2900	2000
	replacements for		150	115 × 47	1450	–	2900	2000
	GLS lamps							
HEGT Tubular halogen			75	109 × 33	1000	–	2900	2000
	single ended		100	109 × 33	1450	–	2900	2000
	opal and clear		500	215 × 46	9500	–	2900	2000
	clear		1000	280 × 46	21000	–	3000	2000
	clear							

Compact fluorescent

ILCOS code	Description	Watts	Size l × Ø	Lumens	Colour K	Life h
FSD	**Single U tube**	5	105 × 28	250	2700 to	10 000
	2 & 4 pin	7	135 × 28	400	4000	10 000
		9	165 × 28	600	depending on	10 000
		11	233 × 28	900	type of lamp	10 000
		18	225 × 38	1200		10 000
		24	320 × 38	1800		10 000
		36	415 × 38	2900		10 000
FSQ	**Double U tube**	10	110 × 28	600	2700 to	10 000
	2 & 4 pin	13	138 × 28	900	4000	10 000
		18	152 × 28	1200		10 000
		26	170 × 28	1800		10 000
FSM	**Triple U tube**	18	114 × 49	1200	2700 to	10 000
	in triangular	26	131 × 49	1800	4000	10 000
	arrangement	32	153 × 49	2400		10 000
FBT	**Double U tube**	7	125 × 45	460	2700 to	10 000
	with E27 & B22	11	125 × 45	600	6000	10 000
	caps*	15	152 × 45	900		10 000
		20	165 × 45	1200		10 000
FSS	**2D**	10	140 × 140	650	2700 to	10 000
	2 & 4 pin	16	140 × 140	1050	6000	10 000
		21	140 × 140	1350		10 000
		28	205 × 205	2050		10 000
		38	205 × 205	2850		10 000
F	**Globe**-compact	15	175 × 110	720	2700	10 000
	fluorescent	20	200 × 125	960		10 000
F	**Self-ballasted**	9	151 × 73	450	2700 to	8000
		13	161 × 73	650	4000	8000
		18	171 × 73	900		8000
		25	181 × 73	1200		8000

*as direct replacement for GLS lamps without need for adaptor

Fluorescent lamps and tubes

single U tube

2D

self ballasted

double U tube

compact
fluorescent globe

triple U tube

circular

7 mm sub-miniature

16 mm miniature

26 mm standard tube

double U tube (for GLS replacement)

38 mm standard tube

Fluorescent tubes

ILCOS code	Description	Watts	Size l × Ø	Lumens	Colour K	Life h
FD	**7 mm Ø**	6	219 × 7	310	3000 to	8000
	sub-miniature	8	320 × 7	600	4000	8000
		11	422 × 7	680		8000
		13	523 × 7	860		8000
FD	**16 mm Ø**	4	136 × 16	115	2950 to	5000
	miniature	6	212 × 16	240	6500	5000
		8	288 × 16	340		5000
		13	517 × 16	750		5000
FD	**26 mm Ø**	15	438 × 26	1050	2700 to	15000
	tri-phosphor	18	590 × 26	1450	6300	15000
		30	895 × 26	2500		15000
		36	1200 × 26	3350		15000
		58	1500 × 26	5400		15000
		70	1778 × 26	6550		15000
FD	**38 mm Ø**	20	590 × 38	1050	2950 to	9000
		40	1200 × 38	2500	6500	9000
		65	1500 × 38	4200		9000
		75	1800 × 38	6400		9000
		85	1800 × 38	6400		9000
		100	2400 × 38	8450		9000
		125	2400 × 38	9300		9000
FC	**Circular**	22	216 × 29	1000	3000	12000
		32	311 × 32	1700	3000	12000
		40	413 × 32	2400	3000	12000
		60	413 × 32	3650	3000	12000

Lamp comparison

	GLS incandescent lamp		FBT double U compact fluorescent lamp		
	Lumens	**Watts**	**Watts**	**Lumens**	
	410	40	7	460	
	700	60	11	600	
	930	75	15	900	
	1350	100	20	1200	

High-intensity discharge lamps

ILCOS code	Description	Watts	Size l × Ø	Lumens	Colour K	Life h
	Metal halide					
MC	**Compact elliptical** metal halide	75	138 × 54	5000	3200	15000
ME	low wattage clear and coated	100	138 × 54	8000	3200	15000
		150	138 × 54	12000	3200	15000
MD	**Double ended** metal halide clear	70	120 × 21	6000	3200	6000
		150	137 × 24	13000	3200	6000
		250	162 × 26	20000	3200	6000
MT	**Single ended** metal halide clear	75	84 × 25	5200	3000	6000
		150	84 × 25	12000	3000	6000
	Mercury vapour					
QE	**Standard Elliptical** mercury coated	50	130 × 56	1800	4000	20000
		80	166 × 71	3800	4000	20000
		125	178 × 76	6300	4000	20000
		250	227 × 91	13000	4000	20000
QR	**Mercury Reflector**	80	168 × 125	3000	4000	24000
		125	168 × 125	5000	4000	24000
		160	168 × 125	2500	4000	24000
	Sodium vapour					
ST	**Tubular** HP sodium (SON) clear	50	156 × 39	4000	2200	24000
		70	156 × 39	6500	2200	24000
		100	211 × 48	9500	2200	24000
		150	211 × 48	17000	2200	24000
		250	260 × 48	32000	2200	24000
SE	**Elliptical** HP sodium (SON) coated	50	165 × 72	3600	2050	24000
		70	165 × 72	6000	2050	24000
		100	186 × 76	9500	2050	24000
		150	227 × 91	15500	2200	24000
		250	227 × 91	31500	2200	24000
STH	**Tubular** HP sodium (white SON) clear	50	150 × 32	2300	2500	5000
		100	150 × 32	4800	2500	5000

High-intensity discharge lamps

single ended metal halide

double ended metal halide

mercury elliptical

mercury reflector

HP sodium elliptical

HP sodium tubular

Sound

Noise levels

The level of hearing is expressed in decibels from 0 dB, the threshold of hearing, to 140 dB, the threshold of pain.

Ears respond to sound frequencies or pitch from around 20 Hz bass to 20 kHz treble. Most people are more sensitive to high rather than low frequencies, but old age reduces the perception of higher frequencies.

Recommended maximum dBA*

- Hospital and general wards   55
- Small consulting rooms   50
- Large offices   45–50
- Private offices   40–45
- Living rooms   40–45
- Small classrooms   40
- Large lecture rooms   35
- Bedrooms   30–40
- Music studios   30

* **dBA** are decibels weighted to simulate the response of our ears as opposed to plain **dB** which do not depend directly on human reaction.

Source: BS 8233: 1999

Sound levels

	dB range
	140
• Threshold of pain	130
• Pneumatic drill	120
• Loud car horn @ 1 m	110
• Pop group @ 20 m	100
• Inside tube train	90
• Inside bus	80
• Average kerbside traffic	70
• Conversational speech	60
• Typical office	50
• Family living room	40
• Library	30
• Bedroom at night	20
• Broadcasting studio	10
• Threshold of hearing	0

Source: Pilkington United Kingdom Ltd

Sound transmission loss of some typical building elements

Material	dB
One layer 9.5 mm plasterboard	25
Cupboards used as partitions	25–35
6 mm single glazing	29
75 mm timber studs with 12.5 mm plasterboard both sides	36
115 mm brickwork plastered one side	43
75 mm clinker concrete block plastered both sides	44
6 mm double glazing with 100 mm air gap	44
100 mm timber studs with 12.5 mm plasterboard both sides & quilt in cavity	46
115 mm brickwork plastered both sides	47
230 mm brickwork plastered one side	48
230 mm brickwork plastered both sides	55

Building Regulations Part E; 2000 effective since 2003. The latest revisions to the Building Regulations require pre completion testing for sound insulation for residential conversions and new buildings. The use of robust details in new houses and flats will be accepted as an alternative to testing.

5
Building Elements

Stairs

Building Regulations requirements

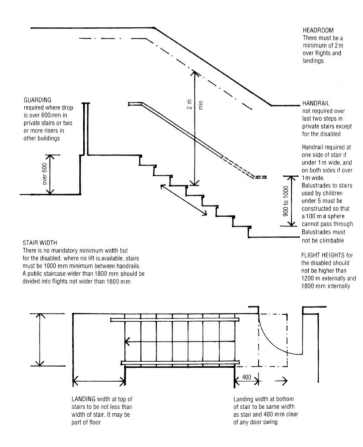

HEADROOM
There must be a minimum of 2 m over flights and landings

GUARDING
required where drop is over 600 mm in private stairs or two or more risers in other buildings

over 600

2 m min

HANDRAIL
not required over last two steps in private stairs except for the disabled

Handrail required at one side of stair if under 1 m wide, and on both sides if over 1 m wide.
Balustrades to stairs used by children under 5 must be constructed so that a 100 m ø sphere cannot pass through. Balustrades must not be climbable

900 to 1000

STAIR WIDTH
There is no mandatory minimum width but for the disabled, where no lift is available, stairs must be 1000 mm minimum between handrails. A public staircase wider than 1800 mm should be divided into flights not wider than 1800 mm

FLIGHT HEIGHTS for the disabled should not be higher than 1200 m externally and 1800 mm internally

400

LANDING width at top of stairs to be not less than width of stair. It may be part of floor

Landing width at bottom of stair to be same width as stair and 400 mm clear of any door swing

Building Regulations requirements – continued

30° minimum

landing width at
least width of stairs

LONG FLIGHTS
Stairs with more than 36 risers in consecutive flights should make at least one change of direction of not
less than 30°. No more than 16 risers in any flight of stairs serving areas used as a shop or for assembly

TAPERED TREADS measurement of going

270

270

going measured
←on this
width

not less
than 50 mm

more than 1 m

ba

ba

going measured
←at this
point

not less
than 50 mm

less than 1 m

ALTERNATING TREADS
may be permitted for
loft conversions where
there is no room for a
proper staircase. They
may only access one
room and must have
handrails both sides
and non-slip surface
to treads

LOFT CONVERSIONS
Headroom may be
reduced if height at
centre of stair is at
least 1900 mm and not
less than 1800 mm at
side of stair

220
min. going for
private stair

max. rise private stair 220

minimum
overlap
16

max. pitch
private
stair = 42°

←pitch→

OPEN RISERS
are allowed except for stairs for the disabled where
no lift is available.
Stairs used by children under 5 must have treads overlapping
a minimum of 16 mm and be constructed so that a 100 mm ø sphere
cannot pass through.

SOURCES:
Building Regulations Approved Documents
K   Stairs, ramps and guards
M   Access for disabled people
B   Fire safety
N   Glazing (for glass balustrades)
BS 6180: 1982 for strength of balustrades
Spiral and helical stairs should be in
accordance with BS 5395: Part 2: 1984

RISE and GOING	max. rise	min. going
Private stair	220	220
External stair for the disabled	150	280
Internal stair for the disabled	170	250
Institutional & Assembly stair	180	280
Assembly building < 100 m²	180	250
Other stair	190	250

normal ratio: twice the rise plus going
(2R + G) should be between 550 mm and 700 mm

Gradients

%	Slope	Application
5%	1:20	maximum uphill gradient preferred by cyclists maximum outdoor slope for pedestrians
6.5%	1:15.4	maximum downhill gradient preferred by cyclists
5.0%	1:20	maximum wheelchair ramp for a maximum length of 10 m and rise of 500 mm
6.7%	1:15	maximum wheelchair ramp for a maximum length of 5 m and rise of 333 mm
8.3%	1:12	maximum wheelchair ramp for a maximum length of 2 m and rise of 166 mm
8.5%	1:11.8	maximum indoor slope for pedestrians
10%	1:10	maximum ramp for lorry loading bays and most car parking garages
12%	1:8.3	any road steeper than this will be impassable in snow without snow tyres or chains maximum for dropped pavement kerbs of less than 1 m long
15%	1:6.7	absolute maximum for multi-storey car parks

Fireplaces

Building Regulation requirements
Fireplace recesses

minimum dimensions of solid non-combustible material

in a solid wall

in a cavity wall

back-to-back in separate dwellings   back-to-back in same dwelling

PREFABRICATED FIREPLACE CHAMBERS
may be used if made of insulating concrete
with the following minimum dimensions:

base	50
side walls	75
rear walls	100
top slab, lintel or throat gather	100

Constructional hearths

minimum dimensions

in fireplace recess

freestanding

CONSTRUCTIONAL HEARTHS are required for an open
fire, a gas flue where the flame is less than 186 mm
above floor finish, a solid fuel or oil burning appliance
where the temperature of the floor may exceed 100°C. If
below this temperature then appliance may sit on a non-
combustible board or tiles – both at least 12 mm thick.

Hearths must be at least 125 mm thick of
solid non-combustible material which
may include the thickness of any non-
combustible decorative surface.

Superimposed hearths

Minimum dimensions from the face of an appliance

Superimposed hearths are optional. They must be made of solid non-combustible material and be placed over a constructional hearth as shown on p. 190. An appliance must be located on a hearth (whether a constructional or superimposed hearth) with the minimum dimensions as shown in the drawings above. The edge of this area of hearth must be clearly marked such as by a change of level.

Minimum distances allowed between COMBUSTIBLE material and hearth. A combustible floor finish may only extend 25 mm under a superimposed hearth.

WALLS ADJACENT TO HEARTHS which are not part of a fireplace recess must have the following thickness and be of solid non-combustible material:

	t
HEARTH abutting a wall	
where **d** is 0–50	200
where **d** is 51–300	75
HEARTH not abutting a wall	
where hearth edge < 150	75

SOURCE:
This is a summary of some of the requirements from
The Building Regulations Approved Document J 2002

Chimneys and Flues

Building Regulations requirements

HEIGHT OF CHIMNEY (H) which includes
terminal should not exceed 4½ times the smallest
width dimension (W) (Bld. Regs. doc A)

MINIMUM WALL THICKNESSES of brick
and block chimneys excluding any liner
100 mm between one flue and another
100 mm between flue and outside air
100 mm between flue and another part of
the same building
200 mm between flue and another
compartment or building

Pitched roofs

Flat roofs with a pitch of less than 10°

CHIMNEY FLUE OUTLETS minimum height above roof

COMBUSTIBLE MATERIAL should be
separated from masonry chimneys by
at least 200 mm from flue OR 40 mm
from the outer face of the chimney
unless it is a floorboard, skirting, dado,
picture rail, mantelshelf or architrave.
Metal fixings in contact with
combustible materials should be at
least 50 mm away from flue.

COMBUSTION AIR will be required
for the correct operation of all flueless
and open flued appliances and some
room sealed models, and to ensure that
the products of combustion are carried
to the outside air.

These requirements are summarized
from The Building Regulations
Approved Document J 2002

Flues in chimneys should be vertical where possible. Maximum permitted offset is 45° to the vertical. Provision must be made to sweep flues, For sizes of flues see Table 2.2 in the Building Regs.

FLUE OFFSETS

Point liner joints with fireproof mortar. Fill void between liner and masonry stack with weak mortar or insulating concrete.

Liner sockets should be positioned uppermost to prevent condensation leaking into stack.

Brick and block chimneys should be lined unless made of refractory material.

FLUE LINERS

non-combustible material

non-combustible shield placed in front of combustible material with at least 12 mm airspace behind shield

UNINSULATED FLUEPIPE — minimum distances away from combustible material

FLUE PIPES should be used only to connect an appliance to a chimney. They should not pass through a roof space, internal wall or floor except to pass directly into a masonry chimney. Horizontal connections to the back of an appliance should not be longer than 150 mm. Flue pipes should have the same diameter or cross-sectional area as that of the appliance outlet.

Flue pipes may be made of:
Cast iron to BS 41
Mild steel at least 3 mm thick
Stainless steel at least 1 mm thick
Vitreous enamelled steel to BS 6999

BALANCED FLUES (room sealed) are mandatory for gas appliances fitted in bathrooms, shower rooms and gas fires or heaters of more than 14 kW (gross) in bedrooms. For positioning of balanced flues, see the numerous dimensional limitations as shown in diagram 3.4 of the Building Regs.

FLUES FOR GAS BOILERS – all new gas and oil boilers are required to be high efficiency condensing models under Building Regulations Part L. The majority of these will have fan assisted balanced flues with a concentric flue pipe where combustion air is delivered via the outer pipe and flue gases are discharged via the inner pipe; fan assistance allows these pipes to run horizontally for up to 10 metres or to include a number of bends. Alternatively, inlet and outlet pipes can be separated and, due to the very low flue temperatures, can be formed in plastic waste pipes. Condensing boilers often cause significant plumes of water vapour at their flue outlets, which needs to be considered in flue location alongside the limits in the Building Regulations diagram J 3.4.

Flueless instantaneous gas water heaters should not be installed in rooms less than 5 m³.

FACTORY-MADE insulated chimneys should conform to BS 4543 and be fitted to BS 7566.

SOURCE:
These requirements are summarized from The Building Regulations Approved Document J 2002.

Doors

Standard doors are still manufactured primarily in imperial sizes. The manufacturers claim that this is because of demands by the building trade. There is also a need for replacement doors in older properties and the apparently odd size 2'8" × 6'8" is still produced for this reason. There is more demand for metric sizes for large scale building projects but the choice is still limited. Unless a large quantity of doors is ordered, standard sized doors are still significantly cheaper than specials.

Because of the need to accommodate wheelchair users, wider doors are now more in demand. An 800 mm clear opening is considered the absolute minimum for a wheelchair user. Sixty mm should be deducted from the actual door width to arrive at the clear opening size. This dimension takes into account the thickness of the door and hinges standing open at one side and the rebate or stop on the other side.

Typical sizes of single leaf standard doors (metric)

	926 × 2040	826 × 2040	807 × 2000	726 × 2040	626 × 2040	526 × 2040	Thickness (mm)
Exterior							
Solid panelled			*				44
Glazed panelled			*				44
Flush		*	*				44
Steel faced			*				44
Framed and ledged			*				44
Ledged and braced			*				36
Interior							
Solid panelled				*			35
Glazed panelled		*	*	*			40
Flush	*	*		*	*	*	40
Moulded panelled	*	*		*	*	*	35 and 40
Fire							
½ hour	*	*	*	*	*	*	44
1 hour		*		*			54

Typical sizes of single leaf standard doors (imperial)

	838 × 1981 2'9" × 6'6"	813 × 2032 2'8" × 6'8"	762 × 1981 2'6" × 6'6"	686 × 1981 2'3" × 6'6"	610 × 1981 2'0" × 6'6"	Thickness (mm)
Exterior						
solid panelled	*	*	*			44
glazed panelled	*	*	*			54
Flush	*	*	*	*	*	44
steel faced	*		*			44
framed and ledged	*	*	*	*	*	44
ledged and braced	*	*	*	*	*	36
Interior						
solid panelled	*		*	*	*	35 & 40
glazed panelled	*	*	*	*	*	35 & 40
Flush	*	*	*	*	*	35 & 40
moulded panelled	*	*	*	*	*	35 & 40
Fire						
1/2 hour	*	*	*	*	*	44
1 hour	*	*	*	*		54

Other types of doors

Fire doors

Fire doors are available in most standard sizes in flush doors, and some are also available in internal moulded panelled doors. Half-hour and one-hour fire doors are only rated FD 30(S) and FD 60(S) when used with appropriate door frames which are fitted with intumescent strip (combined with smoke seal). The intumescent strips and smoke seals may also be fitted to the top and a long edges of the fire door. Existing panelled doors, particularly in listed buildings, can be upgraded to give 30 and 60 minutes fire protection, using intumescent papers and paints.

Source: Environmental Seals Ltd

French doors

Two-leaf glazed doors, opening out, are manufactured in hardwood and softwood in the following typical sizes:

Metric: 1106 wide × 1994 mm high; 1200, 1500 and 1800 wide × 2100 mm high

Imperial: 1168 wide × 1981 mm high (3'10" × 6'6") and 914 wide × 1981 mm high (3'0" × 6'6").

Sliding and sliding folding glazed doors

These are available in hardwood, softwood, softwood with external aluminium cladding, uPVC and aluminium in hardwood frames in the following metric nominal opening sizes typically:

2 leaf:	1200, 1500, 1800, 2100, 2400 wide × 2100 mm high	OX and XO
3 leaf:	2400 to 4000 wide in 200 mm increments × 2100 mm high	OXO
4 leaf:	3400 to 5000 wide in 200 mm increments × 2100 mm high	OXXO

Opening configurations are often labelled:

O = fixed panel and X = sliding panel when viewed from outside.

Some manufacturers offer all panels sliding.

Many manufacturers will make bespoke sizes to suit the height and width of openings dependent on the weight of the leaves.

Garage doors

Garage doors are manufactured in hardwood, softwood, plywood, steel and GRP. Doors can be hinged, or up and over, and can be electrically opened. The following typical sizes exclude the frame which is recommended to be a minimum of ex 75 mm timber.

	W mm	h mm
Single:	1981 × 1981	(6′6″ × 6′6″)
	1981 × 2134	(6′6″ × 7′0″)
	2134 × 1981	(7′0″ × 6′6″)
	2134 × 2134	(7′0″ × 7′0″)
	2286 × 1981	(7′6″ × 6′6″)
	2286 × 2134	(7′6″ × 7′0″)
	2438 × 1981	(8′0″ × 6′6″)
	2438 × 2134	(8′0″ × 7′0″)
Double:	4267 × 1981	(14′0″ × 6′6″)
	4267 × 2134	(14′0″ × 7′0″)
	other double doors available in widths up to 4878 (16′0″)	

Louvre doors

Hardwood open louvre doors suitable for cabinet and wardrobe doors.

28 mm thick and still made in imperial sizes:

Widths (mm):	305 (1'0")	530 (1'9")
	380 (1'3")	610 (2'0")
	457 (1'6")	
	also in 1981 (6'6") heights only	
	686 (2'3")	762 (2'6")

Heights (mm):	457 (1'6")	1524 (5'0")
	610 (2'0")	1676 (5'6")
	762 (2'6")	1829 (6'0")
	915 (3'0")	1981 (6'6")
	1219 (4'0")	

Bi-fold doors

Narrow full height doors, hinged in pairs, suitable for wardrobes. Supplied complete with sliding/folding gear. Typically moulded panelled doors but other larger sizes available with mirrored finishes.

Sizes per pair:	610 mm (2'0") × 1981 (6'6")
(mm)	762 mm (2'6") × 1981 (6'6")
	914 mm (3'0") × 1981 (6'6")

Sources: JELD-WEN UK, Premdor

Door handing

The traditional way of describing the configuration of a door is by the 'hand' – see **1**. There is also the ISO coding method **2** which describes a door's action as clockwise or anticlockwise. Despite its name it is not international and not widely used. Different components for a door sometimes conflict as, for instance, a door which requires a right-hand rebated mortice lock may need a left-hand overhead door closer. When in doubt, the specifier should draw a diagram.

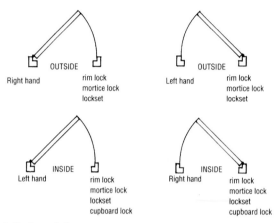

Right hand   OUTSIDE   rim lock
mortice lock
lockset

Left hand   OUTSIDE   rim lock
mortice lock
lockset

Left hand   INSIDE   rim lock
mortice lock
lockset
cupboard lock

Right hand   INSIDE   rim lock
mortice lock
lockset
cupboard lock

1   Handing method
The definition of an OUTSIDE FACE of a door is:
the external side of a door in an external wall;
the corridor side of a room door;
the side of a communicating door on which the hinge knuckles are not seen when the door is closed;
the space between them in the case of twin doors;
the room side of a cupboard, wardrobe or closet.

clockwise closing 5

anticlockwise closing 6

2   ISO coding method

	CODE		
clockwise closing	= 5	e.g. 5.0 =	clockwise closing/opening face
anticlockwise closing	= 6	5.1 =	clockwise closing/closing face
opening face	= 0	6.0 =	anticlockwise closing/opening face
closing face	= 1	6.1 =	anticlockwise closing/closing face

Direction of CLOSING and DOOR FACE are given to identify the door configuration as examples above.

Traditional wooden doors definitions and typical sections

The rails are fixed to the full height styles with haunched tenons & wedged.

Muntins are tenoned to rails

Dowels, as shown on LHS, can also be used for a stronger joint which withstands well uneven shrinkage.

All frame sections are grooved at least 9 mm to house the panels.

Stiles are normally ex 100 × 50 or 125 × 50

Bottom & lock rails are deeper, typically ex 200 × 50

Panels should be min 6 mm ply for internal doors and min 9 mm ply for external doors

Door made up of ex 150 × 32 ledges and ex 100 × 32 braces with ex 25 mm t+g 'V' jointed boarding not more than ex 125 mm wide.

Ledges are screwed to the boards and the boards are nailed to the ledges.

Door hung with steel Tee hinges or with stronger wrought iron strap hinges and fastened with a suffolk latch.

Four–panelled door

Ledged & braced boarded door

ex 100 × 75 head

ex 100 × 50 top rail with stuck (integral) moulding

9 mm ply panel

ex 200 × 50 bottom rail

ex 75 × 50 hardwood weather mould best morticed into door

Rebate in door frame for ms weather bar

ex 125 × 50 hardwood cill carried under side frames with min 9° slope

External door frame
for inward opening door

bolection moulding which projects outside frame
Raised and fielded panel

outside face

stuck mould inside with glass secured with putty outside   glazing beads   stuck mould outside with planted bead inside
Glazed door

architraves master joint between plaster & lining and provide stop-end for skirting

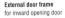

Door frame
ex 100 × 75 with rebate for door stop. Can be erected before walls or built into opening

Door lining
ex 32 mm with width to suit wall
Linings are thinner than door frames and for internal doors only. They have planted stops and are fitted to finished opening

Windows

Standard windows

Standard windows listed below are manufactured in softwood, softwood with aluminium cladding, hardwood, thermally broken aluminium and steel, and in PVC in a wide range of sizes and types. The sizes are approximate. Standard sized windows are less significant on smaller projects and most windows are made to order from standard sections or purpose-made.

Side hung casements
This is by far the most common type of standard window. They are available as single sashes or in twos, threes and fours. There are numerous combinations of fully-opening side hung sashes, one or more fixed lights and smaller top hung vents, with or without glazing bars. Side hung sashes can be fitted with concealed friction stays fixed over the top and under the bottom of sashes, in lieu of conventional hinges, for easier cleaning from inside.

Widths: 630, 915, 1200, 1770 and 2340 mm.
Heights: 750, 900, 1050, 1200 and 1350 mm.

Bay windows
Square, splayed at 45° semi-circular and shallow curved bay windows are available using combinations of fixed lights, side and top hung casements and double hung sashes to suit structural opening widths of approximately 1200 to 3500 mm with projections as little as 130 mm for shallow curved bays and up to 1000 mm for semi-circular bays.

Top hung casements
Top hung sashes generally without glazing bars.

Widths: 630, 915 and 1200 mm singles;
          1770 mm single with fixed side light.

Heights: 450, 600, 750, 900, 1050 and 1200 mm.

Standard windows – continued

Also vertical configurations with central horizontal transom and top hung opening sash to top half mimicking traditional double hung sashes.

Widths: 480, 630, 915, 1200 mm singles;
1700 and 2340 mm doubles.

Heights: 750, 900, 1050, 1200, 1350, 1500 and 1650 mm.

Fixed lights
A range of fixed light windows sometimes referred to as *direct glazed*.

Widths:	300, 485, 630 and 1200 mm.
Heights:	450, 600, 750, 900, 1050, 1200 and 1350 mm.
Circular:	600 mm Ø 'Bullseye'.
Semi-circular:	630, 915 and 1200 mm Ø fanlights with or without two 60° glazing bars.

Double hung sashes
Softwood double hung sashes with spiral balances, some fitted with a tilting mechanism allowing for easier cleaning from the inside. With and without glazing bars.

Widths: 410, 630, 860, 1080 mm singles;
1700 and 1860 mm combinations.
Heights: 1050, 1350 and 1650 mm.

Traditional double hung sashes hung on lead weights in boxes can be made to any size.

H-Windows
High performance softwood windows with complex hinge mechanism allowing partial projection for ventilation and complete reversal for cleaning. Available also as a side hung escape window.

Widths: 450, 600, 900, 1200, 1350, 1500 and 1800 mm.
Heights: 600, 900, 1050, 1200, 1350, 1500 and 1600 mm.

Sources: JELD-WEN UK, Premdor

Tilt and turn windows

High performance windows with two opening configurations: bottom hung inwards tilt for relatively secure ventilation, and side hung inwards turn for cleaning.

Standard windows – typical specification

Glazing

Most windows have rebates suitable for double glazing units (as required under Building Regulations) up to a thickness of 20 mm or 24 mm for high performance. Double glazed units are available with a choice of plain, obscured, annealed, laminated or toughened glass. To meet Building Regulations Part L, double glazing has to be thermally upgraded, usually by a low-e coating applied to the outer face of the inner pane. Hard coatings are more robust for handling, but soft coatings are more efficient thermally. Inert gas filling and the use of non-metallic insulating spacers to the perimeter maximize thermal performance, with triple glazing the next step to bring window U-values down to well below 1, as appropriate for Level 5 or 6 houses, for example.

Leaded lights are windows made up of small panes of glass, either regular or patterned as in stained glass, which are set in lead cames – 'H' section glazing bars.

Protection

The Building Regulations require that all glazing below 800 mm above floor level in windows and below 1500 mm above floor level in doors and sidelights, and sidelights which are within 300 mm of a door, should be fitted with safety glass. See p. 212. Small panes should have a maximum width of 250 mm and an area not exceeding $0.5 \, m^2$ and should be glazed with glass a minimum 6 mm thick. See diagrams on p. 204.

Weather stripping

Weather stripping should always be provided as standard to all opening lights.

Finishes

Timber windows are normally supplied primed for painting or with a base coat for staining. Options may include complete painting or staining with guarantees available up to 10 years.

Ventilation

Most windows are now fitted with ventilators in the head-frame providing either 4000 mm^2 in the narrower windows or 8000 mm^2 controllable secure ventilation to suit current Building Regulations in the wider windows.

Fittings

Fasteners, peg stays, hinges, etc. all supplied with the windows in aluminium, chrome, stainless steel, gold spray, lacquered brass, brown, white or other colour finishes, at extra cost.

Swept heads

Elliptical curves for the tops of panes available factory fitted or supplied loose.

Traditional wooden windows, definitions and typical sections

Casement window (left labels):
- head
- jamb
- top hung
- ventilator
- mullion
- transom
- top rail
- stile
- meeting stiles
- side hung sash
- bottom rail
- cill

Double hung window (right labels):
- outside lining to cased frame
- top rail
- stile
- glazing bars
- top sash
- meeting rail
- horn
- bottom sash
- bottom rail
- flush cill

Casement window

Double hung window

- cast iron weights
- plywood lining
- 21 × 8 parting bead
- 41 × 22 glazing bar
- Spring balances fixed in groove in 24 mm thick frame (modern alternative to pulleys weights & sash cords)

Nordan detail
Inward opening Alu-clad window

- 94 × 70 head & jambs
- 45 × 45 top rail and stiles
- 120 × 70 transom
- 70 × 45 bottom rail
- 165 × 70 cill

- 92 × 21 outside lining
- 116 × 21 pulley head
- 70 × 21 inside lining
- 19 × 14 removable staff bead
- 48 × 41 sash top rail and stiles
- 41 × 24 splayed and rebated meeting rails
- 70 × 41 bottom rail (deeper for larger sashes)
- 136 × 70 flush cill

92 · 31 · 94 · 57 · 88 · 57 · 101 · 41

Roof windows

Horizontally-pivoted roof windows

Designed for roof pitches between 15° and 90°. Pine or polyurethane frames, double glazed with a choice of glass: clear, obscured, toughened, laminated and low-e coated. Glass cavities can be gas filled to achieve U-values of 1.7 down to 1.1 W/m²K:

Standard sizes, overall frame w × h mm

550 × 700				1140 × 700	
550 × 780*					
550 × 980*+	660 × 980	780 × 980*+	940 × 980		1340 × 980
	660 × 1180*	780 × 1180*	940 × 1180	1140 × 1180*+	
		780 × 1400*	940 × 1400	1140 × 1400	1340 × 1400
		780 × 1600	940 × 1600*	1140 × 1600	1340 × 1600
		780 × 1800			

* = ex stock
+ = can be combined with tilted insulated kerb for flat roofs

Finishes: externally – grey aluminium as standard, other metals available.
internally – lacquered or white painted timber frames; polyurethane frames finished white.

Fittings: Control bar at head operates window and ventilation flap; friction hinges; barrel bolt for locking in two positions; security bolts.

Flashings: Available to suit most roofing materials.
If required they can enable windows to be fitted side-by-side or one-above-the-other and in groups.

Accessories: External awning blinds; roller shutters.
Internal insect screens; interior linings.
Roller, black-out, pleated or venetian blinds.
Cord, rod and electronic controls for operating sashes, blinds, etc.
Break-glass points.
Smoke ventilation system to automatically open window in the event of fire.
Pre-installed electric system to operate high level skylights via an infra-red remote control.

Top hung roof windows

Designed for low roof pitches where a pivoted window might interfere with headroom. Suitable for pitches between 15° and 55° (and up to 77° with special springs). Can be rotated 180° for cleaning. Some versions are available for an escape/access door. Sizes similar to pivoted windows.

Additional fixed light windows

These may be fitted directly above or below a roof window, within the same plane, to extend the view and increase daylight.

Balcony system

A top hung roof window opens out horizontally and is combined with a bottom hung lower sash fixed in the same plane. The lower sash opens out to a vertical position and railings automatically unfold to close the sides and create a small balcony.

Roof terrace system

This system combines a top hung roof window with a vertical side hung opening out sash fixed below with no intermediate transome, allowing access to a balcony or terrace.

Additional vertical windows

Where floor level is below the eaves and more light and view is required, bottom hung or tilt-and-turn windows may be fixed in the vertical plane directly below roof windows fixed in the sloping roof above.

Conservation Area roof windows

Horizontal pivot windows with a central vertical glazing bar, recessed installation and black aluminium external finish suitable for Listed Buildings and Conservation Areas.

Sizes:	550 × 980*	660 × 1180	780 × 1400

* A version of this window is available as a side hung escape/access roof window.

Source: Velux Company Ltd

Rooflights

Individual rooflights are typically square, rectangular or round on plan and come as flat glass sheets, domes or pyramids. Plastic rooflights to be suitable for any space except a protected stairway must be rated TP(a) rigid.

Typical sizes nominal clear roof openings
Square: 600, 900, 1200, 1500, 1800 mm.
Rectangular: 600 × 900, 600 × 1200, 900 × 1200,
                      1200 × 1500, 1200 × 1800 mm.
Round: 600, 750, 900, 1050, 1200, 1350, 1500,
                      1800 mm Ø.

Materials
Wired glass: Polished or cast glass, single or double glazed
                      Fire rating: Class 0
Polycarbonate: Clear, opal and tinted. Almost unbreakable,
                      good light transmission, single, double or
                      triple skins
                      Fire rating: TP(a) Class 1
                      Average U-values: single skin $5.3 \text{W/m}^2\text{K}$
                                                double skin $2.8 \text{W/m}^2\text{K}$
                                                triple skin $1.9 \text{W/m}^2\text{K}$
PVC: Clear, opal and tinted. Cheaper than
                      polycarbonate but will discolour in time.
                      Single and double skins
                      Fire rating: TP(a) Class 1
                      U-values: single skin $5.05 \text{W/m}^2\text{K}$
                                          double skin $3.04 \text{W/m}^2\text{K}$

Curbs
Curbs are generally supplied with rooflights, but they may also be fitted directly to builder's timber or concrete curbs. Curbs typically have 30° sloping sides, are made of aluminium or GRP and stand up 150–300 mm above roof deck.

They may be uninsulated, insulated or topped with various forms of ventilators, normally fixed or adjustable louvres, hand or electrically operated.

Access hatch: Hinged rooflight, manually or electrically operated, typically 900 mm sq.

Smoke vent: Hinged rooflight linked by electron magnets to smoke/heat detecting systems.

Optional extras: Bird and insect mesh for vents in curbs.
                    Burglar bars – hinged grille fixed to curb or in-situ upstand.

Sources: Cox Building Products, Duplus Domes Ltd, Ubbink (UK) Ltd

Sunpipes

A mirror-coated tube which transfers daylight from a diamond faceted dome, or flush square rooflight, at roof level to an internal space. It can suit any roof profile and bend to suit the geometry. Diameters range from 230–530 mm and can be combined with solar powered ventilation.

UV protected poly-carbonate top-dome

Nylon condensation trap

Under-felt support plate

560 x 560 overall flashing plate

Adjustable elbow

Plywood fixing panel

Ceiling diffuser

230 d
Sunpipe

250 d
Required ceiling opening

Sunpipe diameters range from 230 to 530 mm (d)

Source: Monodraught Sunpipe

Patent glazing A system of puttyless glazing normally used for roofs but can also be used for curtain walling. The glazing bars, usually aluminium, can be several metres long and are normally spaced at 600 mm centres. The bars have concealed channels to drain the moisture out at the eaves of the roof or the bottom of the wall glazing. Double glazed with sealed units or single glazed over external spaces.

Security fittings

Security against intruders is becoming ever more sophisticated with new electronic technology. However, it is important to ensure the physical protection of buildings and particularly to have a secure perimeter.

External doors

External doors must be sufficiently strong and properly installed to resist shoulder charges and kicking. Doorframes should have minimum 18mm rebates and be firmly fixed to openings at 600mm centres. Doors should have a minimum thickness of 44mm with stiles at least 119mm wide to accommodate locks. Panels should not be less than 9mm thick. Flush doors should be of solid core construction. Meeting styles of double doors should be rebated.

Door ironmongery

Front doors should be fitted with a *high security cylinder lock* for use when the building is occupied, with an additional five- or seven-lever *mortice deadlock* to BS 3621. Back and side doors should be fitted with a similar deadlock with two *security bolts* at the top and bottom. Deadlocks should have *boxed striking plates* to prevent jemmy attack and *hardened steel rollers* to resist hacksawing. Doors should be hung on three (1½ pairs) metal broad *butt hinges*. Outward opening doors should have *hinge bolts* to prevent doors being levered open on the hinge side. Position *letter plates* at least 400mm from any lock. Fit *door viewers* and *door chains* to any door likely to be opened to strangers. Chains should be fixed with 30mm long screws to prevent being forced open. Entrance doors should be lit so that callers can be seen at night. Burglars are wary of breaking glass, so glass doors are not necessarily vulnerable providing the glass is fixed from the inside. However, sliding glass doors are particularly vulnerable. The main mortice lock bolt should be supplemented by a pair of key-operated locking bolts fixed at the top and bottom. *Anti-lift devices* should be fitted in the gap between the door panel and frame to prevent the outer door being lifted off the runners.

Windows

Rear windows are most at risk, as are windows accessible from balconies or flat roofs. Sliding windows should be designed so that it is impossible to remove sashes or glass from the outside. External hinge pins and pivots should be secured by burring over. Avoid rooflights which have domes fixed with clips that can be broken from outside. Where escape from fire is not required, fix *metal bars* or *grilles* below rooflights.

Window ironmongery

All ground floor, basement and any upper floor vulnerable windows should be fitted with two *security bolts* to each casement sash and to the meeting rails of double hung sashes. Upper floor sashes should have at least one security bolt. For greater safety choose locks with a *differ key* rather than those with a common key, which experienced intruders will own. Many window handles include locks as standard.

Other physical devices

Collapsible grilles, sliding shutters and, where appropriate, *blast and bullet-proof screens* and *ram stop bollards*.

Safes for domestic use can be as small as 'two brick' *wall safes* or *floor safes* let into floors. Larger floor safes weigh from 370 kg to 2300 kg and must be anchored to floors. Locks may be key, combination or electronic.

Electronic devices include the following:

- Access control –   voice/video, keypad, card reading entry, phone systems
- Intruder detection – intruder alarms, CCTV surveillance, security lighting
- Fire protection –   smoke and heat detection, fire alarms, 'break glass' switches, automatic linking to fire stations.

Sources: *A Guide to the Security of Homes*
Home Security and Safety
Banham Patent Locks Ltd
Chubb Physical Security Products

Protection for glazing indoors and windows Based on Building Regulations Approved Document N

1. Dotted areas show critical locations in internal and external glazing in doors, side panels, screens and windows.

There are certain areas of glazing which can prove hazardous, particularly to children.

1. Shows the extent of these areas which should be glazed with safety glass or safety plastic to BS 6206:1981.

2. Alternatively glass in these areas should be in small panes **OR**

3. If glazed with standard annealed glass these areas should be protected inside and out with a permanent screen.

2. If annealed glass is used, it should be in small panes not larger than 0.5 m² with a maximum width of 250 mm. The glass should be at least 6 mm thick.

4. Annealed glass thickness/dimension limits. Some annealed glass is considered suitable for use in public buildings for showrooms, offices, etc. and will conform providing it does not exceed the thickness/dimension limitations shown above.

Large areas of glass in non-domestic buildings should 'manifest' themselves with a line of pattern, logo, etc. at 1500 mm above FFL, unless the presence of the glass is made obvious by the use of mullions, transoms, wide frames, large handles or something similar.

3. If annealed glass is used for low level glazing then it must be protected inside and out with permanent screens. These should be at least 800 mm high, unclimbable, i.e. not horizontal rails and designed so as to prevent a 75 mm ø sphere touching the glazing.

6
Materials

Brickwork and Blockwork

Brick sizes

The work (actual) size of the standard brick is

$$215 \times 102.5 \times 65\,mm$$

For the co-ordinating size, which includes the width of one mortar joint, add 10 mm, i.e.

$$225 \times 112.5 \times 75\,mm$$

Metric modular sizes:

$$190 \times 90 \times 65\,mm$$

Other less available brick sizes:

$$215 \times 102.5 \times 50\,mm$$
$$215 \times 102.5 \times 73\,mm$$
$$215 \times 102.5 \times 80\,mm$$

Weights of bricks

	kg/m³
Blue	2405
Engineering	2165
Sand cement	2085
Fire brick	1890
London stock	1845
Sand lime	1845
Flettons	1795
Red facings	1765
Diatomaceous	480

Compressive strengths and percentage water absorption

Brick	N/mm²	water absorption % by mass
Engineering Class A	>70	<4.5
Engineering Class B	>50	<7.0
Flettons	14–25	15–25
London stocks	3–18	20–40
Hand moulded facings	7–60	10–30

Frost resistance and soluble-salt content of bricks

Designation	Frost resistance	Soluble-salt content
FL	frost resistant	low salt content
FN	frost resistant	normal salt content
ML	moderate frost resistance	low salt content
MN	moderate frost resistance	normal salt content
OL	not frost resistant	low salt content
ON	not frost resistant	normal salt content

Spacing of wall ties

65–90 mm leaf thickness   = 450 horizontally/450 mm vertically
Over 90 mm leaf thickness = 900 horizontally/450 mm vertically
For wider caivities spacing may decrease

Cavity wall ties

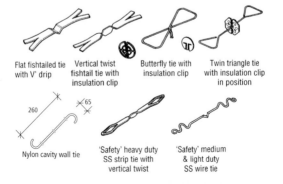

Flat fishtailed tie
with 'V' drip

Vertical twist
fishtail tie with
insulation clip

Butterfly tie with
insulation clip

Twin triangle tie
with insulation clip
in position

Nylon cavity wall tie

'Safety' heavy duty
SS strip tie with
vertical twist

'Safety' medium
& light duty
SS wire tie

Cavity Wall ties are made in stainless steel (wire diameters from 2.5–4.5 mm) or reinforced plastic for reduced thermal bridging, which can be equivalent to 50 mm of cavity insulation. Lengths are from 150–300 mm depending on wall thickness and cavity width. Extra long ties are available for insulated cavities up to 250 mm wide.

Traditional fish tailed ties are now largely superseded because of their sharp edges by SS 'safety' ties as less wire is used in their manufacture. Most ties are fitted with clips to retian partial cavity insulation boards. Outer leaf moisture/drips from central twists and kinks.

Block sizes

The standard block face dimensions are:
440 × 215 mm and 440 × 140 mm, with thicknesses of 75, 90, 100, 140, 150, 190, 200 and 215 mm.

Health & safety restrictions on site manual lifting limit block weights to no more than 20 kg, which restricts the use of

SOLID
440 × 140 × 215 h (most used size)
Load bearing and good for external fair-faced work

HOLLOW
Voids open at both ends
Can be used for vertical reinforcement

CELLULAR
Voids closed at one end
Voids normally laid uppermost
Lighter and therefore easier to lay
Slightly cheaper than solid blocks

THERMAL
Light weight concrete blocks
to give lower U values

SOUND ABSORBING
Slots in one face connect to voids filled
with mineral wool
Unplastered & fair faced. Useful for
sports halls, sound studios, etc.

CONCRETE BLOCKS are generally available in four main grades:

Architectural:	'The Best'; precision made and consistent in colour for fair faced work
Fair faced:	Good quality for unplastered or painted walls
Paint quality:	Suitable for a direct paint finish
Standard:	Cheapest and suitable for plastering and rendering

dense solid blocks in standard formats to 100 mm thickness, or their substitution by lightweight aggregate or hollow blocks; hollow dense blocks up to 190 mm thick are within the 20 kg limit.

Typical foundation block sizes are:
440 × 215 mm and 440 × 140 mm, with thicknesses of 224, 275, 305 and 355 mm. Unless these are mechanically handled, lightweight blocks are used.

Compressive strength:
Blocks range from 2.8 to 7.0 N/mm^2 depending on composition. 4.0 N/mm^2 is average.

There is a wide range of medium and lightweight blocks available from most block manufacturers; the most effective thermal insulating blocks are made from aerated concrete and can achieve conductivities as low as 0.11, which can make a significant contribution to wall insulation.

Several aerated concrete block makers have ranges of thin joint 'glued' masonry which speeds construction, improves accuracy and thermal performance.

For environmental reasons, unfired clay blocks and bricks alongside hemp-lime and similar materials are available for less structurally demanding conditions.

Concrete paving slabs

Type	Nominal size (mm)	Thickness	Number/m^2
A	600 × 450	50 + 63	3.70
B	600 × 600	50 + 63	2.77
C	600 × 750	50 + 63	2.22
D	600 × 900	50 + 63	1.85

Brickwork bonds

ENGLISH BOND
A strong bond which is easy to lay but is somewhat monotonous in appearance.

FLEMISH BOND
This bond with its even, readily understood pattern is generally considered more attractive than English bond.

ENGLISH GARDEN WALL BOND
This bond reduces the numbers of headers making it easier to build both faces of the wall as fair faced.

FLEMISH GARDEN WALL BOND
This requires a fairly large area of wall for the pattern to be appreciated. Careful laying is needed to keep the perpends true, especially if the headers are a different colour from the stretchers.

BOND STRENGTH
In any bond, it is important that the perpends (vertical joints) should not be less than one quarter of the brick length from those in the adjacent course.

STRETCHER BOND
Sometimes called *running* bond, this is the bond for half brick walls.

Mortar mixes for brickwork and blockwork

Grade desig-nation	Cement: lime: sand	Masonry cement: sand	Cement: sand with plasticiser	Compressive strengths N/mm^2 preliminary site	
I	1 : ¼ : 3	–	–	16.0	11.0
II	1 : ½ : 4 to 4½	1 : 2½ to 3½	1 : 3 to 4	6.5	4.5
III	1 : 1 : 5 to 6	1 : 4 to 5	1 : 5 to 6	3.6	2.5
IV	1 : 2 : 8 to 9	1 : 5½ to 6½	1 : 7 to 8	1.5	1.0

Notes:

1   Mortar designation I is strongest, IV is weakest.

2   The weaker the mix the more it can accommodate movement.

3   Where sand volume varies, use the larger quantity for well graded sands and the smaller quantity for coarse or uniformly fine sands.

4   Grade I and II for high strength bricks and blocks in walls subject to high loading or walls subject to high exposure such as retaining walls, below DPC, parapets, copings and free standing walls.

5   Grade III and IV for walls between DPC and eaves not subject to severe exposure.

Pure lime mortars, using lime putty or hydraulic lime without cement, are widely used for historic building work and for new work where expansion joints are to be avoided; for weaker bricks and stones, lime mortars offer a longer life and better weather resistance.

Joints

Flush
Maximum bearing area
Useful for coarse textured bricks
Evens out run-off and absorption;
best for long life and weather resistance

Bucket handle
More visual joint emphasis than flush and almost as strong and weather resistant

Struck or weathered
Gives a shadow line to joint. If correctly made is strong and weather resistant

Recessed
This can allow rain to penetrate and should be confined to frost-resistant bricks and sheltered situations.

Special bricks

BULLNOSE

single bull-
nose

bullnose internal
return
on flat

cownose

double
bullnose

bullnose external
return
on edge

cownose
stop

single
bullnose
stop

bullnose external
return
on flat

double
bullnose
stop

bullnose
mitre

Bullnose, angle, cant and
plinth brick dimensions are
based on the standard brick
215 × 115 × 65 mm.

bullnose
header on
flat

bullnose double
header
on flat

bullnose
stretcher
on flat

bullnose double
stretcher
on flat

ARCH

tapered
header

bullnose internal
return
on end

stop end
to
double
bullnose

tapered
stretcher

bullnose internal
return
on edge

double bullnose
external
return
on edge

Arch bricks are available with
four different tapers to suit
diameters at approximately
900 to 2700 mm.

Special bricks – continued

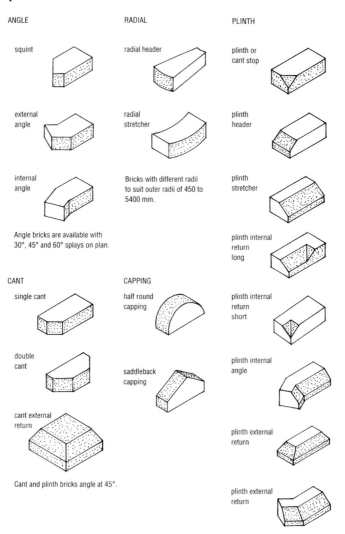

ANGLE

squint

external angle

internal angle

Angle bricks are available with 30°, 45° and 60° splays on plan.

RADIAL

radial header

radial stretcher

Bricks with different radii to suit outer radii of 450 to 5400 mm.

PLINTH

plinth or cant stop

plinth header

plinth stretcher

plinth internal return long

plinth internal return short

plinth internal angle

plinth external return

plinth external return

CANT

single cant

double cant

cant external return

Cant and plinth bricks angle at 45°.

CAPPING

half round capping

saddleback capping

Dotted shading indicates faced surfaces as standard.

Source: Ibstock Brick Ltd

Brick paving patterns

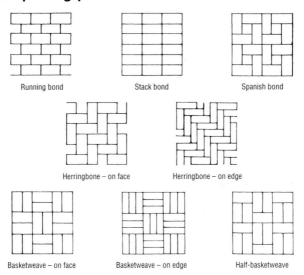

Running bond

Stack bond

Spanish bond

Herringbone – on face

Herringbone – on edge

Basketweave – on face

Basketweave – on edge

Half-basketweave

Clayware – definitions

earthenware Pottery made from brick earth; softer than stoneware. Exposed surfaces are often glazed.

firebrick Bricks made from any clay which is difficult to fuse and generally has a high quartz content. Used for fire backs and boiler liners for temperatures up to 1600°C.

stoneware Highly *vitrified clayware* used for sanitary fittings and drainpipes.

vitreous china A strong high-grade ceramic ware made from white clays and finely ground minerals. All exposed surfaces are coated with an impervious non-crazing vitreous glaze. Used for sanitary ware, it is easy to clean but brittle compared with *glazed stoneware*.

vitrified clayware Clay which is hard-burnt to about 1100°C and therefore vitrified throughout. It has low water absorption, and can be used unglazed for floor tiles, drainpipes, etc. Can be fair cut with an angle grinder.

Concrete – some types and treatments

aerated concrete A lightweight concrete with no coarse aggregates, made of cement, lime, sand and chemical admixtures which cause bubbles to make a cellular consistency. It has low strength but good insulation properties. It is easily cut and nailable. There are many grades, some unsuitable below ground. Water absorption will impair its thermal performance.

bush hammering Tooling concrete or stone with a compressed air hammer to remove 1 to 6 mm of the outer skin to reveal a surface texture that improves its appearance.

granolithic finish A thin topping of cement, granite chippings and sand laid over a concrete slab, preferably as a monolithic screed to provide a good wearing surface. Can be made non-slip by sprinkling carborundum powder over the surface before final trowelling.

glass-reinforced concrete (GRC) Precast concrete, reinforced with glass fibre to make thin panels with improved strength and impact resistance.

polymer-impregnated concrete Concrete made with a polymer to improve the strength by filling all the voids normally left in conventional concrete. Water absorption is thus reduced and the concrete has greater dimensional stability.

refractory concrete Concrete made with high alumina cement and refractory aggregate, such as broken firebrick, to withstand very high temperatures.

Stonework

Building stone comes from three rock types:
- **Igneous** rocks formed from cooled molten rock, e.g. granite
- **Metamorphic** rocks formed from the re-crystallization of previous rocks after heat and pressure, e.g. slate and marble
- **Sedimentary** rocks formed from ancient sediments deposited on sea or river beds and then compacted or naturally cemented, e.g. limestone or sandstone.

Typical building stones

Stone	County	Colour	Dry weight kg/m^3	Compressive strength kN/m^2
Granites				
Cornish	Cornwall	silvery grey	2610	113 685
Peterhead	Grampian	bright red	2803	129 558
Rubislaw	Grampian	bluish-grey	2500	138 352
Sandstones				
Bramley Fell	W Yorks.	grey to buff	2178	42 900
Darley Dale	Derbys.	light grey	2322	55 448
Forest of Dean	Glos.	grey to blue	2435	67 522
Kerridge	Derbys.	buff	2450	62 205
Runcorn red	Cheshire	red & mottled	2082	27 242
Limestones				
Ancaster	Lincs.	cream to brown	2515	23 380
Bath	Wilts/ Somerset	lt. brown to cream	2082	24 024
Clipsham	Leics.	pale cream to buff	2322	29 172
Mansfield	Notts.	creamy yellow	2242	49 550
Portland	Dorset	lt. brown to white	2210	30 780

Mortar mixes for stonework

Typical mix			Application
cement	: lime : sand	1 : 3 : 12	dense stones (granite, etc.), not limestones
Putty/hydraulic	: lime : sand	2 : 5	most building stones
cement	: lime : sand	1 : 2 : 9	exposed details, not limestones
cement	: lime : sand	1 : 1 : 6	most sandstones

Joints	mm thickness
internal marble cladding	1.5
external cladding	2 to 3
slate cladding	3
large slabs	4.5
polished granites	4.5
fine ashlar	6 maximum
rubble walls	12 to 18

Sources: *Building Construction, Stone in Building*

Damp-proof courses (DPCs)

DPCs provide an impermeable barrier to the passage of moisture from below, from above or horizontally. They can be flexible, semi-rigid or rigid. Rigid DPCs are only suitable for rising damp. Soft metal DPCs are expensive but safest for intricate situations. Cavity trays are needed above elements that bridge cavities to direct water to outside. DPCs should be bedded *both* sides in mortar. Seal DPCs to floor membranes. Upper and vertical DPCs should always lap over lower or horizontal ones. DPCs must not project into cavities where they may collect mortar and bridge the cavity.

Type	Material	Minimum thickness mm	Joint	Application	Remarks
Flexible polymer based	polyethylene	0.46	100 mm min lap and sealed	H at base of walls, under cills, vertical jambs	appropriates lateral movement; tough, easy to seal, expensive, can be punctured
	bitumen polymer	1.5	100 mm min lap and sealed	H at base of walls, stepped; CT; V at jambs	
Flexible bitumen based	bitumen/hessian base	3.8	100 mm min lap and sealed	H at base of walls, under copings, cills; CT, V at jambs	hessian may decay, but OK if bitumen not disturbed. If cold, warm DPC before use, may extrude under high loads or temperatures
	bitumen/hessian base/lead	4.4	100 mm min lap and sealed	H at base of walls, under copings, cills; CT, V at jambs	lead lamination gives extra tensile strength
Semi-rigid	mastic asphalt	12.0	none	H under copings	grit should be added for key, liable to expand
	lead	1.8	100 mm min, welted against damp from above	H under copings, chimney stacks	corrodes in contact with mortar, protect by coating both sides with bitumen
	copper	0.25	100 mm min, welted against damp from above	H under copings, chimney stacks	good against corrosion, difficult to work, may stain masonry green
Rigid	slate	two courses 4.0	laid to break joint	H at base of free-standing and retaining walls	very durable, bed in 1 : 3 sand cement
	brick to BS 3921	two courses 150	laid to break joint	H at base of free-standing and retaining walls	good for freestanding walls

H = horizontal; V = vertical; CT = cavity tray.

Damp-proof membranes (DPMs)

DPMs are sheet or liquid membranes designed to resist damp caused by capillary action. They do not have to perform as well as tanking membranes, which must resist water pressure. DPMs may be positioned under site slabs providing the hardcore is smoothed with 25 mm minimum rolled sand or preferably 25 mm smooth blinding concrete. This position is more vulnerable to damage than placing them over smooth finished site slabs. In this position the membrane can prevent satisfactory bonding between slab and screed, so a thick screed is needed, ideally at least 63 mm.

DPMs must be carried up to lap or join DPCs in walls. Brush-applied membranes are better than sheets in this respect.

Care must be taken not to penetrate membranes when laying. Any pipe ducts must be in position before screeds are poured, as any subsequent chasing could well damage the DPM.

Type	Description
Low density polyethylene film (LDPE)	Min 0.3 mm thick. Cheapest DPM, protects against methane and radon gas. No good against any water pressure. Joints must be rigorously taped. Easy to penetrate on site
Cold-applied bitumen solutions; coal tar; pitch/rubber or bitumen rubber emulsions	Ideally three coats. Must be carefully applied to avoid thin patches and pinholes
Hot-applied pitch or bitumen	Ideally three coats. Must be carefully applied to avoid thin patches and pinholes
LDPE plus bitumen sheet	Not as easily displaced as LPDE film and easier to overlap. Small perforations less likely, as will 'self heal'
High density polyethylene (HDPE) with bitumen to both faces	High performance PE core is coated both sides with bitumen, with upper surface bonded to this PE film. Underside has film which is released before laying
Epoxy resin	Two-coat system for newly laid concrete slabs which have not fully dried out. Second coat scattered with fine sand. Suitable for moisture-sensitive flooring, e.g. PVC, cork, lino, wood
Mastic asphalt	12–16 mm thick, not often used under screeds but more often as a combined DPM/floor finish 20–25 mm thick and layed on a glass fibre isolating membrane
Ethylene propylene di-monomer (EPDM)	1.2 and 1.4 mm synthetic rubber sheet (Pirelli), strong and not affected by chemicals, exposure to ozone, UV light, continuous wet, freeze–thaw cycles, microbe attack. Used for foundations, dams, reservoirs, single ply roofing, etc.

Sources: *Specification 94*
Ruberoid Building Products IKO Group

Dampness in buildings

Typical causes

WATER PENETRATION
1 Defective haunching to chimney top
2 Defective chimney flashing
3 Slipped or cracked slates
4 Lack of DPC under parapet coping
5 Defective flashing to valley gutter
6 Lack of cavity tray over window head
7 Cracked RWP and blocked hopper
8 Cracked asphalt to flat roof
9 No asphalt upstand at junction of flat roof to wall
10 Cracked rendering
11 Mortar droppings on cavity ties transmitting water to inner skin
12 Cracked window sill
13 Defective paint and putty to window frame
14 Lack of door threshold letting in driving rain
15 Damp patch on wall from defective sealant round bath edge above

RISING DAMP
16 Earth bridging damp proof course
17 No vertical tanking to earth retaining wall
18 No DPC under timber joists on sleeper walll
19 Faulty DPM under floor

CONDENSATION
20 No vapour barrier in flat roof causing interstitial condensation
21 Blocked eaves ventilation to roof space
22 Lack of ridge ventilator to ventilate roof space
23 Lack of air brick to blocked up flue
24 Cold spot condensation showing inside solid concrete lintel
25 Damp low down on external walls in unventilated cupboards and behind pictures

Source: *Dampness in Buildings*

Plaster and render

External rendering

Rendering mortars are essentially the same as those for laying masonry, but should be made with clean washed plastering sand.

Where possible, use the same mix for undercoats as for finishing coats, otherwise the undercoat should be stronger than the finishing coat.

Strong backgrounds, such as concrete or engineering brick, may need an initial keying coat or spatterdash such as 1:1½ or 1:3 cement : sand thrown on and not trowelled.

For severe exposures, two undercoats are preferable.

On metal lathing, two undercoats are invariably needed.

It is particularly important to reduce the chances of rendering cracking and increase the possibility of moisture evaporating through it to the exterior; these factors are crucial for the rendering of existing buildings that may have poor DPCs or none.

Since strong cement mixes increase shrinkage cracking and prevent evaporation, they should be avoided. Traditional buildings should be rendered using hydraulic or putty lime without cement; render for modern buildings should preferably be carried out with weak cement : hydrated lime : sand mixes for improved flexibility, or with proprietary render mixes. Undercoats can have polypropylene fibres included in the mix to minimize cracking.

Rendering mixes for different backgrounds and exposures

Use	Background	Severe	Moderate	Sheltered
First and subsequent undercoats	dense, strong	II	II	II
	moderately strong, porous	III	III	III
	moderately weak, porous	III	IV	IV
	metal lathing	I / II	I / II	I / II
Final coats	dense, strong	III	III	III
	moderately strong, porous	III	IV	IV
	moderately weak, porous	III	IV	IV
	metal lathing	III	III	III

Plaster and render glossary

aggregate Sand particles or crushed stone that form the bulk of a mortar or render.

binder A component that hardens to bind aggregates together; normally lime and Portland cement.

browning Undercoat plaster made from *gypsum* and *sand*. It replaced lime and sand 'coarse stuff'. Now generally superseded by pre-mixed *lightweight plasters*.

cement Usually Portland cement, so called because it resembles Portland stone when set. It is a mixture of chalk and clay burnt in a kiln. When mixed with water it hardens in a process known as hydration.

dash External rendering thrown onto a wall by hand or applicator.

dry dash Coarse aggregate thrown onto a wet *render* coat, giving an exposed aggregate finish.

dry hydrated lime Ordinary (non-hydraulic) lime produced as a dry powder by adding just enough water to slake the quicklime (adding more water produces *lime putty*). Hydrated lime is typically used in cement : lime : sand mixes to improve workability and flexibility.

gypsum A solid white mined mineral, the main constituent of which is calcium sulphate, used as a *binder* in gypsum plaster.

gypsum plaster Plaster made of gypsum with lightweight aggregates and a *retarder*. It is unsuitable for external work or damp areas. It is used as a smooth finishing coat.

hemihydrate plaster A plaster made by gently heating gypsum to drive off most of its chemically combined water to become half-hydrated. In its pure form it is plaster of Paris, but with the addition of *retarders*, such as keratin, it becomes the basic material for all gypsum plaster, and is known as retarded hemihydrate plaster.

hydrated lime *Quicklime* slaked with water.

hydraulic lime Lime that can set in the absence of air under water. It is made by burning lime with up to 22 per cent clay. It is widely available in bagged powdered form and conveniently similar in handling to cement for masons unused to lime putties.

Keene's cement Hard-burnt anhydrous (water-free) gypsum mixed with alum to form a plaster, which can be trowelled to a smooth, intensely hard finish.

lightweight plaster Plaster with lightweight aggregates such as expanded perlite combined with *retarded hemihydrate plaster*. It has low shrinkage and is thermally insulating.

lime Chalk or limestone burnt in a kiln to 825°C or more.

lime putty *Hydrated lime* soaked to give it plasticity. Used for lime plasters, renders, mortars, grouts and limewash.

mortar A mixture of sand, cement and water, used primarily for bedding and pointing brickwork, laying floor tiles, and as undercoats to plaster and final coats of external walls.

non-hydraulic lime High calcium lime made by slaking relatively pure limestone. Mortars and renders made from this lime set slowly and are relatively soft, but accommodate normal building movement well and have high levels of vapour permeability and porosity.

pebble dash A dry dash finish in which clean washed pebbles are pushed into wet render and left exposed.

plaster Usually gypsum plaster for interiors, or cement render for exterior work.

pozzolana A natural volcanic silica dust originally from Pozzuoli, Italy. When mixed with lime it sets hard, even under water, making Roman cement. The term *pozzolanic additive* now includes other aggregates, such as pulverized fuel ash (PFA) and brick dust, which have similar hydraulic properties.

quicklime *Lime* before it has been slaked. It reacts strongly with water to produce *hydrated lime*.

rendering *Mortar* undercoats and finishing coats for external walls and to receive tiling in wet areas.

retarder Added to cement, plaster or mortar to slow down the initial rate of setting by inhibiting hydration.

spatter dash Cement and sand in a very wet mix, sometimes with a binding agent, flicked on in small blobs with an applicator. Used to create a key for backgrounds with poor suction.

stucco Smooth rendering, originally lime and sand but now cement lime mortar. Often with decorative mouldings shaped to imitate rusticated masonry or column embellishments.

Tyrolean finish A spattered textured render achieved by being thrown against a wall with a hand-operated applicator.

Sources: *The Penguin Dictionary of Building*
Illustrated Dictionary of Building

Pre-mixed plasters

Pre-mixed plasters are made from gypsum, which is a natural mineral deposit – calcium sulphate dihydrate. They should conform to BS 1191 Part 2: 1973 *Specification for gypsum building plasters*.

Pre-mixed plasters should not be used in continuously damp or humid places, nor should they be used where the temperature exceeds 43°C. Gypsum plasters are unsuitable for external work because gypsum is partially soluble in water.

British Gypsum have two brand names, 'Carlite' and 'Thistle', which they keep for historical rather than functional significance:

Carlite Browning   An undercoat plaster for solid backgrounds of moderate suction with an adequate mechanical key.

Carlite HSB Browning An undercoat plaster for solid backgrounds of high suction with an adequate mechanical key.

Carlite Bonding Coat An undercoat plaster for low suction backgrounds such as plasterboard, concrete or other surfaces treated with a PVAC agent.

Carlite Finish A final coat plaster for all three Carlite undercoat plasters.

Thistle Hardwall An undercoat plaster with high impact resistance and quicker drying surface. May be applied by hand or machine.

Thistle Multi-Finish A final coat plaster for a wide range of backgrounds.

Thistle Board Finish A final coat plaster for plasterboard.

Thistle Dri-Coat A cement-based undercoat plaster for old walls, where plaster has been removed and a chemical DPC inserted.

Thistle Renovating An undercoat plaster containing perlite and additives to promote early surface drying when applied to structures containing residual moisture.

Thistle Renovating Finish Final coat plaster for use with Thistle Renovating plaster. Contains a fungicide and should be applied as soon as the undercoat is set.

Thistle Universal One Coat One coat plaster suitable for most backgrounds with a smooth white finish. May be applied by hand or machine.

Source: British Gypsum Ltd

Pre-mixed plasters
Selection guide and coat thickness in mm

Background	Carlite Browning	HSB Browning	Bonding Coat	Finish	Thistle Hardwall	Multi-Finish	Board Finish	Dri-Coat	Renovating	Renovating Finish	Univ. One-Coat
Plasterboard			8+	2		2	2				5
Dry lining foil-backed & thermal laminate boards						2	2				
Brick walls	11 or	11+		2	11+	2			11+	2	13
Dense concrete blocks			11+	2	11+	2			11+	2	13
Lightweight concrete blocks	11 or	11+		2	11+	2			11+	2	13
Normal ballast concrete*			8+	2	8+	2					10
Expanded metal lathing			11+	2	11+	2					13
Stone & brick walls injected with a DPC						2 or	2	11+			

* Concrete which is exceptionally smooth will require a PVAC agent. Very level surfaces may be plastered with a single 2 mm coat of Thistle Multi-Finish or Board Finish.

Source: British Gypsum Ltd

Gypsum plasters can be badly affected by damp: lime or cement based plasters may perform better in such situations.

Metals

Metals commonly used in the construction industry

Name	Symbol	Atomic number*	Description
Aluminium	Al	13	Lightweight, fairly strong metal normally used as an alloy for castings, sheet or extrusions
Brass	–	–	An alloy containing zinc and more than 50% copper. Easily formed, strong and corrosion resistant
Bronze	–	–	An alloy of copper and tin, sometimes combined with other elements. Hard and corrosion resistant
Copper	Cu	29	A durable, malleable metal, easy to form but hardens quickly when worked and needs annealing. Good electrical and thermal conductivity
Iron	Fe	26	A heavy metal, the fourth most abundant element on the earth's crust. Almost always alloyed with other elements
Lead	Pb	82	The heaviest of the heavy metals, dull blue grey, easily fusible, soft, malleable and very durable
Stainless steel	–	–	An alloy of steel and up to 20% chromium and 10% nickel. Corrosion resistant but more difficult to fashion than carbon steel
Steel	–	–	An alloy of iron and a small, carefully controlled proportion of carbon, normally less than 1%
Tin	Sn	50	A metal nearly approaching silver in whiteness and lustre, highly malleable and taking a high polish. Used to form alloys such as bronze, pewter, etc.
Titanium	Ti	22	Relatively light, strong transitional metal found in beach sands. As strong as steel but 45% lighter, and twice as strong as aluminium but 60% heavier
Zinc	Zn	30	A hard, brittle, bluish white metal, malleable and ductile between 95° and 120°C obtained from various ores. Corrodes 25 times more slowly than steel

*A ratio of the average mass of atoms in a given sample to one-twelfth the mass of a carbon 12 atom.

Bi-metal compatibility

Contact between dissimilar metals should be avoided where possible.

Where contact cannot be avoided and moisture may be present, metals should be separated as shown in the table below.

	Stainless steel	Mild steel	Copper/bronze	Cast iron	Aluminium
Stainless steel	✔	✗	✔	✗	✗
Mild steel	✗	✔	✗	✔	✗
Copper/bronze	✔	✗	✔	✗	✗
Cast iron	✗	✔	✗	✔	✗
Aluminium	✗	✗	✗	✗	✔

✔ = may be in contact; ✔ = may be in contact in dry conditions; ✗ = should not be used in contact.

Metals – some commonly used industrial techniques

aluminium extrusions Aluminium sections made by pushing aluminium through a series of dies until the required intricate shapes are obtained.

brazing A simple, inexpensive way of joining two pieces of hot metal with a film of copper-zinc alloy, a hard solder also referred to as the *filler*. Brazed steel joints are less strong than welded joints.

cast iron An alloy of iron and carbon containing more than 1.7 per cent carbon (normally 2.4–4 per cent). Components are made by casting from remelted pig (ingot) iron with cast iron and steel scrap. It has low melting point and flows well, and is useful for more intricate shapes than steel or wrought iron.

forging (smithing) The act of hammering metal into shape when it is red-hot, traditionally on an anvil. Formerly referred to iron, but now includes steel, light alloys and non-ferrous metals worked with power hammers, drop stamps and hydraulic forging machines.

shot blasting Cleaning metal surfaces by projecting steel shot with a jet of compressed air. Used as a preparation for painting or metal coating.

sweating Uniting metal parts by holding them together while molten solder flows between them, as in a capillary joint, which is a spigot and socket joint in metal tubing.

tempering Reducing the brittleness of steel by heating and slow cooling (annealing).

welding Joining pieces of metal made plastic or liquid by heat and/or pressure. A filler metal whose melting temperature is the same as that of the metal to be jointed may also be used. Arc welding fuses metals together with an electric arc, often with a consumable metal electrode.

wrought iron Iron with a very low carbon content (0.02–0.03 per cent). It is very malleable and cannot be hardened by tempering. It is soft, rusts less than steel but is more expensive, so it has largely been replaced by mild steel. Used for chains, hooks, bars and decorative ironwork.

Metal finishes

anodizing A protective durable film of oxide formed by dipping an aluminium alloy object into a bath of chromic or sulphuric acid through which an electric current is passed. The film may be coloured with dyes.

chromium plating The electrolytic deposition of chromium onto other metals to produce a very hard, bright finish. When applied to iron or steel, chromium adheres best if a layer of nickel or copper is first deposited.

galvanizing A coating for steel which is quite durable and gives good protection against corrosion in moderate conditions. Components are hot dipped in molten zinc or coated with zinc electrolytically.

powder coating Polyester, polyurethane, acrylic and epoxy plastics sprayed and heat-cured onto metals such as aluminium or galvanized steel for a 50–100-micron thick film. Finished components can also be hot dipped in polyethylene or nylon for a 200–300-micron thick film.

sherardizing A protective coating of zinc on small items such as nuts and bolts, which are rolled for 10 hours in a drum containing sand and zinc dust heated to 380°C. The coating is thin but the zinc diffuses into the steel to form a zinc alloy. It does not peel off, distorts less and is more durable than galvanizing.

stove enamelling Drying of durable enamel paints by heat, normally over 65°C, either in a convection oven or by radiant heat lamps.

vitreous enamelling A glazed surface finish produced by applying powdered glass, dry or suspended in water, which is fused onto metal. This is a true enamel – not enamel paint.

Sources: *The Penguin Dictionary of Building*
Illustrated Dictionary of Building

Insulation

Thermal insulation

Next to a vacuum, trapped air or inert gas is the most effective way to trap heat, so all insulants work in this way from the most natural, like sheep's wool, to the most technologically sophisticated oil-based materials like phenolic foam.

Construction insulants have to perform in different circumstances – wet and dry for example – so different materials are appropriate.

Some 'insulants' also function in other ways such as aerated concrete blockwork walls; others such as multi-foils, combine air-trapping technology with reflectance to resist heat transfer – though some of the multi-foil manufacturers' performance claims have been shown to be exaggerated.

The relative performance of insulants is measured either by their conductivity ('K-value') – the lower the better – or by their resistivity ('R-value') – the higher the better. In the UK, K-values and their relatives, U-values (thermal transmittance, see p. 149), are used, whereas in the US, R-values (resistivity) and R-values (thermal resistance of particular thicknesses of a material) are the norm.

Table of insulation materials

| | CHARACTERISTICS AS INSULANTS | | | | | | | | | | |
Insulants	K-value	Vapour permeability	Moisture tolerance	Rigidity	For masonry walls	For timber frames/roofs	Structural use	Origin	Embodied energy	CO$_2$ impact	Relative cost
Aerated Concrete	0.16	medium	High	high	wall blocks	no	yes	mineral	high	high	medium
Hemp & Limecrete	0.15?	high	medium	medium	infill	infill	semi-structural	plant & mineral	medium	very low	high
Softwood	0.14	medium	Low	high	no	yes	yes	plant	low	very low	medium
Woodwool slabs	0.11	high	medium	high	no	yes	yes	plant & mineral	medium	low	medium
Vermiculite granules	0.065	high	good/LiV*	none	no	yes	no	mineral	high	medium	low
Multi-foils	0.035/CbS*	low	High/LiV*	none	protected cavity insul.	yes	no	oil	very high	high	very high
Glass wool	0.033–0.04	high	Med/LiV*	none	cavity insul.	yes	no	mineral	high	high	low

Material										
Mineral wool	0.033–0.04	high	Med/LiV*	varies	cavity insul.	yes	no	mineral	high	low
Sheep's wool	0.035	high	High	none		yes	no	animal	low	high
Cellulose fibre	0.038	high	Very poor	none		no	no	plant & recycled	low	low to medium
Expanded polystyrene	0.032–0.04	low	Med/LiV*	low	cavity insul.	yes	no	oil	high	low
Extruded polystyrene	.028–0.036	none	High	medium	cavity insul.	yes	no	oil	high	medium
Polyeurethane foams	.022–0.028	none	High	medium	protected cavity insul.	yes	no	oil	high	medium to high
Isocyanurate foams	.022–0.028	none	medium	medium	protected cavity insul.	yes	no	oil	high	high
Phenolic	0.02	none	high	medium	protected cavity insul.	yes	no	oil	high	high

Notes: LiV: Loss in insulating value when wet; quilts permanently if saturated; batts and slabs recover when dried out.
CbS: Assumes cavities both sides: including these, typical 30 mm thick multi-foils occupy approx 60 mm and perform as well as 60 mm mineral fibre.
Protected: These insulants not yet marketed for full fill cavity insulation, so require cavity, membrane or polystyrene cavity board protection.

Although there are substantial differences in insulating performance between, say, phenolic foam (k : 0.02) and sheep's wool (k: 0.039), other factors such as vapour permeability and moisture control in relation to adjacent materials make comparison more complex.

In many situations, especially in existing buildings, the space or cost implications of using more environmentally benign insulants such as recycled cellulose fibre or sheep's wool may be prohibitive and the long-term environmental value of using a much higher performance, oil-based insulant with high embodied energy may be worthwhile.

In new buildings, materials such as hemp–lime concrete or aerated concrete which combine thermal insulation, acoustic insulation, thermal mass and structural function may prove ideal, whereas for thermal dry lining to an existing building, minimizing thickness – with maximum insulation – may be the overriding criteria for selection.

Insulation and condensation

One of the most critical details for successfully insulating buildings, beyond the selection of the insulant itself, is the control of water vapour from human activities within the building, i.e., breathing, sweating, washing, cooking, etc. As buildings have been better sealed to save energy, this has become even more crucial.

Since extract facilities, whether passive or fan-powered, cannot be relied upon to be either wholly effective or correctly controlled, it is important that there is a rising 'gradient of permeability' towards the building's outside skin so that the building can 'breathe' without causing – or at least without trapping – condensation at its cold exterior.

The worst examples of this problem occur with an impermeable outer skin such as flat roofing or sheet metal cladding and the best examples of its avoidance are in fully permeable traditional lime-mortared masonry or earth walling, or in open-vented timber cladding to framed structures.

There are two ways to deal with the problem (for the least permeable outer skins as in flat roofing, both are needed). The first is to ventilate an air space between the insulation and the external skin so that the vapour and condensation has a chance to evaporate; the second is to introduce a 'vapour check' – most commonly sheet polythene but sometimes integral with lining materials – on the warm side of the insulation to reduce the amount of vapour reaching the cold surface. It is important that the vapour check is not expected to be perfect: although 'vapour barriers' are theoretically possible, they require careful design and thorough and conscientious workmanship on site, which cannot realistically be expected in most circumstances.

Acoustic insulation

Soundproofing of construction requires three conditions to be fulfilled:
1. Airtight construction to prevent sound transmission in air.
2. Heavyweight construction to reduce low frequency sound transmission.
3. Lightweight insulation to reduce high frequency sound transmission.

Better quality or more primitive methods of traditional construction tended to achieve good acoustic insulation between most buildings, through substantial masonry walls, but tended to have poor insulation between storeys due to air leaky timber floors; with heavy lath and plaster ceilings, sound transfer is much reduced.

Modern construction usually aims to minimize weight and thickness for economic reasons; for smaller buildings this usually means precast concrete or multi-layer timber floors and either double skin/double thickness masonry, or else double-leaf timber frame party walls.

In timber construction, air gaps or 'floating layers' are critical to reducing transmission while in masonry construction, which is more reliant on weight, similar performance is achieved by building either double skin or double thickness walls. In both types of construction, workmanship has to be careful and thorough to achieve effective acoustic insulation.

Building Regulations Part E includes 'Robust Standard Details' for party walls and party floors that have been field tested; new construction requires either use of such details or field testing.

Roofing

Tiles, slates and shingles
Typical minimum pitches

Bituminous shingles	17°
Cedar shingles	14°
Cedar shakes	20°
Clay tiles – plain	35°
Clay tiles – interlocking	25°
Concrete tiles – plain	35°
Concrete tiles – interlocking	17.5°
Fibre cement slates	20°
Natural slates	22.5°
Stone slates – sandstone and limestone	30°

Note: In areas of high winds and driving rain, these minimum pitches may not be advisable.

Roofing slates

Type	Size mm	No./m²	Batten gauge	No./m²	Batten gauge	No./m²	Batten gauge
		50 mm lap		**75 mm lap**		**100 mm lap**	
Princesses	610 × 355	10.06	280	10.55	267	11.05	255
Duchesses	610 × 305	11.71	280	12.28	267	12.86	255
Small Duchesses	560 × 305	12.86	255	13.55	242	14.26	230
Marchionesses	560 × 280	14.01	255	14.76	242	15.53	230
Wide Countesses	510 × 305	14.26	230	15.11	217	15.99	205
Countesses	510 × 255	17.05	230	18.07	217	19.13	205
Wide Viscountesses	460 × 255	19.13	205	20.42	192	21.79	180
Viscountesses	460 × 230	21.21	205	22.64	192	24.15	180
Wide ladies	405 × 255	22.16	177	23.77	165	25.80	152
Ladies	405 × 205	27.56	177	29.56	165	32.09	152

Grade	Thickness	Weight
Best	4 mm	31 kg/m²
Medium Strong	5 mm	35 kg/m²
Heavies	6 mm	40 kg/m²

Slates are now more commonly available in metric sizes and 6, 7, 8 and 10 mm thicknesses.

Source: Alfred McAlpine Slate Ltd

Roofing tiles

	Clay PLAIN	Clay interlocking SINGLE PANTILE	Concrete interlocking DOUBLE ROMAN	Concrete interlocking DOUBLE PANTILE	Concrete interlocking FLAT SLATE
Size mm	265 × 165	380 × 260	418 × 330	420 × 330	430 × 380
Pitch min	35°	22.5°	17.5°	22.5°	17.5°
Pitch max	90°	90°	90°	44°	44°
Headlap min	65 mm	65 mm	75 mm	75 mm	75 mm
Gauge max	100 mm	315 mm	343 mm	345 mm	355 mm
Cover width	165 mm	203 mm	300 mm	296 mm	343 mm
Coverage	60/m²	15.6/m²	9.7/m²	9.8/m²	8.2/m²
Weight @ max gauge	77 kg/m²	42 kg/m²	45 kg/m²	46 kg/m²	51 kg/m²
Weight per 1000	1.27 tonnes	2.69 tonnes	4.69 tonnes	4.7 tonnes	6.24 tonnes

Coverage relates to tiles laid at the maximum gauge. The number of tiles will increase as gauge decreases.
Weights are approximate and relate to tiles laid at maximum gauge. Weights will increase as gauge decreases.

Sarkings

Sarkings are weatherproof membranes laid over rafters and below battens to draught-proof and weatherproof the roof against driving rain or powder snow that may penetrate the tiles or slates.

Traditional sarkings of reinforced bitumen felt have been largely superseded by lighter, breathable sarkings that can be laid to form an effectively draught-proofed roof but still allow free dispersal of water vapour to avoid roof space condensation; such materials generally avoid the need for eaves, ridge and roof slope ventilators. Where they are laid directly over insulation between rafters, or over a permeable sarking board, tiling battens are raised clear of the sarking by 25 × 50 counter battens nailed down to the tops of the rafters.

Battens

All tiles and slates may be fixed to 50 × 25 mm battens with supports at maximum 600 mm centres. Battens for plain clay tiles may be reduced to 38 × 19 mm when fixed at 450 mm centres.

Matching accessories

Accessories made in materials to match the tiles include the following: Universal angle ridge tiles, mono ridge tiles, specific angle ridge and hip tiles, ornamental ridge tiles, block-end ridge tiles, cloaked verge tiles, ridge ventilation tiles, ridge gas flue tiles, vent tiles for soil pipes and fan ducts.

uPVC accessories

These include devices for fixing ridge and hip tiles without mortar and for providing under-eaves ventilation and abutment ventilation for lean-to roofs.

Sources: Redland Roofing, Marley Building Materials Ltd, Klober Ltd

Shingles

Shingles are taper sawn from blocks of western red cedar or, less often, oak and sweet chestnut.

No. 1 grade Blue Label is the premium grade for roofs and walls.

Size
The standard size is 400 mm long in varying widths from 75 to 350 mm. The thickness tapers from 3 mm at the head to 10 mm at the butt, or tail, end.

Colour
Reddish-brown, fading to silver-grey when weathered.

Treatment
Shingles are available untreated, tanalized, or with fire retardants. Tanalizing is recommended for external use. Some local authorities may insist on a fire-retardant treatment depending on the nature of the location.

Fancy butt
These are shingles with shaped butt ends such as diamond, half round, arrow, fish scale, hexagonal, octagonal, etc. These are suitable for pitches over 22°.

Accessories
Pre-formed cedar hip and ridge units 450 mm long are available which are normally fixed over 150 mm wide strip of F1 roofing felt.

Pitch
14° minimum pitch
14° to 20° maximum recommended gauge   = 95 mm
Over 20° maximum recommended gauge   = 125 mm
Vertical walling maximum recommended gauge = 190 mm

Coverage
Shingles are ordered by the bundle. One bundle covers approximately 1.8 m^2 @ 100 mm gauge.

Weight
400 mm long @ 95 mm gauge

untreated	8.09 kg/m^2
tanalized	16.19 kg/m^2
with fire retardant	9.25 kg/m^2

Battens
Shingles are fixed to 38 × 19 mm battens with a 6 mm gap between adjacent shingles using silicon bronze nails – two nails to each shingle. Nails are positioned 19 mm in from side edge and 38 mm above the butt line of the course above.

Underlays are not normally recommended except in cases of severe exposure. For warm roofs, counter battens will be required between the shingle batten and the insulation board.

Flashing
Bituminous paint should be applied to metal flashings to avoid contact between shingles and metal and subsequent staining. As an alternative, GRP valleys and flashings may be more suitable.

Source: John Brash & Co Ltd

Thatch

Water reed
Phragmites communis, grown in British and Continental rivers and marshes. Norfolk reed is the finest thatching material. Water reed thatch is found in East Anglia, the South Coast, S Wales and NE Scotland.

Combed wheat reed
Winter wheat straw, nowadays 'Maris Huntsman', which is passed through a comber. Butt ends are aligned to form face of thatch. Found in the West Country. Sometimes called *Devon Reed*.

Long wheat straw
Threshed wheat straw, wetted and prepared by hand. Ears and butts are mixed up and a greater length of stem is exposed. Found in central, southern and SE regions of England.

Pitch
Recommended pitch is 50°, minimum 45° and maximum 60°.

Weight
Approximately 34 kg/m^2.

Netting
This is essential to preserve the thatch from bird and rodent damage. 20 or 22 gauge galvanized wire mesh should last 10 to 15 years.

Sedge
Cladium mariscus is a marsh plant with a rush-like leaf. It is still used in the fens and for ridges to Norfolk reed thatch.

Heather
Calluna vulgaris was once in general use in non-corn growing areas such as Dartmoor and the NE and can still occasionally be seen in Scotland.

Thatching data

	Water reed	Combed wheat reed	Long wheat straw
Length	0.9 m–1.8 m	1.2 m	1.2 m
Coat thickness	300 mm	300–400 mm	400 mm
Coverage	80–100 bundles / 9.3 m² (1 bundle = 300 mm Ø)	1 tonne / 32 m²	1 tonne / 36.6 m²
Lifespan	50–70 years	20–40 years	10–20 years
Battens (38 & 25 mm) centres	255 mm	150–230 mm	150 mm

Sources: *Thatch, A Manual for Owners, Surveyors, Architects and Builders*
The Care and Repair of Thatched Roofs, SPAB

Lead

Lead sheet for the building industry may be either *milled lead sheet* to BS 1178 : 1982 or *machine cast lead sheet* covered by Agrément Certificates 86/1764 and 91/2662.

Cast lead sheet is also still made by specialist firms using the traditional method of running molten lead over a bed of prepared sand. This is mainly used for replacing old cast lead roofs and ornamental leadwork.

Milled lead sheet is the most commonly available having about 85 per cent of the market. There are no significant differences in the properties, performance or cost between cast and milled lead sheet. Cast lead sheet at first appears slightly darker and less shiny than milled, but is indistinguishable six months after installation.

Thickness
Choice of thickness depends upon use. Additional thickness will cope better with thermal movement, mechanical damage and resist windlift. It will also provide more material for dressing and bossing into shape.

Sizes
Lead sheet is specified by its BS code number or its thickness in millimetres. The range of metric sizes corresponds closely to the former imperial sizes which were expressed in lb/sq.ft. The ends of lead coils may also carry colour markings for easy recognition as shown below.

BS Code no.	Thickness mm	Weight kg/m^2	Colour code	Application
3	1.32	14.99	green	soakers
4	1.80	20.41	blue	soakers, flashings
5	2.24	25.40	red	soakers, flashings, gutters, wall and roof coverings
6	2.65	30.05	black	gutters, wall and roof coverings
7	3.15	35.72	white	gutters, roof coverings
8	3.55	40.26	orange	gutters and flat roofs

Sheet size

Lead sheet may be supplied cut to size or as large sheets 2.4 m wide and up to 12 m long.

For flashings, coils are available in code 3, 4 and 5 lead and in widths from 150 to 600 mm in steps of 50 mm, and 3 m or 6 m in length.

Weight

To determine the weight of a piece of lead, multiply the length $\times$ width (m) $\times$ thickness (mm) $\times$ 11.34 = kgs.

Joints
Maximum spacing

BS Code no.	Flat Roof 0–3°		Pitched Roof 10°–60°		Pitched Roof 60°–80°		Wall Cladding	
	Joints with fall	Joints across fall	Joints with fall	Joints across fall	Joints with fall	Joints across fall	Vertical joints	Horizontal joints
4	500	1500	500	1500	500	1500	500	1500
5	600	2000	600	2000	600	2000	600	2000
6	675	2250	675	2250	675	2250	600	2000
7	675	2500	675	2400	675	2250	650	2250
8	750	3000	750	2500	750	2250	700	2250

Parapet and tapered gutters

BS Code no.	maximum spacing of drips mm	maximum overall girth mm
4	1500	750
5	2000	800
6	2250	850
7	2700	900
8	3000	1000

Flashings

To ensure long life flashings should never exceed 1.0m in length for code 3 lead and 1.5m in length for codes 4 and 5. Flashings should lap a minimum of 100mm horizontally. Vertical laps should be a minimum as shown below.

Roof pitch	Lap mm	Roof pitch	Lap mm
11°	359	40°	115
15°	290	50°	100
20°	220	60°	85
30°	150	90°	75

DPCs
Code 4 lead sheet is suitable for most DPCs. This may be increased to code 5 where a 50mm cavity is exceeded.

Lead DPCs should be covered both sides with bituminous paint to avoid the risk of corrosion from free alkali in fresh Portland cement.

Condensation
In well heated buildings, warm moist air may filter through the roof structure and condense on the underside of the lead covering, leading in the long term to serious corrosion. Ensure that there is ventilation between the timber decking supporting the lead and any insulation.

Corrosion
Lead may be used in close contact with copper, zinc, iron and aluminium. It may be attacked by organic acids from hardwoods and cedar shingles.

Sources: Lead Sheet Association
Lead Development Association
Midland Lead Manufacturers Ltd

Copper roofing

Copper is classified as a noble material. It has a long life (75–100 years), is corrosion resistant and is lightweight and workable. It is more resistant to creep on vertical surfaces than lead and can cover flat or curved surfaces.

Copper for roofing, flashings and DPCs should conform to BS 2870: 1980.

Copper strip = 0.15 to 10 mm thickness, of any width and not cut to length. It is usually supplied in 50 kg coils. It is cheaper than sheet.

Copper sheet = 0.15 to 10 mm thick flat material of exact length and over 450 mm wide.

Copper foil = 0.15 mm thick or less.

Normal roofing thickness is 0.6 mm; 0.45 mm is now considered sub-standard. 0.7 mm is used for pre-patinated copper sheet and for sites with exposure to high winds.

Pre-patinated copper was first used in Germany in the late 1980s. 0.7 mm thick copper sheets have a chemically induced copper chloride patina. This produces the blue/green appearance which is more even than the streaky appearance of some naturally induced patinas. The sheet size is limited to 3 m in length so is not suited for longstrip roofing.

Longstrip copper roofing

This method was introduced to the UK from the Continent in 1957. Factory or site formed copper trays are attached to a fully supporting deck with standing seams or roll joints. The copper used has a harder temper and special expansion clips at seams allow longitudinal movement. The main advantage is absence of cross joints on sloping roofs and drips on flat roofs, which saves labour and reduces cost. Suitable for pitches from 6° to 90°.

Bay size = 525 mm centres × 10.0 m. In exposed sites bay widths should be reduced to 375 mm centres.

After 10 m in length, 50 mm high drips should be placed across fall.

Weight
0.6 mm @ 525 mm centres = 5.7 kg/m^2

Falls
Minimum fall for any copper roof 1 : 60 (17 mm in 1 metre)
Minimum fall for copper gutters 1 : 80 (12 mm in 1 metre)

Parapet gutters
Maximum length of any one sheet is 1.8 m. Thereafter 50 mm minimum deep drips should be introduced. Continuous dripping of rainwater from tiled or slated roofs may perforate gutter linings. Sacrificial strips should be placed in gutters and replaced when worn.

Step flashing
Maximum 1.8 m long with welted joints. Single step flashings, with each end overlapping 75 mm, may be easier to repair where small areas corrode.

Laying

Lay with underfelt of impregnated flax felt with ventilation to space or voids under decking to avoid condensation. Fixings are copper clips (cleats) secured by copper nails or brass screws to decking. Avoid any use of soft solder to prevent electrolytic action. Use mastic between apron flashings and pipes.

DPCs

Copper is highly suitable for DPCs as it is flexible and not attacked by cement mortar. Joints should overlap 100 mm.

Corrosion

Copper can be corroded by sulphur dioxide from chimneys unless stacks rise well clear of roof. Copper will corrode when in contact with damp wood impregnated with some fire retardants and from the run-off from western red cedar cladding. Ammonia (from cats' urine) may cause cracking. Copper will corrode aluminium, zinc and steel if in direct contact or indirect contact from water run-off. Copper may leave green stains on masonry.

Patina

This takes 5 to 20 years to form, depending on location. It is a thin, insoluble layer of copper salts which protects the underlying material from atmospheric attacks. It is generally green but may look buff or black in soot-laden air.

Traditional copper roofing

There are two traditional methods of copper roofing:

Batten rolls
40mm high shaped wooden rolls are laid parallel to bay slope. Bay sheets are turned up sides of roll and covered with copper capping strip. Ridge rolls are 80mm high. Suitable for flat and pitched roofs.

Bay size = 500mm centres × 1.8m.

Standing seams
These are suitable for side joints on roofs which are not subject to foot traffic, and may be used for roofs over 6°. The seams are double welted joints 20–25mm high.

Bay size = 525mm centres × 1.8m.

Cross joints
At right angles to wood rolls or standing seams. They should be *double* lock cross welts. Above 45° pitch, *single* lock cross welts may be used. Stagger cross joints in adjacent bays to avoid too much metal at seams. On flat roofs, drips 65mm deep should be introduced at maximum 3m centres (see Falls above).

Maximum sheet sizes
Sheet sizes should not exceed $1.3\,m^2$, reduced to $1.10\,m^2$ where 0.45mm thick sheet is used.

Sources: Copper Development Association
Broderick Structures Ltd

Aluminium roofing

Aluminium is strong but lightweight and malleable, has a long life and low maintenance. A high proportion of recycled material is used in its manufacture.

The most readily available recommended roofing grade is 1050A, which is 99.5 per cent pure aluminium, with H2 temper. 0 temper (fully soft) is suitable for flashings or intricate shaping. See CP 143 Part 15 1973 (1986) for application.

Aluminium is normally available in 'mill finish' which weathers to a matt grey, staying light in unpolluted areas but darkening in industrial atmospheres. It can also be supplied with a factory applied PVF2 paint in a limited range of colours. Avoid dark, heat-absorbing shades.

Thickness
0.8 mm is recommended roofing gauge.

Sheet width
450 mm standard.

Bay width
Typically 380 mm; longstrip typically 525 mm; batten roll typically 390 mm.

Bay length
Traditional standing seam – 3 m maximum rising to 6 m for roofs pitched above 10°.
Longstrip – 10 m maximum is typical but is available up to 50 m.

Weight
0.8 mm @ 525 mm centres = 2.6 kg/m^2.

Falls
Minimum 1 : 60.

Fixings
All aluminium, including adjacent flashings and gutters.

Joints
Traditional standing seam, longstrip standing seam and batten roll.

Corrosion
Aluminium is corroded by contact with brass and copper. Direct contact with and run-off from lead should be protected with a barrier of bituminous paint. Zinc is sacrificial to aluminium which can lead to premature failure of zinc-coated steel fixings. Avoid contact with wood preservatives and acidic timbers by the use of polythene barrier membranes.

Source: Hoogovens Aluminium Building Systems Ltd

Zinc roofing

Zinc is versatile, ductile, economical, has moderate resistance to atmospheric corrosion and is suitable for marine locations.

During the 1960s zinc alloys replaced commercial zinc for roofing. The material is 99.9 per cent pure zinc alloyed with titanium and copper. There are two types, A and B, which should conform to BS 6561 : 1985. For installation see CP 143 Part 5 : 1964.

Type A
Fine, even grain structure with good resistance to creep and thermal movement. Primarily used for roofing. Available in sheets and coils.

Recommended roofing thicknesses are 0.65, 0.70 and 0.80 mm.

Typical sheet size: 2438 × 914 mm (8' × 3') in thicknesses from 0.50 to 1.0 mm.

Typical coil size: 500, 610, 686, 914 and 1000 mm widths up to 21 m long.

Zinc can also be supplied pre-patinated in 0.70 mm thickness with blue-grey colour.

Type B

Rolled to a soft temper and used mainly for flashings – also for coverings to small balconies, canopies, dormer windows and for DPCs. Available in coils.

Typical coil size: 150, 240, 300, 480 and 600 mm widths by 10 m long.

Bay sizes

From 500 to 900 mm.
Typical longstrip bay: 525 mm centres with standing seam and 540 mm centres with batten roll.
Maximum bay length: 10 m.

Weight

0.7 mm @ 525 mm centres = 5.1 kg/m^2.

Falls

Minimum 3° but ponding may occur so 7° is the minimum recommended pitch, particularly for longer bays.

Side joints

Standing seam and batten roll – similar to copper.

Cross joints

Between 3° and 10° – 75 mm high drips.
Between 10° and 25° – single lock welt with additional soldered undercloak.
Between 25° and 90° – single lock welt with 25 mm undercloak and 30 mm overcloak.

Fixings

Nails	= galvanized steel or SS.
Screws	= galvanized or zinc anodized steel or SS.
Clips	= zinc to match roofing type.
Solder	= 60 : 40 lead/tin alloy.
Liquid flux	= Bakers fluid or killed spirits of salt.

Corrosion

Zinc is non-staining and contact is possible with iron, steel, aluminium, lead and stainless steel. Run-off from unprotected iron and steel may cause staining but no harm. Zinc should not be used directly or indirectly from run-off with copper which will cause corrosion. Zinc may be corroded by contact with western red cedar, oak, sweet chestnut, certain fire retardants and soluble salts in walling materials. Titanium zinc has a long life.

Sources: Zinc Development Association
               Metra Non-Ferrous Metals Ltd

Stainless steel roofing

Stainless steel is lightweight, can be pre-formed, has a low coefficient of expansion, high tensile strength, can be worked at any time of year, is resistant to corrosion attack by condensation, and has good environmental credentials, being substantially recycled and very long-lasting; it can match and be used alongside lead. Stainless steel for roofing should conform to BS 1449 Part 2: 1983.

There are two grades normally used for roofing:

Type 304:   (Austenitic) Suitable for most UK situations but *not* within 15 miles of the sea or in aggressively industrial atmospheres – 0.38 mm thick.

Type 316:   (Austenitic Molybdenum) Highest grade which is now the standard grade recommended, suitable for all atmospheres – 0.4 mm thick.

Stainless steel is naturally reflective but low reflectivity is achieved by:

Mechanical rolling   – Rolling sheets under pressure through a set of engraving tools.

Terne coating   – Coated with tin which weathers to form a mid-grey patina similar to lead.

Sheet width

Coils vary typically 500 mm and 650 mm wide but sometimes still imperial 457 mm (18″) and 508 mm (20″).

Bay width

385 mm and 435 mm centres with standing seams, 425 mm and 450 mm centres with batten rolls.

Bay length

Maximum is normally 9 m but is available up to 15 m. Over 3 m expansion clips must be used.

Weight

0.4 mm @ 435 mm centres = 4 kg/m^2.

Falls

Minimum 5° up to 90°. 9° minimum recommended for exposed sites.

Joints

Traditional standing seam, longstrip standing seam and batten roll.
Cross joints between 5° and 12° should be lap lock welt.
Cross joints between 13° and 20° double lock welt.
Cross joints between 21° and 90° single lock welt.

Fixings

Stainless steel throughout for all clips, nails and screws.

Corrosion

Resistant to most chemicals. Hydrochloric acid, used to clean masonry, will cause corrosion. Contact with copper may cause staining but otherwise no harm. Migrant rust marks can occur from the sparks of carbon steel cutting/grinding machines. It is not attacked by cement alkalis, acids in timber or run-off from lichens.

Sources: Broderick Structures Ltd
Lee Steel Strip Ltd

Profiled metal sheet

Profiled metal sheet may be used for both roofing and cladding. Profiling thin metal sheet gives stiffness, providing greater strength. The deeper the profile, the stronger the sheet and greater the span. Bolder profiles cast darker shadows and may therefore be preferred aesthetically. Coated steel is lowest in cost but limited in life to the durability of the finish. Aluminium develops its own protective film but is less resistant to impact. Cladding to lower parts of buildings should be protected by guard rails or other devices. Avoid complex building shapes to simplify detailing. Profiled sheets are quick to erect, dismantle and repair. The most common profile is trapezoidal.

Curved profiled sheet

Radiused corners may be achieved by using crimped profiled sheets. Typical minimum external radius is 370 mm. Non-crimped profiled sheets may be pre-formed to a minimum radius of 3 m which may be useful for barrel vaulting. Ordinary profiled sheets may be curved slightly on site. As a rule of thumb, the depth of the trough in mm gives the maximum curve in metres. Mitred units are available for both internal and external corners with flashings purpose-made to match.

Thickness
0.5 to 1.5 mm.

Sheet width
500 to 1000 mm.

Trough depth
20 to 70 mm for roofing – depths up to 120 mm are normally used for structural decking.

Weight
0.9 mm – 3.7 kg/m^2.

Falls
1.5° (1 : 40) minimum.

Finishes
Hot dip galvanizing, stove and vitreous enamelling, terne coating, mill finish aluminium, PVC and PVF2 colour coatings, composite bitumen mineral fibres, etc.

Source: Rigidal Systems Ltd

Flat roofs – non-metallic

A flat roof is defined as having a fall not greater than 10° (1 : 6). BS 6229: 1982 *Flat roofs with continuously supported coverings* deals with design principles.

Design considerations
A flat roof must be *structurally rigid*, and have substantial and *continuous support* for the membrane, provision for *movement joints, rainwater* disposal, *thermal* design, *condensation* avoidance, *wind* resistance, consideration for roof *penetrations* and appropriate *protection* of the membrane.

Rainwater
Flat roofs should have a minimum fall of 1 : 80. However, to allow for construction tolerances, a design fall of minimum 1 : 50 is desirable.

The fail safe drainage of flat roofs is to fall to external gutters; less good is via scuppers in parapet walls to external RWPs.

Where internal RWPs are planned, position them away from parapet edges where debris will collect and it is difficult to make a watertight seal. Ideally they should be sited at points of maximum deflection.

Avoid only one outlet in a contained roof as this may block, causing water to rise above upstands and cause damage from water penetration or from overloading the structure.

Where roofs meet walls, upstands must be a minimum of 150 mm high. They should be protected with lead, copper or super purity aluminium flashing tucked 30 mm minimum into the wall.

Condensation

Condensation is the major cause of failure leading to blistering and decay. Moisture laden rooms below flat roofs should have good ventilation, extra insulation and vapour control layers which can withstand accidental damage during construction.

Avoid thermal bridges which can result in localized condensation.

Wind

All layers must be properly secured to substrate to resist wind uplift.

Penetration

Keep roof penetration to a minimum. Where available, use proprietary components such as flanged roof outlets and sleeves for cables.

Sunlight

Ultra-violet light will damage bituminous felts, asphalts and some single ply materials. They should be protected with a layer of stone chippings bonded in hot bitumen or a cold bitumen solution. Alternatively, mineral reinforced cement tiles or glass reinforced concrete tiles laid in a thick coating of hot bitumen will provide a good surface for pedestrian traffic.

25 mm thick concrete pavings provide a more stable walking surface and should be bedded on proprietary plastic corner supports which have the advantage of making up irregularities of level and the separation of the promenade surface from the membrane with rapid drainage of surface water.

Light coloured top surfaces and reflective paints reflect the sun's energy but provide only limited protection against damage from ultra-violet light.

Vapour control layer

Proprietary felts incorporating aluminium foil when laid fully supported are the best type of vapour control layer. They are essential in cold and warm roofs but are not required in inverted warm roofs. Over profiled metal decking, two layers bonded together may be required because of lack of continuous support.

Mastic asphalt

Asphalt is a blend of fine and coarse aggregates bonded with bitumen. The ingredients are heated and blended in batches and either delivered hot in bulk or cast into blocks for re-heating on site.

Roofing grade asphalts are described in BS 6925: 1988 and BS 6577. For specification and application of asphalt roofing see CP 144: Part 4: 1970.

Recent developments include the addition of polymers which claim to make the material more flexible. These are not yet covered by a British Standard.

Asphalt is laid over a *separating layer* of inodorous black felt to BS 747 type 4A(i), and laid in two layers of a combined thickness of 20 mm. Application in two layers allows the joints to be staggered. The final surface is trowelled to produce a bitumen rich layer which is then dressed with fine sand to mask surface crazing in cold weather. This should then be protected with chippings or paving. See **Sunlight** above.

Bituminous felt

Formerly roofing felts were made of rag, asbestos or glass fibre cores coated with bitumen. Over the last 15 years or so, most felts have been made with cores of polyester fleece which give increased stress resistance. BS 747: 1977 (1986) has been amended to include this type. See CP 144 Part 3 for specification and application.

Newer felts are often made with polymer modified bitumen producing greater flexibility and better performance.

Roofing felts are applied in two or more layers, bonded in hot bitumen, and bonded by gas torch or by means of a self-adhesive layer incorporated onto one side of the felt.

First layer felts, often perforated, bind directly to the substrate.

Intermediate felts are smooth faced for full bonding.

Top layer felts may have the top surface prepared for site-applied protection such as chippings.

Cap sheet felts, designed to be left exposed without further protection, incorporate a surface coating of mineral chippings or metal foil.

Single ply membranes

Developed in Europe and the USA, these are now increasingly available in the UK (as yet not covered by a British Standard though both BBA and BRE certification is available on some products), and are made of plastics, synthetic rubber-based materials and some modified bitumen materials.

There are thermoset and thermoplastic type plastics:

Thermoset includes all synthetic rubbers. These have fixed molecular structures which cannot be reshaped by heat or solvents and are joined by adhesives.

Thermoplastic materials are those whose molecular structure is not permanently set and welds may be formed by heat or solvents. Welding is more satisfactory than glueing but requires greater skill.

Sheets may be attached mechanically to the substrate with screw fasteners and disc washers set in seams or by welding membrane to disc washers fixed to substrate, or by adhesive. On inverted warm roofs, the membrane is loose laid and ballasted. The main advantage of sheets is that they are flexible and have a very long life.

Some single ply materials may not be used in conjunction with expanded polystyrene insulation.

Sources: *Flat Roofing – A Guide to Good Practice*

Glass

Glass used in buildings is composed of silica (sand) 70 per cent, soda 14 per cent, lime 10 per cent and various other oxides. These are added to recycled glass and heated in a furnace to around 1550°C, refined, then cooled before floating the molten liquid onto molten tin to form a perfectly flat surface. This is then cooled from 620°C to 250°C in the annealing chamber before the continuous cold glass ribbon is cut into sheets measuring 6000 × 3210 mm. This material is then used to make a variety of glass sheets with thicknesses from 2 mm to 25 mm and many different properties and coatings, which can be used as follows.

Environmental control

Solar control

The increased use of glass in architecture today makes it imperative to consider the comfort of a building's occupants. Solar control glass can be an attractive feature of a building whilst at the same time reducing the demand on air conditioning systems, reducing running costs of the building and saving energy.

In hot climates, solar control glass can be used to minimize solar heat gain and help control glare.

In temperate regions, it can be used to balance solar control with high levels of natural light.

Solar control glass can be specified for any situation where excessive solar heat gain is likely to be an issue, from large conservatories to glass walkways, and building façades to atria.

The Pilkington range of solar control glass offers a range of performance options to suit most building applications: Suncool; Eclipse Advantage; Optifloat tinted; Arctic Blue; Insulight Sun; Optilam.

All products are available in toughened or laminated form for safety and security requirements and can be combined with other benefits such as noise control.

Thermal insulation

With increasing environmental awareness, more emphasis is now being placed on ways to save energy in any building, domestic or commercial. In recent years, new regulations have been introduced specifying minimum requirements for energy efficiency. Glass can play an important role in this. Heat loss is normally measured by the thermal transmittance or U-value, usually expressed in W/m^2K. In its most basic terms, the lower the U-value, the greater the thermal insulation. Insulating glass units incorporating low-emissivity glass can significantly improve the thermal insulation values.

Pilkington products

K Glass (hard coat low-e): this coating is applied during man-ufacture. The glass can be easily toughened or laminated and has a higher passive solar gain than Optitherm SN.

Optitherm SN (soft coat low-e): a high quality clear glass with a specially formulated 'off-line' ultra low-emissivity coating applied to one surface after glass manufacture; is available in toughened and laminated form.

Environmental control glass properties

Examples of double glazed units with two panes of clear float glass and 16mm argon filled cavity.

		Maximum* unit sizes annealed/ toughened mm	Light % transmit- tance	Light % reflec- tance	Solar radiant heat % transmit- tance	Shading coeffi- cient	U-Value W/m²**
	6mm Clear Float 6mm toughened	3000 × 1600 4500 × 2500	79	14	72	0.82	2.6

Examples of double glazed units with 6mm Pilkington Optifloat clear inner pane, 16mm cavity and an outer pane of solar control glass

Solar control glass	Optifloat 6mm Bronze	3000 × 1600 4500 × 2500	44	8	48	0.56	2.6
	Eclipse Advantage 6mm clear	3000 × 1600 2000 × 4000	60	29	55	0.64	1.6
	Suncool Brilliant 6mm 66/33	3000 × 1600 4200 × 2400	65	15	36	0.42	1.1
	Suncool High Performance 6mm 70/40 neutral	3000 × 1600 4200 × 2400	70	10	43	0.50	1.1
	Activ Suncool HP 6mm 53/40	3000 × 1600 4200 × 2400	49	14	39	0.45	1.3

Examples of double glazed units with 6mm Pilkington Optitherm SN inner pane coating to the inside (cavity) face of the inner pane and 16mm argon filled cavity***

Thermal Insulation	Pilkington Optifloat 6mm clear	3000 × 1600 4200 × 2400	77	11	61	0.71	1.2
	Activ 6mm	2200 × 3600 2000 × 3600	72	17	58	0.67	1.2
	Eclipse Advantage 6mm clear	3000 × 1600 3100 × 2500	58	27	47	0.55	1.1

* Maximum sizes are for guidance only and are **not** recommended glazing sizes. Upper figure is for annealed glass, lower figure for toughened glass.

** U-value for air-filled cavity approx 15 per cent higher. Where cavity width is limited, Krypton filling gives a lower U-value than Argon but is not readily available and is more expensive. Warm edge spacer bars instead of aluminium will also reduce the U-value.

*** U-value for K Glass inner pane approx. 15 per cent higher.

Acoustic

Pilkington **Optilam™** Phon glass gives sound control in situations where there is excess noise from roads, rail, air traffic and other sources. Using a PVB (polyvinyl butyral) specific interlayer, Pilkington **Optilam™** Phon is a high quality acoustic laminated glass that offers excellent noise reduction.

Pilkington **Optilam™** is produced by combining two or more sheets of glass with PVB interlayers, and it is this lamination that enables it to offer impact protection and safety. By varying the number of layers and thickness of the glass, it can offer wide-ranging benefits and be used in various applications.

Fire

A range of fire-resistant glass types is available offering increasing levels of protection, which is measured in defined time periods (30, 60, 90, 120 and 180 minutes) and in terms of 'integrity and insulation' or 'integrity only' as designated by the European Standards.

It should be noted that fire-resistant glass must always be specified as part of a tested and approved glazing system, and installation should be carried out by specialists in order to ensure that the expected fire performance is achieved should it be called upon. Areas of glazing are limited by the Building Regulations Part B.

Pilkington Pyrostop™ A clear multi-laminated fire-resistant glass that both retains its integrity and insulates against all heat transfer from fire.
30–60 minutes' insulation, 60 minutes' integrity, thicknesses from 15–51 mm.

Pilkington Pyrodur™ Clear integrity fire barrier – plus protection against radiant heat.
Less than 30 minutes' insulation, 30–60 minutes' integrity, thicknesses 10–13 mm.

Pilkington Pyrodur™ Plus Clear integrity only fire-resistant glass with a narrow profile and impact resistance ideal for fire doors and partitioning.
Less than 30 minutes' insulation, 30–60 minutes' integrity, 7 mm thickness.

Pilkington Pyroshield™ Achieving over 60 minutes' integrity in suitable glazing systems.
Wired glass, clear or textured. 30–60 minutes' integrity, 6–7 mm thick.

Safety and Security
From security to fire-resistance, safety glass can be used to protect a building's occupants in many ways, while also allowing the creation of bold and attractive designs. The main categories in which glass can be used for protection are outlined here.

Safety glass
Requirement N1 of the Building Regulations concerns glazing in critical locations. In such places glass should either (1) break safely, (2) be robust, i.e. adequately thick, or (3) be permanently protected. See p. 212.

Glass which is deemed to break safely must conform to BS 6206 : 1981. Manifestations may need to be incorporated in the glazing or applied afterwards to satisfy the Buildings Regulations Part M.

Toughened and laminated glass can meet these requirements.

Toughened glass
Toughened glass is normal annealed glass subjected to heating and rapid cooling. This produces high compression in the surface and compensating tension in the core. It is about 4–5 times stronger than annealed glass and is highly resistant to thermal shock. When it breaks it shatters into relatively harmless pieces. It *cannot* be cut, drilled or edge-worked after toughening. Any such work must be done prior to toughening. The 'strain' pattern of toughening, i.e. horizontal

bands about 275 mm apart, may be noticed in bright sunlight. Can be made to incorporate designs for decoration or obscuration.

Thicknesses	4–19 mm
Maximum sizes	2550 × 1550 mm; 2720 × 1270 mm
Minimum size	305 × 200 mm

Laminated glass
Laminated glass is made from two or more panes of various glasses with interlayers of polyvinyl butyral bonded between each pane. Normal thickness is 3 ply, i.e. two panes of glass and one interlayer. On impact the glass adheres to interlayers.

Unlike toughened glass it can be cut, drilled and edge-worked after manufacture. Screen printed designs can be incorporated during manufacture.

Anti-Bandit glasses have thicker interlayers and are designed to resist manual attack.

Bullet-resistant glasses are made from thicknesses from 20 mm up. They are designed to meet specific bullets from 9 mm automatics up to 5.56 mm military rifles or solid slug shotguns. They can also provide protection against bomb blast.

Thicknesses	from 4.4 mm to 45 mm
Maximum size	3200 × 2000 mm depending on glass used

Glass beams, posts and balustrades can be formed from laminated sheets.

Structural
Structural glazing enables the creation of a complete glass envelope for buildings with frameless façades on any plane.

Support structures, located internally or externally, can use glass mullions, a conventional steel construction or the Pilkington **Planar™** Tension Structure design to be as subtle or dominant as appropriate.

Pilkington Profilit™ is an alkaline cast glass in U-shaped form. The profiled glass with its installation system offers many interesting and varied architectural solutions. Its main application is in exterior glazing where it is suitable for large glass façades.

'Self Cleaning'

An applied coating uses the forces of nature to help keep the glass free from organic dirt, providing not only the practical benefit of less cleaning, but also clearer, better-looking windows. The performance of the coating varies according to orientation and pitch.

Decorative

A variety of textured, satin, reflective, etched, screen printed, coloured, stained and handmade glasses are available.

Source: Pilkington United Kingdom Ltd

Glass blocks

Glass blocks are now no longer made in the UK but are imported from Germany and Italy. Metric and imperial sizes are made, imperial being used not only for new work but also for renovation and the US market.

Metric sizes   115 × 115 × 80 mm; 190 × 190 × 80 and 100 mm; 240 × 240 × 80 mm; 240 × 115 × 80 mm; 300 × 300 × 100 mm.

Imperial sizes   6″ × 6″ × 3$^1/_8$″ and 4″; 8″ × 8″ × 3$^1/_8$″ and 4″; 8″ × 4″ × 3$^1/_8$″ and 4″; 8″ × 6″ × 3$^1/_8$″.

Colours   Clear as standard; bronze, azure, blue, turquoise, pink, green, grey.

Patterns   Waves, chequers, ribs, sand blasted, etc.

Specials   Fixed louvre ventilator (190 mm sq), corner blocks, bullet resistant, end blocks with one side mitred for unframed edges to free standing panels.

Radii   Minimum internal radii for curved walls for block widths as follows:
115 mm = 650 mm; 6″ (146 mm) = 1200 mm; 190 mm = 1800 mm; 240 mm = 3700 mm

Weight   80 mm thick = 100 kg/m^2;
100 mm thick = 125 kg/m^2.

U-values   80 mm thick = 2.9 W/m^{2}K;
100 mm thick = 2.5 W/m^{2}K.

Light transmission   Clear blocks = 80%; bronze = 60% approx.

Fire rating   Class O – fixing systems for both half-hour and one-hour fire rating

Sound insulation   37–42 db over 100–3150 Hz.

Structure	Glass blocks are self-supporting but not load bearing.
	Mortar jointed panels should not exceed 5 m long × 3.5 m high (3 m for fire-resisting panels) in any direction, nor be greater than 17.5 m².
Fixing	Glass blocks are generally fixed on site but can be prefabricated in panels. The normal joint is 10 mm but can be wider to suit dimensional requirements.
	Blocks are laid in wet mortar with 6 or 8 mm Ø SS reinforcing bars fixed horizontally or vertically, normally about every other block. Joints are then pointed up.
	Silicone sealants are applied at perimeters.
	Intumescent mastics are applied to internal and external perimeter joints for fire-resisting panels.
	There is also a 'Quiktech' dry fix system using plastic profiles to space and centre the blocks and a special adhesive to bond the system together; 5 mm joints are grouted and perimeter joints filled with a silicone seal.
Pavement lights	100 × 100 square, 117 dia., can be supplied separately or set in concrete ribs for foot or vehicular traffic.
Colours	Clear, sandblasted, blue, amber.

Source: Luxcrete Ltd

Timber

Timber sustainability

The world's forests are under threat from illegal logging, clearance for agricultural expansion and poor management. However, timber can be a most energy efficient material. A tree grows to maturity in the space of one human lifetime, whereas stocks of oil, fossil fuels and minerals take millennia to produce and are therefore not *renewable* resources. The growth of trees fixes carbon and actually reduces the amount of CO_2 in the atmosphere. This advantage is only realized in well-managed forests where trees are replaced. Timber has seven times less embodied energy (by weight) than that of steel and 29 times less than aluminium, as it needs no heat for manufacture and extraction is relatively cheap compared to mining. How do architects obtain information from suppliers as to whether timber comes from renewable resources?

The **Forest Stewardship Council** (FSC) was founded in 1993 and is an international non-profit and non-governmental organization. It is an association of environmental and social groups, timber trade organizations and forestry professionals from around the world.

Its objectives are to provide independent certifiers of forest products and to provide consumers with reliable information about these materials.

It evaluates, accredits and monitors timber all round the world, whether it is tropical, temperate or boreal (northern). Certification is the process of inspecting forests to check they are being managed according to an agreed set of principles and criteria. These include recognition of indigenous people's rights, long-term economic viability, protection of biodiversity, conservation of ancient natural woodland, responsible management and regular monitoring. Timber from FSC-endorsed forests will be covered by a 'chain-of-custody-certificate'.

Consult the FSC for their lists of suppliers and certified timber and wood products.

Sources: Forest Stewardship Council, Friends of the Earth
Forests Forever, *The Culture of Timber*

Timber nomenclature

'Softwood' and 'Hardwood' are botanical terms and do not necessarily reflect the density of the species. Softwoods are coniferous (cone-bearing) trees of northern climates and are relatively soft with the exception of Pitch Pine and Yew (670kg/m^3). Hardwoods are deciduous trees and vary enormously in density from Balsa (110kg/m^3) to Lignum Vitae (1250kg/m^3).

Moisture

Moisture content of newly-felled trees can be 60 per cent and higher. Air drying will reduce the moisture content to approximately 18 per cent. Further kiln drying can reduce the moisture content to six per cent.

Recommended average moisture content for timbers from BS 1186 : Part 1

External joinery		16°
Internal joinery	Buildings with intermittent heating	15°
	Buildings with continuous heating from 12–16°C	12°
	Buildings with continuous heating from 20–24°C	10°

Durability

This relates to fungal decay. It is expressed in the five durability classes described below and numbered in the tables on pp. 280–1 and 282–4. Sapwood of all species is non-durable and should not be used in exposed situations without preservative treatment.

1 = very durable	–	more than 25 years
2 = durable	–	15–25 years
3 = moderately durable	–	10–15 years
4 = non-durable	–	5–10 years
5 = perishable	–	less than 5 years

Classes of timber for joinery

These are effectively appearance classes and make no reference to durability and workability, stability or surface absorbency. The four classes characterize the quality of timber and moisture content after machining, at the time it is supplied to the first purchaser. They describe the presence (or absence) of knots, splits, resin pockets, sapwood, wane, straightness of grain, exposed pith, rot, joints (in long timbers), plugs or filler (of knots).

Class CSH Clear softwood and hardwood, i.e. free from knots or other surface defects. Difficult to obtain in softwoods with the possible exception of selected Douglas fir, hemlock, parana pine and western red cedar.

Class 1 This is suitable for both softwood and hardwood components, particularly small mouldings such as glazing bars and beads.
Also for joinery which will receive a clear finish.

Class 2 Suitable for general purpose softwood joinery and laminated timber. Commonly used for window casements.

Class 3 As class 2 but with greater latitude in knot size and spacing.

Timber sizes

Softwoods and hardwoods are usually available in sizes as shown in the tables on p. 279 and p. 285.

European softwoods are generally supplied in 1.8 m lengths in increments of 300 mm up to about 5.7 m.

North American softwoods are normally supplied in 1.8 m lengths up to 7.2 m in 600 mm increments. Other lengths to special order up to a maximum of 12.0 m.

Hardwoods which are imported in log form may be cut to specified sizes and are available in 19, 25, 32, 38, 50, 63 and 75 mm thicknesses; widths from 150 mm up and lengths from 1.8 m to typically 4.5 m and sometimes 6 m.

Softwood – standard sawn sizes (mm)

Thickness	25	38	50	75	100	125	150	175	200	225	250	300	
12	•	•	•	•	•		•						
16			•	*	*	*	*						
19	•	•	•	*	*	*	*						
22				*	*	*	*						
25	•	•	•	*	*	*	*	*	*	*	*	*	These
32				*	*	*	*	*	*	*	*	*	sizes
36				*	*	*	*						generally
38			•	•	*	*	*	*	*	*	*		from
44				*	*	*	*	*	*	*	*	*	Europe
47				*	*	*	*	*	*	*	*	*	
50			•	*	*	*	*	*	*	*	*		
63					*	*	*	*	*	*			
75				•	*	*	*	*	*	*	*	*	
100					*		*		*		*	*	These
150							*		*			*	sizes
200									*				generally
250											*		from
300												*	N America

• = sizes that may be available from stock or sawn from larger standard sizes
* = sizes laid down in BS 4471 : 1996

Reduction from sawn sizes by planing

Structural timber	3 mm up to	100 mm
	5 mm over	100 mm
Joinery and cabinet work	7 mm up to	35 mm
	9 mm over	35 mm
	11 mm up to	150 mm
	13 mm over	150 mm.

Softwoods

Species	Place of origin	Appearance	Density kg/m³	Durability class	Veneer	Uses (remarks)
Cedar of Lebanon* *Cedrus Libani*	Europe UK	light brown	580	2	✓	garden furniture, drawer linings (aromatic smell)
Douglas Fir *Pseudotsuga menziesii*	N America UK	light, reddish brown	530	3	✓	plywood, construction (long lengths), joinery, vats
Hemlock, western *Tsuga heterophylla*	N America	pale brown	500	4		construction (large sizes), joinery (uniform colour)
Larch, European *Larix decidua*	Europe	pale, reddish	590	3	✓	boat planking, pit props, transmission poles
Larch, Japanese *Larix kaempferi*	Europe	reddish brown	560	3		stakes, construction
Parana Pine *Araucaria angustifolia*	S America	golden brown and red streaks	550	4	✓	interior joinery, plywood (may distort)
Pine, Corsican *Pinus nigra maritima*	Europe	light yellow-brown	510	4		joinery, construction
Pine, maritime *Pinus pinaster*	Europe	pale brown to yellow	510	3		pallets, packaging
Pine, pitch *Pinus palustris*	South USA	yellow-brown to red-brown	670	3		heavy construction, joinery
Pine, radiata *Pinus radiata*	S Africa Australia	yellow to pale brown	480	4		packaging, furniture
Pine, Scots *Pinus sylvestris*	UK	pale yellow-brown to red-brown	510	4		construction, joinery
Pine, yellow *Pinus strobus*	N America	pale yellow to light brown	420	4		pattern-making, doors, drawing boards
Spruce Canadian *Picea* spp	Canada	white to pale yellow	450	4		construction, joinery

Species	Place of origin	Appearance	Density kg/m^3	Durability class	Veneer	Uses (remarks)
Spruce, sitka *Picea sitchensis*	UK	pinkish-brown	450	4		construction, pallets, packaging
Spruce, western white *Picea glauca*	N America	white to pale yellow-brown	450	4		construction (large sizes), joinery
Western Red Cedar *Thuja plicata*	N America	reddish-brown	390	2	✓	exterior cladding, shingles, greenhouses, beehives
Whitewood, European *Picea abies* and *Abies alba*	Europe Scandina via USSR	white to pale yellow-brown	470	4	✓	interior joinery, construction, flooring
Yew *Taxus baccata*	Europe	orange-brown to purple-brown	670	2	✓	furniture, cabinetry, turnery (good colour range)

* = limited availability

Source: Trada Technology Ltd

Hardwoods

Species	Place of origin	Appearance	Density kg/m³	Durability class	Veneer	Uses (remarks)
Afrormosia *Pericopsis elata*	W Africa	light brown, colour variable	710	1	✓	joinery, furniture, cladding
Agba *Gossweilero dendron balsamiferum*	W Africa	yellow-brown	510	2	✓	joinery, trim, cladding (may exude gum)
Ash, European *Fraximus exelsior*	UK Europe	pale white to light brown	710	5	✓	interior joinery (may be bent), sports goods
Balsa* *Ochroma pyramidale*	S America	pinky-white	160	5		insulation, buoyancy aids, architectural models
Beech, European *Fagus sylvatica*	UK Europe	pale pinkish brown	720	5	✓	furniture (bends well), flooring, plywood
Birch, European* *Betula pubescens*	Europe Scandinavia	white to light brown	670	5	✓	plywood, furniture, turnery (bends well)
Cherry, European* *Prunus avium*	Europe	pink-brown	630	3	✓	cabinet making (may warp), furniture
Chestnut, sweet* *Castanea sativa*	Europe	honey-brown	560	2	✓	joinery, fencing (straight grained)
Ebony* *Diospyros* spp	W Africa India	black with grey stripes	1110	1	✓	decorative work, inlaying, turnery (small sizes only)
Elm, European* *Ulmus* spp	Europe UK	reddish-brown	560	4	✓	furniture, coffins, boats (resists splitting)
Gaboon* *Aucoumea klaineana*	W Africa	pink-brown	430	4	✓	plywood, blockboard
Greenheart *Ocotea rodiaei*	Guyana	yellow-olive green to brown	1040	1		heavy marine construction, bridges etc. (very large sizes)

Species	Place of origin	Appearance	Density kg/m^3	Durability class	Veneer	Uses (remarks)
Hickory＊ *Carya* spp	N America	brown to red-brown	830	4		tool handles, ladder rungs, sports goods (bends well)
Iroko *Chlorophora excelsa*	W Africa	yellow-brown	660	1	✓	joinery, work-tops, construction
Keruing *Dipterocarpus* spp	SE Asia	pink-brown to dark brown	740	3		heavy and general construction, decking, vehicle flooring
Lignum Vitae＊ *Guaicum* spp	Central America	dark green-brown	1250	1		bushes, bearings, sports goods (small sizes only)
Lime, European＊ *Tilia* spp	UK Europe	yellow-white to pale brown	560	5		carving, turnery, bungs, clogs (fine texture)
Mahogany, African *Khaya* spp	W Africa	reddish-brown	530	3	✓	furniture, cabinetry, joinery
Mahogany, American *Swietenia macrophylla*	Brazil	reddish-brown	560	2	✓	furniture, cabinetry, boats, joinery (stable, easily worked)
Maple, rock *Acer saccharum*	N America	creamy-white	740	4	✓	flooring, furniture, turnery (hardwearing)
Meranti, dark red *Shorea* spp	SE Asia	medium to dark red-brown	710	3	✓	joinery, plywood (uniform grain)
Oak, American red *Quercus* spp	N America	yellow-brown with red tinge	790	4	✓	furniture, interior joinery (bends well)
Oak, European *Quercus robur*	UK Europe	yellow to warm brown	690	2	✓	construction, joinery, flooring, cooperage, fencing (bends well)

Hardwoods – continued

Species	Place of origin	Appearance	Density kg/m³	Durability class	Veneer	Uses (remarks)
Obeche *Triplochiton scleroxylon*	W Africa	white to pale yellow	390	4	✓	interior joinery, furniture, plywood (very stable)
Plane, European* *Platanus hybrida*	Europe	mottled red-brown	640	5	✓	decorative work, turnery, inlays
Ramin *Gonystylus* spp	SE Asia	white to pale yellow	670	4	✓	mouldings, furniture, louvre doors (easily machined)
Rosewood* *Dalbergia* spp	S America India	purplish-brown with black streaks	870	1	✓	interior joinery, cabinetry, turnery, veneers
Sapele *Entandophragma cylindricum*	W Africa	red-brown with stripe figure	640	3	✓	interior joinery, door veneers, flooring
Sycamore* *Acer pseudoplatanus*	Europe UK	white to creamy yellow	630	5	✓	furniture, panelling, kitchen ware (does not taint or stain)
Teak *Tectona grandis*	Burma Thailand	golden brown	660	1	✓	furniture, joinery, boats (chemical and termite resistant)
Utile *Entandophragma utile*	W Africa	reddish-brown	660	2	✓	joinery, furniture, cabinetry
Walnut, European* *Juglans regia*	Europe UK	grey-brown with dark streaks	670	3	✓	furniture, turnery, gun stocks (decorative)

* = limited availability

Hardwood – standard sawn sizes (mm)

Thickness	50	63	75	100	125	150	175	200	225	250	300
19			*	*	*	*	*				
25	*	*	*	*	*	*	*	*	*	*	*
32			*	*	*	*	*	*	*	*	*
38			*	*	*	*	*	*	*	*	*
50				*	*	*	*	*	*	*	*
63						*	*	*	*	*	*
75						*	*	*	*	*	*
100						*	*	*	*	*	*

* = sizes laid down in BS 5450 : 1977.

Reduction from sawn sizes by planning

Structural timber	3 mm up to	100 mm
	5 mm for	101–150 mm
	6 mm for	151–300 mm
Flooring, matchings	5 mm up to	25 mm
	6 mm for	26–50 mm
	7 mm for	51–300 mm
Wood trim	6 mm up to	25 mm
	7 mm for	26–50 mm
	8 mm for	51–100 mm
	9 mm for	101–105 mm
	10 mm for	151–300 mm
Joinery and cabinet work	7 mm up to	25 mm
	9 mm for	26–50 mm
	10 mm for	51–100 mm
	12 mm for	101–150 mm
	14 mm for	151–300 mm

Softwood mouldings

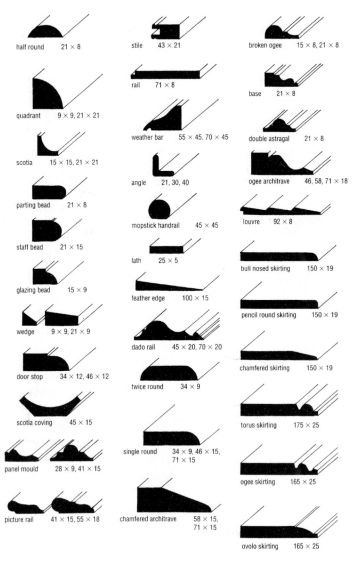

half round	21 × 8	
quadrant	9 × 9, 21 × 21	
scotia	15 × 15, 21 × 21	
parting bead	21 × 8	
staff bead	21 × 15	
glazing bead	15 × 9	
wedge	9 × 9, 21 × 9	
door stop	34 × 12, 46 × 12	
scotia coving	45 × 15	
panel mould	28 × 9, 41 × 15	
picture rail	41 × 15, 55 × 18	

stile	43 × 21
rail	71 × 8
weather bar	55 × 45, 70 × 45
angle	21, 30, 40
mopstick handrail	45 × 45
lath	25 × 5
feather edge	100 × 15
dado rail	45 × 20, 70 × 20
twice round	34 × 9
single round	34 × 9, 46 × 15, 71 × 15
chamfered architrave	58 × 15, 71 × 15

broken ogee	15 × 8, 21 × 8
base	21 × 8
double astragal	21 × 8
ogee architrave	46, 58, 71 × 18
louvre	92 × 8
bull nosed skirting	150 × 19
pencil round skirting	150 × 19
chamfered skirting	150 × 19
torus skirting	175 × 25
ogee skirting	165 × 25
ovolo skirting	165 × 25

Some sections are available in a range of sizes.
The dimensions given are those most often available.

Hardwood mouldings

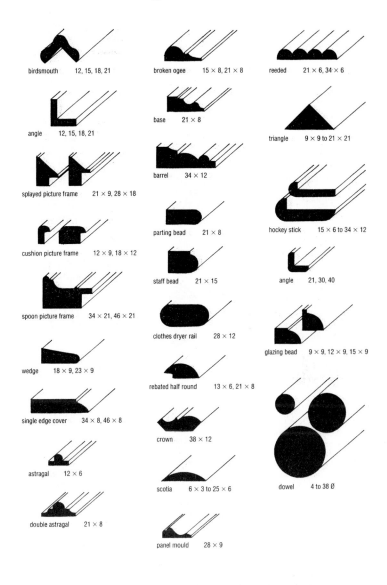

birdsmouth   12, 15, 18, 21

angle   12, 15, 18, 21

splayed picture frame   21 × 9, 28 × 18

cushion picture frame   12 × 9, 18 × 12

spoon picture frame   34 × 21, 46 × 21

wedge   18 × 9, 23 × 9

single edge cover   34 × 8, 46 × 8

astragal   12 × 6

double astragal   21 × 8

broken ogee   15 × 8, 21 × 8

base   21 × 8

barrel   34 × 12

parting bead   21 × 8

staff bead   21 × 15

clothes dryer rail   28 × 12

rebated half round   13 × 6, 21 × 8

crown   38 × 12

scotia   6 × 3 to 25 × 6

panel mould   28 × 9

reeded   21 × 6, 34 × 6

triangle   9 × 9 to 21 × 21

hockey stick   15 × 6 to 34 × 12

angle   21, 30, 40

glazing bead   9 × 9, 12 × 9, 15 × 9

dowel   4 to 38 Ø

Wood veneers

QUARTER CUT veneers are cut at right angles to the growth rings in the logs. The variations in colour brought about by summer/winter growth produce a straight grain effect. This is thought to be an advantage in veneers such as sapele.

CROWN CUT/FLAT CUT veneers are produced by slicing through logs, giving a less straight grained veneer with more figure and in general a more decorative finish.

ROTARY CUT is made by mounting a log on a lathe and rotating it against a sharp fixed knife. The cut follows the annular growth rings producing a bold variegated grain. Rotary cut veneer is exceptionally wide.

BURR/BURL VENEERS are made from the enlarged trunk of certain trees, particularly walnut. The grain is very irregular with the appearance of small knots grouped closely together. Small sections of this veneer are normally joined together to form a larger sheet.

Source: James Latham plc

Wood rotting fungi

Dry rot *Serpula lacrimans*

This is the most damaging of fungi. Mainly attacks softwoods and typically occurs in wood embedded in damp masonry. It needs wood with only 20 per cent moisture content and thrives in dark, humid conditions and so is seldom seen externally. It is able to penetrate bricks and mortar and thus can transport moisture from a damp source to new woodwork.

Fruit body	Tough, fleshy pancake or bracket. Yellow ochre turning to rusty-red with white or grey margins.
Mycelium (fungal roots)	Silky white sheets, cotton wool-like cushions or felted grey skin showing tinges of yellow and lilac. Strands sometimes 6 mm thick, becoming brittle when dry.
Damage	Darkens wood with large cuboidal cracking and deep fissures. Wood lightweight and crumbly. No skin of sound wood. Wood may be warped and give off distinctive musty mushroomy smell.

Wet rots

These can only grow on timber with a 40 to 50 per cent moisture content and tend not to spread much beyond the source of dampness.

Coniophora puteana (cellar fungus)

A brown rot occurring in softwoods and hardwoods. Most common cause of decay in woodwork soaked by leaking water.

Fruit body	Rare in buildings. Thin greenish olive-brown plate. Spores on minute pimples.
Mycelium	Only present in conditions of high humidity. Slender thread-like yellowish becoming deep brown or black.
Damage	Darkens wood, small cuboidal cracks, often below sound veneer.

Fibroporia vaillantii (mine fungus)

A brown rot which attacks softwood, particularly in high temperature areas.

Fruit body Irregular, white, cream to yellow lumpy sheets or plates with numerous minute pores.

Mycelium White or cream sheets of fern-like growths.

Damage Resembles dry rot in cuboidal pieces but wood lighter in colour and cracks less deep.

Phellinus contiguus

A white rot which attacks softwoods and hardwoods and is frequently found on external joinery.

Fruit body Only found occasionally. Tough, elongated, ochre to dark brown, covered in minute pores.

Mycelium Tawny brown tufts may be found in crevices.

Damage Wood bleaches and develops stringy fibrous appearance.
Does not crumble.

Donkioporia expansa

A white rot which attacks hardwood, particularly oak, and may spread to adjacent softwoods. Often found at beam ends bedded in damp walls and associated with death watch beetle.

Fruit body Thick, hard, dull fawn or biscuit coloured plate or bracket. Long pores, often in several layers.

Mycelium White to biscuit felted growth, often shaped to contours in wood. Can exude yellow-brown liquid.

Damage Wood becomes bleached and is reduced to consistency of whitish lint which will crush but does not crumble.

Asterostroma

A white rot usually found in softwood joinery such as skirting boards.

Fruit body   Thin, sheet-like, without pores rather like mycelium.
Mycelium   White, cream or buff sheets with strands which can cross long distances over masonry.
Damage   Wood is bleached and becomes stringy and fibrous.
No cuboidal cracking and does not crumble.

Treatment

Timber suffering from fungal or woodworm damage should only be treated if really necessary. Very often the damage is old, as when the sapwood has been destroyed but the remaining heartwood is sufficient for structural stability.

Many defects can be cured by eliminating the source of the damp and improving ventilation. The use of unjustified treatment is contrary to the Control of Substances Hazardous to Health (COSHH) Regulations and is not acceptable.

The person or company applying the treatment could be liable to prosecution.

However, when there is no alternative to chemical treatment, the following action should be undertaken:

Identify fungus. Rapidly dry out any moisture sources and improve ventilation.

Remove all affected timber (about 400 mm from visible signs for dry rot) and ideally burn on site.

Avoid distributing spores when handling.

Treat all remaining timbers with approved fungicide. Replace with pre-treated timber.

Woodworm

Wood boring insects do not depend on damp and humid conditions, although certain species prefer timber which has been decayed by fungi.

The life cycle of a woodworm is egg, larva, pupa and adult. First signs of attack are the exit holes made by the adults who emerge to mate and usually die after reproduction.

The following insects can all cause serious damage and the death watch and longhorn beetle can cause structural damage. Other beetles only feed on damp wood rotted by fungi and, since they cannot attack sound dry wood, remedial action to control wood rot will limit further infestation.

Common furniture beetle (*Anobium punctatum*)
Attacks both softwoods and European hardwoods and also plywood made with natural glues. It is the most widespread beetle and only affects sapwood if wood rot is present. Commonly found in older furniture, structural timbers, under stairs, cupboards and areas affected by damp.

Beetle 2–6 mm long, exit hole 1–2 mm, adults emerge May–September.

Wood boring weevils
(*Pentarthrum huttonii* and *Euophryum confine*)
Attacks decayed hard and softwoods in damp situations, typically poorly ventilated cellars and wood in contact with wet floors and walls.

Beetle 3–5 mm long, exit hole 1.0 mm with surface channels, adults emerge at any time.

Powder post beetle (*Lyctus brunneus*)
Attacks tropical and European hardwoods, not found in softwoods. Veneers, plywood and blockboard are all susceptible.

Beetle 4–7 mm long, exit hole 1–2 mm.

Death watch beetle (*Xestobium rufovillosum*)

Attacks sapwood and heartwood of partially decayed hard-woods and occasionally adjacent softwoods. Often found in old churches with oak and elm structures. Typically found in areas prone to dampness such as wall plates, ends of joists, lintels and timbers built into masonry.

Beetle 6–8 mm long, exit hole 3 mm, adults emerge March–June.

Longhorn beetle (*Hylotrupes bajulus*)

Attacks softwood, particularly in roof timbers. May be over-looked in early stages as there are few exit holes. Scraping noises audible on hot days with large infestations. Prevalent only in Surrey and SW London. Outbreaks should be reported to BRE Timber & Protection Division.

Beetle 10–20 mm long, exit hole 6–10 mm oval, adults emerge July–September.

Treatment

Fresh exit holes and bore dust on or below timbers are signs of active infestation, although vibrations may dislodge old bore dust. Chemical treatment however may not be necessary. See paragraph on Treatment on p. 291.

Identify beetle and treat timbers with appropriate insecticidal spray, emulsion or paste to destroy adults and unhatched eggs on the surface of the wood and larvae before they develop into pupae. Solvent-based products penetrate timber very effectively but have health and safety problems associated with them. Some water-based products claim to be as effective but more environmentally friendly; of these, boron-based products are likely to be least toxic in the environment at large.

If associated with fungal decay, treat as for wood rot and use a dual-purpose remedy (i.e. anti-rot and beetle). Do not use dual purpose products where woodworm is present in timbers which are dry and expected to remain so.

Source: *Recognising Wood Rot and Insect Damage in Buildings*

Wood boring beetles

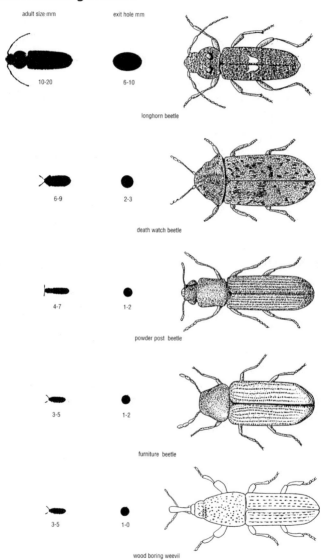

adult size mm   exit hole mm

10-20   6-10

longhorn beetle

6-9   2-3

death watch beetle

4-7   1-2

powder post beetle

3-5   1-2

furniture beetle

3-5   1-0

wood boring weevil

Building boards

Chipboard

Particle board with a variety of woodchips bonded with resin adhesives.

No chipboard is completely moisture resistant and should not be used externally.

Six classes identified in BS 5669 Part 2: 1989

C1	= general purpose use	C3	=	moisture resistant
C1A	= slightly better quality for furniture	C4	=	moisture resistant flooring quality
C2	= flooring quality	C5	=	moisture resistant structural quality

Sheets can be supplied wood veneer and melamine faced; with low formaldehyde rating, or bonded to polystyrene for insulated flooring.

Thicknesses   12, 15, 18, 22, 25, 28, 30 and 38 mm.
Sheet sizes   1220 × 2440 mm, 1830 × 2440 mm,
            1220 × 2745 mm, 1830 × 3050 mm,
            1220 × 3050 mm, 1830 × 3660 mm
            also
            600 × 2440 mm for 18 and 22 mm flooring

Wood veneer and melamine faced shelves
Thickness   15 mm
Widths   152 (6″), 229 (9″), 305 (12″), 381 (15″),
          457 (18″), 533 (21″), 610 (24″), 686 (27″), 762
          (30″); 914 mm (36″)
Lengths   1830 (6′) and 2440 mm (8′)

Source: Norbord Ltd

Blockboard

Composite board with one or two veneers applied to solid core of timber blocks 7–30 mm wide, also available with decorative wood or laminate veneers, commonly 18 mm thick.

Thicknesses   13, 16, 18, 22, 25, 32, 38 and 45 mm
Sheet sizes   1220 × 2440 mm; 1525 × 3050 and 3660 mm;
1830 × 5200 mm

Source: James Latham plc

Hardboard

Thin, dense boards with one very smooth face and mesh textured reverse. Grainless, knotless, and will not easily split or splinter. It can be bent, is easy to machine, has high internal bond strength for glueing and good dimensional stability. Two types available:

Standard hardboard	= general internal linings and door facings
Oil tempered hardboard	= structural purposes (higher strength and moisture resistance), flooring overlays

Thicknesses   3.2, 4.8 and 6.0 mm
Sheet sizes   1220 × 2440 and 3050 mm

Also available:
Perforated hardboard with
4.8 mm Ø holes @ 19 mm centres × 3.2 mm thick and
7.0 mm Ø holes @ 25 mm centres × 6.0 mm thick

Hardboard with painted finishes.

Source: Masonite CP Ltd

Laminboard

A composite board with veneers applied to a core of narrow timber strips (as opposed to wider blocks in blockboard). It is heavier, flatter and more expensive than blockboard but is less likely to warp.

Thicknesses   13, 16, 19, 22, 25, 32, 38 and 44 mm
Sheet sizes   1220 × 2440 mm, 1525 × 3050 and 3660 mm.

MDF (Medium Density Fibreboard)

Homogenous board of softwood fibres bonded with synthetic resins producing a very dense, fine textured uniform material which can be machined to great accuracy. Normal grades are not moisture resistant but moisture resistant grades are available. Low and zero formaldehyde (Medite, etc.), flame-retardant and integrally coloured boards are also available.

Thicknesses   6, 9, 12, 15, 18, 22, 25 and 30 mm (smaller and larger thicknesses also made by a few manufacturers).
Sheet sizes   1220 × 2440 mm 1525 × 2440 mm 1830 × 2440 mm
1220 × 2745 mm 1525 × 2745 mm 1830 × 3660 mm
1220 × 3050 mm 1525 × 3050 mm

Medium hardboard

A board with a density between that of wood fibre insulation board and standard hardboard. It has good thermal and insulation properties with a fine finish. Can be cold and steam bent. Moisture resistant and flame-retardant grades available. Used for notice boards, ceilings, wall linings, shop fittings, display work and pin boards.

Thicknesses   6.4, 9.5 and 12.7 mm
Sheet size   1220 × 2440 mm

Source: Medite Europe Ltd

OSB (Oriented Strand Board)

Made from softwood strands, approximately 75 mm long, placed in layers in different directions, bonded and compressed together with exterior grade water-resistant resins. A 'green' product made from thinnings from managed plantations. Process utilizes 95 per cent of the wood, discarded bark being used for fuel or horticulture. Cheaper than plywood, strong in both directions, with a uniform and decorative appearance.

Two grades available, one suitable for formwork, site hoardings and crating, the other for sheathing, flooring and decorative panels.

Thicknesses	6, 8, 9, 11, 15, 18, 22 and 25 mm
Sheet sizes	1200 × 2400 mm; 1220 × 2440 mm;
	590 × 2400 mm and 2440 mm for
	9 mm thick t & g flooring

Source: Norbord Ltd

Matchboarding

Timber boards, tongued and grooved on opposite sides. Joints can be plain butt joints as for floorboards or moulded with 'V' or quirk (rounded) shoulders for wall cladding.

Typical sizes of matchboards

Nominal size mm	Laid width mm	Finished thickness mm
12.5 × 100	80	10
19 × 75	55	15
19 × 100	80	15
19 × 150	130	15
25 × 75	55	20
25 × 100	80	20
25 × 150	130	20

Plywood

Made from softwood and hardwood veneers placed at right angles, or sometimes 45°, to one another. The veneers are strong in the direction of the grain, weak in the other. Thus structural plywoods have odd numbers of layers so that the grain to the outside faces lies in the same direction. Adhesives used are described as WBP (weather- and boilproof) for external or arduous conditions. BR (boil resistant), MR (moisture resistant) and INT (interior) are progressively less resistant. Since many hardwood plywoods are sourced from unstainable forestry, it is advisable to specify softwood ply in preference.

Plywoods are graded according to species and country of origin and are effectively as follows:

Veneer with minimal imperfections as peeled.
Veneer with imperfections plugged or filled.
Veneer with imperfections which have not been repaired.

Thicknesses	0.8, 1.0, 1.2, 1.5 mm (aircraft specification); 2, 2.5, 3, 4, 5, 6, 6.5, 9, 12, 15, 18, 21, 24 and 27 mm
Sheet sizes	1220 × 1220 mm 1525 × 610 mm (t & g)
	1220 × 2440 mm 1525 × 1525 mm
	1220 × 3050 mm 1525 × 2440 mm
	1220 × 3660 mm 1525 × 3050 mm
	1270 × 1270 mm 1525 × 3660 mm

Source: James Latham plc

Plasterboard

Boards with a core of aerated gypsum plaster bonded between two sheets of strong paper which should comply with BS 1230 Part 1 : 1985.

There are different grades for dry lining and wet plaster. Dry lining boards have tapered edges to allow for jointing tapes.

Boards are available backed with foil, polystyrene, polyurethane foam and phenolic foam. Others have more moisture-resistant and fire-resistant cores.

Thicknesses   9.5, 12.5, 15 and 19 mm (25–50 mm for boards backed with insulation)

Sheet sizes   400 × 1200 mm   600 × 1800 mm
                                   600 × 2400 mm
                 900 × 1200 mm   1200 × 2400 mm
                 900 × 1800 mm   1200 × 2700 mm
                 900 × 2400 mm   1200 × 3000 mm

Source: British Gypsum

Calcium silicate board

Asbestos-free board mainly used for structural fire protection. Cellulose fibres dispersed in water are mixed with lime, cement, silica and fire protective fillers to form a slurry. Water is then removed from the slurry under vacuum to form boards which are transferred to high pressure steam autoclaves for curing. Denser boards are hydraulically compressed before curing. Boards can be easily cut to size and drilled for screw fixing. 9 mm and 12 mm thick boards are available with rebated edges for seamless flush jointing. Boards may be decorated or left untreated.

Thicknesses	6, 9, 12, 15, 20, 22, 25, 30, 35, 40, 45, 50, 55 and 60 mm
Sheet sizes	1220, 1830, 2440, 3050 mm long × 610 and 1220 mm wide
Fire Classification	Class 0 for surface spread of flame
Fire Protection	From 60 to 240 minutes depending on product

Source: Promat

Plastics

Plastics – commonly used in building

Plastics are organic substances mainly derived from by-products of coal–gas manufacture and refining of mineral oil. These are manipulated to form long-chain molecules on which the plasticity and rigidity of the material of the products made from them depend. They are made up of three main groups:

- **thermoplastics**, such as polythene, vinyls and nylon, where the structure is not permanently set and which can therefore be joined by heat or solvents.
- **thermosetting plastics**, such as phenol formaldehyde, melamine and fibreglass, which have fixed molecular structures that cannot be re-shaped by heat or solvents and are joined by adhesives.
- **elastomers**, such as natural rubber, neoprene and butyl rubber, which have polymers in which the helical molecular chains are free to straighten when the material is stretched and recover when the load is released.

Plastics – industrial techniques

glass-reinforced plastic (GRP) Synthetic resin reinforced with glass fibre, used for rooflights, wall panels, etc.

injection moulding Similar to die casting for moulding thermoplastics. Plastic is melted and then forced under pressure into a cooled moulding chamber.

plastic laminate Decorative laminate made up of paper or fabric impregnated with melamine or phenolic resins and bonded together under pressure to form a hard-wearing, scratch-resistant finish used primarily for work surfaces.

solvent welding A permanent joint made between thermoplastics by smearing both sides with an appropriate solvent before joining together.

vacuum forming Making components by evacuating the space between the sheet material and the die so that forming is affected by atmospheric pressure.

Plastics – abbreviations in general use

Abbreviation	Plastic	Uses
ABS	Acrylonitrile butadiene styrene	cold water pipes
CPE	Chlorinated polyethylene	water tanks
CPVC	Chlorinated polyvinyl chloride	Hot water and waste pipes
EPDM	Ethylene propylene di-monomer	gaskets, single ply roofing
EPS	Expanded polystyrene	plastic foam for insulation
ETFE	Ethyl tetra fluoro ethylene	Film for foil roof cushions
EVA	Ethylene vinyl acetate	weather protective films
GRP	Glass-reinforced polyester (fibreglass)	cladding, panels, mouldings
HDPE	High density polyethylene	flooring, piping
HIPS	High impact polystyrene	ceilings, mirrors
LDPE	Low density polyethylene	bins, pipes, fittings
MF	Melamine-formaldehyde	laminated plastics, adhesives
PA	Polyamide (nylon)	electrical fittings, washers, ropes
PB	Polybutylene	pipe fittings
PC	Polycarbonate	anti-vandal glazing
PE	Polyethylene	electrical insulation, flooring, piping
PF	Phenol-formaldehyde (Bakelite)	electrical fittings, door furniture
PMMA	Polymethyl methacrylate (Perspex)	sanitary ware, transparent sheet
PP	Polypropylene	electrical insulation, piping
PS	Polystyrene	insulation, suspended ceilings
PTFE	Polytetrafluoroethylene	pipe jointing, sealing tape
PU	Polyurethane	insulation, paints, coatings
PVA	Polyvinyl acetate (latex emulsion)	emulsion paint, bonding agents
PVC	Polyvinyl chloride	floor and wall coverings
PVB	Polyvinyl butyral	laminated glass
PVF	Polyvinyl fluoride	protective films
UF	Urea-formaldehyde	glues, insulation
UP	Unsaturated polyester	paint, powder coatings, bituminous felt
UPVC	Unplasticised polyvinyl chloride	rainwater, soil and waste pipes, roof sheeting

Nails and screws

Nails

panel pin	round wire nail
hardboard panel pin	purlin nail
lath nail	lost head nail
plasterboard nail	cut floorboard brad
gimp pin for upholstery	cut clasp nail for heavy carpentry
cut lath nail	double head shutter nail for temporary fixing
cedar shake nail	masonry nail
carpet tack	
sprig for fixing glass to timber frames	helical threaded nail for corrugated sheet
escutcheon pin	annular nail for boats and external joinery
clout nail for roofing, felt and fencing	convex head nail for corrugated sheet
large clout nail for roofing felt	chisel point nail for fixing pipes to masonry
clout head peg for roof tiling	

Wood screws

countersunk	
raised head	
raised countersunk	
dome head	
coach screw	
cross head	

Machine screws and bolts

countersunk	
raised countersunk	
round	
binder pan	
pan	
cheese	
fillister	
mushroom	

Source: *Handbook of Fixings and Fastenings*

Standard wire gauge (SWG)
in millimetres and inches

SWG	mm	inches	SWG	mm	inches
1	7.62	0.300	16	1.63	0.064
2	7.00	0.276	17	1.42	0.056
3	6.40	0.252	18	1.22	0.048
4	5.89	0.232	19	1.02	0.040
5	5.38	0.212	20	0.914	0.036
6	4.88	0.192	21	0.813	0.032
7	4.47	0.176	22	0.711	0.028
8	4.06	0.160	23	0.610	0.024
9	3.66	0.144	24	0.559	0.022
10	3.25	0.128	25	0.508	0.020
11	2.95	0.116	26	0.457	0.018
12	2.64	0.104	27	0.417	0.016
13	2.34	0.092	28	0.376	0.015
14	2.03	0.080	29	0.345	0.014
15	1.83	0.072	30	0.315	0.012

Colour

The *colour spectrum* is made up of colour refracted from a beam of light, as through a glass prism or as seen in a rainbow. The bands of colour are arranged according to their decreasing wavelength (6.5×10^{-7} for red to 4.2×10^{-7} for violet), and are traditionally divided into seven main colours: red, orange, yellow, green, blue, indigo and violet. When arranged as segments of a circle, this is known as the *colour circle*. The *primary* colours are red, yellow and blue, as these cannot be mixed from other colours. The *secondary* colours are orange, green and purple, and the *tertiary colours* are produced by adding a primary colour to a secondary colour.

Complementary colours are pairs of colours on opposite sides of the circle, which when mixed together make browns and greys. The term *hue* indicates a specific colour, defined in terms of, say, redness or blueness, but not lightness or darkness. *Tone* is the lightness or darkness of a colour. Adding black, white or grey to a hue reduces its intensity.

Colour systems

British Standards Colour System BS: 4800 1989. Colours are defined by a three-part code consisting of hue, greyness and weight. Hues are divided into twelve equal numbers, from 02 (red/purple) to 24 (purple), with an additional 00 for neutral whites, greys and blacks. The greyness is described by five letters: (A) grey; (B) nearly grey; (C) grey/clear; (D) nearly clear and (E) clear. Weight, a subjective term, describes both lightness and greyness, so each letter is followed by number from 01 to 58. Thus the colour 'heather' 22 C 37 is made up of:

22 (violet) C (grey/clear) 37 (medium weight)

NCS Natural Colour System. The Natural Colour System (NCS), generally referred to in the UK as *Colour Dimensions*, was developed by the Scandinavian Colour Institute in 1978.

It is a colour language system that can describe any colour by notation, and is based on the assumption that human beings are able to identify six basic colours – white W; black S (note *not* B); yellow Y; red R; blue B and green G. These are arranged in a *colour circle*, with yellow, red, blue and green marking the quadrants. These segments are divided into 10 per cent steps, so that orange can be described as Y 50 R (yellow with 50 per cent red). To describe the shade of a colour there is the NCS *triangle*, where the base of the triangle is a grey scale marked in 10 per cent steps from white W to black S. The apex of the triangle represents the pure colour and is similarly marked in 10 per cent steps. Thus a colour can be described as 1080-Y50R for an orange with 10 per cent blackness, 80 per cent chromatic intensity at yellow with 50 per cent red. This system allows for a much finer subdivision of colours than the BS system.

RAL Colour Collection. This system is used within the building industry for defining colours of coatings such as plastics, metals, glazed bricks and some paints and lacquers. It was established in Germany in 1925 and developed over the years, is now designated RAL 840-HR, and lists 194 colours. Colours are defined by four digits, the first being the colour class: 1 yellow; 2 orange; 3 red; 4 violet; 5 blue; 6 green; 7 grey; 8 brown and 9 black. The next three digits relate only to the sequence in which the colours were filed. An official name is also applied to each standard RAL colour, e.g. RAL 6003 olive green.

RAL Design System. This system has 1688 colours arranged in a colour atlas based on a three-dimensional colour space defined by the co-ordinates of hue, lightness and chroma. The colours are coded with three numbers; thus reddish/yellow is 69.9 7.56 56.5. It is similar to the Natural Colour System except that it is based on the mathematical division of the whole visible wavelength spectrum, which is then divided into mostly 10 per cent steps. The system can be easily used by computer programs to formulate colours.

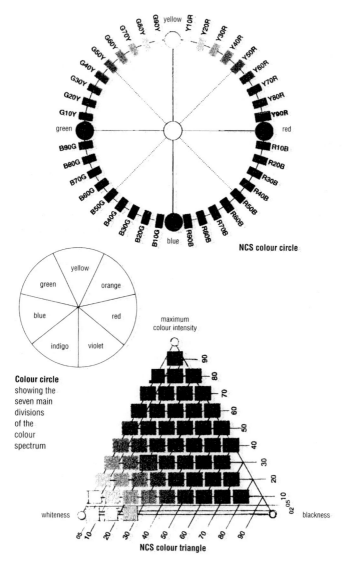

NCS colour circle

Colour circle
showing the
seven main
divisions
of the
colour
spectrum

NCS colour triangle

Source: NCS Colour Centre

Painting

Preparation. Careful preparation is vital if the decorative finish applied is to succeed and be durable. It is important to follow instructions about preparing substrates, atmospheric conditions and drying times between coats. Ensure that the right product is specified for the task, and that primers and subsequent coats are compatible.

Paints

Paints basically consist of pigments, binder, and a solvent or water. Other ingredients are added for specific uses.

Solvent-based paints and stains are now considered environmentally unsound and are increasingly being supplanted by water-based alternatives. These are less glossy and more water-permeable than oil paints, but are quick-drying, odour-free, and tend not to yellow with age.

Organic paints

It is now possible to use totally solvent-free paints and varnishes containing 0.0 per cent volatile organic compounds (VOCs). Most paints currently on sale, both gloss and emulsion, contain solvents and VOCs.

VOCs are a major contributor to low-level atmospheric pollution and the use of these compounds leads to global warming. In addition, the use of solvent-based paints is a major cause of 'sick building syndrome', 'Danish painter's syndrome', asthma, allergies, chemical sensitivities and the general flu-like symptoms reported by many people using conventional paints including matt and silk wall paints.

Organic paints are ideal for children's bedrooms, nurseries, kitchens and anywhere in the home, especially for people who are chemically sensitive or suffer from asthma or allergies.

Source: ECOS Organic Paints Ltd

Primers offer protection to the substrate from corrosion and deterioration, and give a good base for undercoats.

Undercoats, which are often just thinner versions of the finishing coat, provide a base for the topcoats.

Topcoats provide the durable and decorative surface, and come in gloss, satin, eggshell and matt finishes.

In addition to the paints listed overleaf there are specialist paints such as: *flame-retardant* paints, which emit non-combustible gases when subjected to fire; *intumescent coatings*, which expand to form a layer of insulating foam for structural steel; *multi-colour* paints, which incorporate coloured flecks, or two-part systems which use a special roller for the top coat to reveal partially the darker colour of the first coat; *silicone water-repellent* paints for porous masonry; *bituminous* paints for waterproofing metals and masonry; and *epoxy-ester coatings* to resist abrasion, oil and detergent spills.

Paints – typical products

Primers	Use*	Base*	Description
Zinc phosphate acrylic	M	WB	for all metals inside and out, quick-drying, low odour
Red oxide	M	SB	replaces red lead and calcium plumbate for ferrous metals
Etching	M	SB	factory pre-treatment for new galvanized metal
Mordant solution	M	WB	pre-treatment of galvanized metal
Micaceous iron oxide	M	SB	for marine and industrial steelwork, resists pollution and high humidity
Acrylated rubber	M, Ms	BS	for all metals, plaster and masonry, resists moisture
Wood primer	W	SB	non-lead primer for all woods inside and out
Wood primer/undercoat	W	WB	high opacity, quick-drying primer and undercoat
Aluminium wood primer	W	SB	good for resinous woods and as sealer for creosoted and bituminous surfaces
Alkali-resistant	P	SB	for dry walls under SB finishes, seals stains and fire damage
Plaster sealer	P	WB	for dry porous interior surfaces, e.g. plasterboard
Stabilizing primer	Ms	SB	to seal powdery and chalky surfaces

Undercoats			
Exterior flexible	W	SB	long-lasting, flexible, good opacity for exterior wood
Undercoat	all	SB	for use inside and out under solvent-based finishes
Preservative basecoat	W	SB	for new and bare wood to protect against blue stain and fungal decay

Finishes			
High gloss	all	SB	alkyd high gloss for all surfaces inside and out
Satin, eggshell, flat	W, M, P	SB	alkyd paints in three finishes for interior use
Vinyl emulsion	P	WB	matt, soft sheen and silk finishes for interiors
Masonry – smooth	Ms	WB	contains fungicide, for dry masonry, rendering, concrete, etc.
Masonry – textured	Ms	WB	fine granular finish, for dry masonry, etc
Masonry – all seasons	Ms	SB	flexible, smooth and good for applying in cold conditions
Epoxy floor	Ms, C	WB	two-pack mid-sheen paint for interior masonry and concrete floors
Floor	W, C	WB	quick-drying, for interior concrete and wood floors
Ecolyd gloss	W, M, Ms	SB	high quality, mirror-finish gloss, low solvent content
Protective enamel	M	SB	glossy, protective, quick-drying, for machinery
Exterior UPVC	PVC	WB	for redecoration of weathered UPVC surfaces
Acrylated rubber coating	M, Ms	SB	for steelwork and masonry inside and out, good against condensation
Aluminium	W, M	SB	heat resisting to 260°C, for metals and wood
Timber preservative	W	SB	coloured, water-repellent finish for sawn timber, fences, sheds, etc.
Protective wood stain	W	SB	water-repellent, mould-resistant, light-fast translucent colours
Exterior varnish	W	SB	transparent gloss finish for exterior wood
Interior varnish	W	WB	tough, quick-drying, durable clear polyurethane finish
Aquatech basecoat	W	WB	flexible satin finish for bare and new wood
Aquatech woodstain	W	WB	flexible satin coloured finish, resists peeling, blistering
Diamond glaze	W	WB	clear lacquer for interior wood surfaces subject to hard wear

*C = concrete; M = metal; Ms = masonry; P = plaster; SB = solvent-based; W = wood; WB = water based.

Source: ICI Paints

Paint covering capacity

Approximate maximum areas
for smooth surfaces of average porosity

m²/litre

			m²/litre
Preparation	Fungicidal wash		30
	Stabilizing primer		12
	Etching primer		19
	Timber preservative	– solvent based	10
	Timber preservative	– water based	12
Primers	Wood primer	– solvent based	13
	Wood primer	– aluminium	16
	Wood primer	– microporous	15
	Wood primer undercoat	– water based	12
	Metal primer	– solvent based	6
	Metal primer	– water based	15
	Metal primer	– zinc phosphate	6
	Acrylated rubber primer		5
Finishes	Undercoat	– solvent based	16
	Emulsion	– matt	15
	Emulsion	– vinyl silk	15
	Matt finish	– solvent based	16
	Eggshell finish	– solvent based	16
	Eggshell finish	– water based	15
	Microporous gloss	– solvent based	14
	High gloss	– solvent based	17
	Non-drip gloss	– solvent based	13
	Wood stain	– solvent based	25
	Exterior varnish	– solvent based	16
	Interior varnish	– solvent based	16
	Masonry paint	– smooth	10
	Masonry paint	– textured	6
	Acrylated rubber		6

Source: ICI Paints

Wallpaper coverage for walls and ceilings

Approximate number of rolls required

Walls	Measurement around walls (m)	Height of room above skirting (m)						
		2.3	2.4	2.6	2.7	2.9	3.1	3.2
	9.0	4	5	5	5	6	6	6
	10.4	5	5	5	5	6	6	6
	11.6	5	6	6	6	7	7	8
	12.8	6	6	7	7	7	8	8
	14.0	6	7	7	7	8	8	8
	15.2	7	7	8	8	9	9	10
	16.5	7	8	9	9	9	10	10
	17.8	8	8	9	9	10	10	11
	19.0	8	9	10	10	10	11	12
	20.0	9	9	10	10	11	12	13
	21.3	9	10	11	11	12	12	13
	22.6	10	10	12	12	12	13	14
	23.8	10	11	12	13	13	14	15
	25.0	11	11	13	13	14	14	16
	26.0	12	12	14	14	14	15	16
	27.4	12	13	14	14	15	16	17
	28.7	13	13	15	15	15	16	18
	30.0	13	14	15	15	16	17	19

Ceilings	Measurement around room (m)	no. rolls
	12.0	2
	15.0	3
	18.0	4
	20.0	5
	21.0	6
	24.0	7
	25.0	8
	27.0	9
	28.0	10
	30.0	11
	30.5	12

Notes:
Standard wallpaper roll is 530 mm wide $\times$ 10.06 m long (21" $\times$ 33'0")
One roll will cover approximately 5 m^2 (54 ft^2) including waste

Addresses/Sources

RIBA companies

Royal Institute of British Architects
66 Portland Place, London W1N 4AD   tel: 020 7580 5533
email: admin@inst.riba.org   fax: 020 7255 1541
www.riba.org

RIBA Enterprises Ltd, Manufacturer Network
15 Bonhill Street, London EC2P 2EA   tel: 020 7496 8300
email: admin@ribenterprises.com   fax: 020 7374 8200
www.ribaenterprises.com

RIBA Publishing
15 Bonhill Street, London EC2P 2EA   tel: 020 7496 8300
email: enquiry@ribapublishing.com   fax: 020 7374 8500
www.ribapublishing.com

NBS Services
The Old Post Office, St Nicholas Street,   tel: 0845 456 9594
Newcastle upon Tyne NE1 1RH   fax: 0191 232 5714
email: info@theNBS.com
www.nbsservices.co.uk

Technical Indexes Ltd
Willoughby Road, Bracknell RG12 8DW   tel: 01344 426311
email: marketing@techindex.co.uk   fax: 01344 424971
www.techindex.co.uk

RIBA Bookshops
email: sales@ribabookshops.com
website: www.ribabookshops.com
London   66 Portland Place W1B 1AD   tel: 020 7256 7222
Belfast   2 Mount Charles BT2 1NZ   tel: 028 9032 3350
Birmingham   Margaret Street B3 3SP   tel: 0121 233 2321
Manchester   113 Portland Street M1 6FB   tel: 0161 236 7691

Associations, Institutes and other information sources

Ancient Monuments Society
St Anne's Vestry Hall, 2 Church Entry,   tel: 020 7236 3934
London EC4V 5HB   fax: 020 7329 3677
www.ancientmonumentssociety.org.uk

Architects Registration Board (ARB)
8 Weymouth Street, London W1N 3FB   tel: 020 7580 5861
email: info@arb.org.uk www.arb.org.uk   fax: 020 7436 5269

Architectural Association (AA)
36 Bedford Square, London WC1B 3ES   tel: 020 7887 4000
email: info@aaschool.ac.uk www.aaschool.ac.uk   fax: 020 7414 0782

Arts Council of England
14 Great Peter Street, London SW1P 3NQ   tel: 0845 300 6200
email: enquiries@artscouncil.org.uk   fax: 020 7973 5590
www.artscouncil.org.uk

Barbour Index plc
New Lodge, Drift Road, Windsor SL4 4RQ   tel: 01344 884121
email: mso@barbour-index.co.uk   fax: 01344 884113
www.barbour-index.co.uk

Brick Development Association (BDA)
Woodside House, Winkfield, Windsor SL4 2DX tel: 01344 885651
email: brick@brick.org.uk www.brick.org.uk fax: 01344 890129

British Board of Agrément (BBA)
PO Box 195, Bucknalls Lane, Garston,   tel: 01923 665300
Watford WD25 9BA   fax: 01923 665301
email: info@bba.star.co.uk www.bbacerts.co.uk

British Constructional Steelwork Association Ltd (BCSA)
4 Whitehall Court, London SW1A 2ES   tel: 020 7839 8566
email: postroom@steelconstruction.org   fax: 020 7976 1634
www.steelconstruction.org

British Standards Institution (BSI)
389 Chiswick High Road, London W4 4AL   tel: 020 8996 9001
email: cservices@bsi-global.com   fax: 020 8996 7001
www.bsi-global.com

Building Centre
26 Store Street, London WC1E 7BT   tel: 020 7692 4000
email: information@buildingcentre.co.uk   fax: 020 7580 9641
www.buildingcentre.co.uk

Building Centre Bookshop
26 Store Street, London WC1E 7BT
email: bookshop@buildingcentre.co.uk
www.buildingcentre.co.uk

tel: 020 7692 4040
fax: 020 7636 3628

Building Research Establishment (BRE)
Bucknalls Lane, Garston, Watford WD25 9XX
email: enquiries@bre.co.uk www.bre.co.uk

tel: 01923 664000
fax: 01923 664010

Cadw – Welsh historic monuments
Crown Buildings, Cathays Park, Cardiff CF10 3NQ
email: cadw@wales.gsi.gov.uk
www.cadw.wales.gov.uk

tel: 029 2050 0200
fax: 029 2082 6375

Centre for Accessible Environments
70 South Lambeth Road, London SW8 1RL
email: cae@globalnet.co.uk www.cae.org.uk

tel: 020 7840 0125
fax: 020 7840 5811

Centre for Alternative Technology (CAT)
Machynlleth, Powys SY20 9AZ
email: info@cat.org.uk www.cat.org.uk

tel: 01654 705950
fax: 01654 702782

Chartered Institution of Building Services Engineers (CIBSE)
Delta House, 222 Balham High Road,
London SW12 9BS
email: info@cibse.org www.cibse.org

tel: 020 8675 5211
fax: 020 8675 5449

Chartered Institute of Building (CIOB)
Englemere, Kings Ride, Ascot SL5 8BJ
email: reception@ciob.org.uk www.ciob.org.uk

tel: 01344 630808
fax: 01344 630888

CIBSE
222 Balham High Road
London SW12 9BS
www.cibse.org

tel: 020 8675 5211

Civic Trust
Winchester House, 259–269 Old Marylebone Road,
London NW1 5RA
email: civicsocieties@civictrust.org.uk
www.civictrust.org.uk

tel: 020 7170 4299
fax: 020 7170 4298

Commission for Architecture & the Built Environment (CABE)
The Tower Building, 11 York Road,
London SE1 7NX
email: enquiries@cabe.org.uk
www.cabe.org.uk

tel: 020 7960 2400
fax: 020 7960 2444

Concrete Information Ltd (CIL)
Riverside House, 4 Meadows Business Park,   tel: 01276 608700
Station Approach, Blackwater, Camberley,   fax: 01276 608701
Surrey GU17 9AB
email: etrout@concreteinfo.org
www.concreteinfo.org

Construction Industry Council (CIC)
26 Store Street, London WC1E 7BT   tel: 02073997400
email: cic@cic.org.uk   fax: 020 7580 6140
email: info@cic.org.uk www.cic.org.uk

Copper Development Association
1 Brunel Court, Corner Hall, Hemel Hempstead   tel: 01442 275705
HP3 9XX   fax: 01442 275716
email: mail@copperdev.co.uk www.cda.org.uk

Countryside Council for Wales
Maes y Ffynnon, Penrhosgarnedd, Bangor,   tel: 0845 1306 229
Gwynedd LL57 2DW   fax: 01248 355782
www.ccw.gov.uk

Department for Culture, Media and Sport (DCMS)
2–4, Cockspur Street, London SW1Y 5DH   tel: 020 7211 6000
email: enquiries@culture.gov.uk www.culture.gov.uk   fax: 020 7211 6171

Department of Environment, Food & Rural Affairs
Nobel House, 17 Smith Square, London SW1P 3JR   tel: 020 7328 6000
email: helpline@defra.gsi.gov.uk www.defra.gov.uk   fax: 020 7238 6609

Department of Transport
Eland House, Bressenden Place, London SW1E 5DU   tel: 020 7944 3000
www.dtlr.gov.uk

Disabled Living Foundation
380–384 Harrow Road, London W9 2HU   tel: 020 7289 6111
email: dlfinfo@dlf.org.uk www.dlf.org.uk   fax: 020 7266 2922

English Heritage
1 Waterhouse Square, 138–142 Holborn,   tel: 020 7973 3000
London EC1N 3ST   fax: 020 7973 3001
www.english-heritage.org.uk

English Nature
Northminster House, Peterborough PE1 1UA   tel: 01733 455000
email: enquiries@english-nature.org.uk   fax: 01733 455103
www.english-nature.org.uk

Environment Agency
Rio House, Waterside Drive, Aztec West,
Almondsbury, Bristol, BS32 4UD
email: enquiries@environment-agency.gov.uk
www.environment-agency.gov.uk

tel: 01454 624400
fax: 01454 624409

Environment & Heritage Service Northern Ireland
5–33 Hill Street Belfast BT1 2LA
www.ehsni.gov.uk

tel: 028 9054 3037
fax: 028 9054 3111

Federation of Master Builders
Gordon Fisher House, 14–15 Great James Street,
London WC1N 3DP
email: central@fmb.org.uk www.fmb.org.uk

tel: 020 7242 7583
fax: 020 7404 0296

Forests Forever
Floor 4 Clareville House, 26/27 Oxendon Street,
London SW1Y 4EL www.ttf.co.uk

tel: 020 7839 1891
fax: 020 7930 0094

Forest Stewardship Council (FSC)
R8 11–13 Great Oak Street, Llanidloes,
Powys, SY18 6BU
email: info@fsc-uk.org www.fsc-uk.demon.co.uk

tel: 01686 413916
fax: 01686 412176

Friends of the Earth Ltd
26–28 Underwood Street, London N1 7JQ
email: info@foe.co.uk www.foe.co.uk

tel: 020 7490 1555
fax: 020 7490 0881

Glass and Glazing Federation (GGF)
44–48 Borough High Street, London SE1 1XB
email: info@ggf.org.uk www.ggf.org.uk

tel: 0845 257 7963
fax: 0870 042 4266

Guild of Architectural Ironmongers
8 Stepney Green, London E1 3JU
email: info@gai.org.uk www.gai.org.uk

tel: 020 7790 3431
fax: 020 7790 8517

Health and Safety Executive (HSE)
Rose Court, 2 Southwark Bridge, London SE1 9HS
www.hse.gov.uk

tel: 0845 345 0055
fax: 020 7556 2102

Heating & Ventilating Contractors' Association (HVCA)
ESCA House, 34 Palace Court, Bayswater,
London W2 4JG
email: contact@hvca.org.uk www.hvca.org.uk

tel: 020 7313 4900
fax: 020 7727 9268

Historic Scotland
Longmore House, Salisbury Place, Edinburgh EH9 1SH   tel: 0131 668 8642
www.historic-scotland.gov.uk   fax: 0131 668 8669

Institution of Civil Engineers (ICE)
1–7 Great George Street, London SW1P 3AA   tel: 020 7222 7722
www.ice.org.uk   fax: 020 7222 7500

Institute of Engineering and Technology (IET)
Michael Faraday House, Stevenage, Herts, SG1 2AY   tel: 01438 313 311/
email: postmaster@theiet.org   765 526
www.iee.org.uk   fax: 01438 767 339

Institution of Mechanical Engineers
1 Birdcage Walk, London SW1H 9JJ   tel: 020 7222 7899
email: enquiries@imeche.org.uk   fax: 020 7222 4557
www.imeche.org.uk

Institution of Structural Engineers (ISE)
11 Upper Belgrave Street, London SW1X 8BH   tel: 020 7235 4535
email: mail@istructe.org.uk www.istructe.org.uk   fax: 020 7235 4294

Landscape Institute
33 Great Portland Street, London W1W 8QG   tel: 020 7299 4500
email: mail@landscapeinstitute.org   fax: 020 7299 4501
www.landscapeinstitute.org

Lead Development Association International
17a Welbeck Way, London W1G 9YJ   tel: 020 7499 8422
email: enq@ldaint.org www.ldaint.org   fax: 020 7493 1555

Lead Sheet Association
Hawkwell Business Centre, Maidstone Road,   tel: 01892 822773
Pembury, Tunbridge Wells TN2 4AH   fax: 01892 823003
email: leadsa@globalnet.co.uk
www.leadsheetassociation.org.uk

Lighting Industry Federation (LIF)
8 Whitehall Road, Chingford, London E4 6EQ   tel: 020 8529 6909
email: info@lif.co.uk www.lif.co.uk   fax: 020 8529 6909

National Building Specification Ltd (NBS)
The Old Post Office, St Nicholas Street,   tel: 0191 232 9594
Newcastle upon Tyne NE1 1RH   fax: 0191 232 5714
email: info@thenbs.com www.thenbs.com

National Trust
36 Queen Anne's Gate, London SW1H 9AS   tel: 020 7222 9251
www.nationaltrust.org.uk   fax: 020 7222 5097

Ordnance Survey
Romsey Road, Maybush, Southampton SO16 4GU   tel: 0845 605 0505
email: customerservices@ordsvy.gov.uk   fax: 023 8079 2452
www.ordsvy.gov.uk

Planning Appeals Commission (N. Ireland)
Park House, 87 Great Victoria Street,   tel: 028 9024 4710
Belfast BT2 7AG   fax: 028 9031 2536
email: info@pacni.gov.uk www.pacni.gov.uk

Planning Inspectorate (England)
Temple Quay House, 2 The Square, Temple Quay,   tel: 0117 372 8852
Bristol BS1 9PN   fax: 0117 987 8139
email: enquiries@planning-inspectorate.gsi.gov.uk
www.planning-inspectorate.gsi.gov.uk

Planning Inspectorate (Wales)
Crown Buildings, Cathays Park, Cardiff CF10 3NQ   tel: 029 2082 3866
email: wales@planning-inspectorate.gsi.gov.uk   fax: 029 2082 5150
www.planning-inspectorate.gov.uk

Royal Incorporation of Architects in Scotland (RIAS)
15 Rutland Square, Edinburgh EH1 2BE   tel: 0131 229 7545
email: info@rias.org.uk www.rias.org.uk   fax: 0131 228 2188

Royal Institute of British Architects (RIBA)
66 Portland Place, London W1N 4AD   tel: 020 7580 5533
email: info@inst.riba.org   fax: 020 7255 1541
www.riba.org or www.architecture.com

Royal Institution of Chartered Surveyors (RICS)
12 Great George St, Parliament Square,   tel: 0870 333 1600
London SW1P 3AD   www.rics.org   fax: 020 7334 3811

Royal Town Planning Institute (RTPI)
41 Botolph Lane, London EC3R 8DL   tel: 020 7929 9494
email: online@rtpi.org.uk www.rtpi.org.uk   fax: 020 7929 9490

Scottish Civic Trust
Tobacco Merchant's House, 42 Miller Street,   tel: 0141 221 1466
Glasgow, G1 1DT   fax: 0141 248 6952
email: sct@scottishcivictrust.org.uk
www.scottishcivictrust.org.uk

Scottish Natural Heritage
Public Relations Department, Battleby, Redgorten, tel: 0131 447 4784
Perth, Scotland PH1 3EW   fax: 0131 446 2405
email: enquiries@snh.gov.uk www.snh.org.uk

Society for the Protection of Ancient Buildings (SPAB)
37 Spital Square, London E1 6DY   tel: 020 7377 1644
email: info@spab.org.uk www.spab.org.uk   fax: 020 7247 5296

The Stationery Office (formerly HMSO)
St Crispins, Duke Street, Norwich NR3 1PD   tel: 01603 622211
www.tso.co.uk

The Stationery Office Bookshops
email: esupport@tso.co.uk www.tsoshop.co.uk
16 Arthur Street, Belfast BT1 4GD   tel: 028 9023 8451
71 Lothian Road, Edinburgh EH3 9AZ   tel: 0870 606 5566

Stone Federation Great Britain
Channel Business Centre, Ingles Manor,   tel: 01303 856123
Castle Hill Avenue, Folkestone, Kent, CT20 2RD   fax: 01303 221095
email: jane.buxey@stone-federationgb.org.uk
www.stone-federationgb.org.uk

Timber Trade Federation
Clareville House, 26–27 Oxendon Street,   tel: 020 7839 1891
London SW1Y 4EL   fax: 020 7930 0094
email: ttf@ttf.co.uk www.ttf.co.uk

Timber Research and Development Association (TRADA)
Stocking Lane, Hughenden Valley,   tel: 01494 569600
High Wycombe HP14 4ND   fax: 01494 565487
email: information@trada.co.uk www.trada.co.uk

Town and Country Planning Association (TCPA)
17 Carlton House Terrace, London SW1Y 5AS   tel: 020 7930 8903
email: tcpa@tcpa.org.uk www.tcpa.org.uk   fax: 020 7930 3280

Water Regulations Advisory Service (WRAS)
Fern Close, Pen-y-fan Industrial Estate Oakdale   tel: 01495 248454
NP11 3EH   www.wras.co.uk   fax: 01495 249234

Water Research Centre plc
PO Box 16, Henley Road, Medmenham,   tel: 01491 636500
Marlow SL7 2HD   fax: 01491 636501
email: solutions@wrcplc.co.uk www.wrcplc.co.uk

Which?
PO Box 44, Hertford X, SG14 1SH   tel: 01992 822800
email: which@which.net www.which.net   fax: 020 7830 8585

Zinc Information Centre
6 Wrens Court, 56 Victoria Road,   tel: 0121 362 1201
Sutton Coldfield B72 1SY   fax: 0121 355 8727
email: zincinfo@hdg.org.uk

Manufacturers – referred to in the text

ACP (Concrete) Ltd
Risehow Industrial Estate, Flimby,
Maryport CA15 8PD
email: sales@acp-concrete.co.uk
www.acp-concrete.co.uk

tel: 01900 814659
fax: 01900 816200

Applied Energy Products Ltd
Morley Way, Peterborough PE2 9JJ
www.applied-energy.co.uk

tel: 01733 456789
fax: 01733 310606

Autopa Ltd
Cottage Leap, off Butlers Leap, Rugby,
Warwickshire CV21 3XP
email: info@autopa.co.uk www.autopa.co.uk

tel: 01788 550556
fax: 01788 550265

Banham Burglary Prevention
233–235 Kensington High Street, London W8 6SF
email: security@banham.com www.banham.com

tel: 020 7622 5151
fax: 020 7376 1232

Brash, John & Co Ltd
The Old Shipyard, Gainsborough DN21 1NG
email: jbltdinfo@johnbrash.co.uk
www.johnbrash.co.uk

tel: 01427 613858
fax: 01427 810218

British Gypsum Ltd
East Leake, Loughborough LE12 6JT
www.british-gypsum.bpb.com

tel: 0870 545 6123
fax: 0870 545 6356

Buckingham Nurseries
Tingewick Road, Buckingham MK18 4AE
www.bucknur.com

tel: 01280 822133
fax: 01280 815491

Caradon Ideal Ltd
PO Box 103, National Avenue,
Kingston-upon-Hull HU5 4JN
www.idealboilers.com

tel: 0870 849 8056
fax: 0870 849 8058

CSI Security Ltd
Ronald Close, Kempston, Bedford MK42 7SH
email: sales@csisec.com www.csisec.com

tel: 01234 840840
fax: 01234 840841

Concord Marlin
Avis Way, Newhaven BN9 0ED
email: sales@concordmarlin.com
www.concordmarlin.com

tel: 0870 606 2030
fax: 01273 512688

Corus Tubes
PO Box 101, Welson Road, Corby NN17 5UA
www.corustubes.com

tel: 01536 402121
fax: 01536 404111

Corus Building Systems, Kalzip Division
Haydock Lane, Haydock, St Helens WA11 9TY
email: kalzip-uk@corusgroup.com www.kalzip.com

tel: 01925 825100
fax: 01925 852944

Cox Building Products Ltd
Unit 1, Shaw Road, Bushbury,
Wolverhampton WV10 9LA
email: sales@coxbp.com www.coxbp.com

tel: 01902 371800
fax: 01902 371810

Duplus Architectural Systems Ltd
370 Melton Road, Leicester LE4 7SL
email: sales@duplus.co.uk www.duplus.co.uk

tel: 0116 261 0710
fax: 0116 261 0539

Ecos Organic Paints
Unit 34, Heysham Business Park, Middleton Road,
Heysham, LA3 3PP
www.ecospaints.com

tel: 01524 852371
fax: 01524 858978

Envirograf
Environmental Seals Ltd, Envirograf House,
Barfrestone, Dover CT15 7JG   www.envirograf.com

tel: 01304 842 555
fax: 01304 842666

GE Lighting Europe
153 Lincoln Road, Enfield, EN1 1SB
www.gelighting.com

tel: 020 8626 8500
fax: 020 8626 8502

Hepworth Building Products
Edlington, Doncaster, South Yorkshire DN12 1BY
www.hepworthbp.co.uk

tel: 01709 856 300
fax: 01709 856 301

Ibstock Brick Ltd
Leicester Road, Ibstock LE67 6HS
email: marketing@ibstock.co.uk www.ibstock.co.uk

tel: 01530 261999
fax: 01530 261888

ICI Paints Division
Wexham Road, Slough SL2 5DS
www.duluxtrade.co.uk

tel: 01753 550000
fax: 01753 578218

Ideal-Standard Ltd
The Bathroom Works, National Avenue,
Kingston-upon-Hull HU5 4HS
email: brochures@ideal-standard.co.uk
www.ideal-standard.co.uk

tel: 01482 346461
fax: 01482 445886

I G Lintols Ltd
Ballyreagh Industrial Estate, Cookstown,
Co Tyrone BT80 9DG   www.igltd.co.uk

tel: 02886 762184
fax: 02886 761011

JELD-WEN UK Ltd
Watch House Lane, Doncaster DN5 9LR
www.jeld-wen.co.uk

tel: 01302 394000
fax: 01302 787383

Klober Ltd
Ingleberry Road, Shepshed,
Loughborough LE12 9DE   www.klober.co.uk

tel: 01509 500660
fax: 01509 600061

Lafarge Roofing Ltd
Regent House, Station Approach,
Dorking RH4 1TG
email: roofing@lafarge-roofing.co.uk
www.lafarge-roofing.co.uk

tel: 0870 560 1000
fax: 0870 564 2742

Latham, James plc
Unit 3, Swallow Park, Finway Road,
Hemel Hempstead HP2 7QU
www.lathamtimber.co.uk

tel: 01442 849100
fax: 01442 267241

Luxcrete Ltd
Premier House, Disraeli Road, Park Royal,
London NW10 7BT   www.luxcrete.co.uk

tel: 020 8965 7292
fax: 020 8961 6337

Marley Eternit Ltd (Roofing)
Station Road, Coleshill, Birmingham B46 1HP
email: roofinginfo@marleyeternit.co.uk
www.marleyeternit.co.uk

tel: 01283 722588
fax: 01283 722219

Masonite Beams (UK) Ltd
Maple House, 5 Over Minnis, New Ash Green,
Longfield, DA3 8JA
email: beams@panelagency.com

tel: 01474 879158
fax: 01474 872426

McAlpine Slate, Alfred Ltd
Penrhyn Quarry, Bethesda, Bangor LL57 4YG
email: slate@alfred.mcalpine.com
www.amslate.com

tel: 01248 600656
fax: 01248 601171

Medite Europe Ltd
Maitland House, Warrior Square,
Southend-on-Sea SS1 2JY
email: www.medite-europe.com

tel: 01702 619044
fax: 01712 617162

Metra Non-Ferrous Metals Ltd
Pindar Road, Hoddesden EN11 0DE
email: enquiries@metra-metals.co.uk
www.metra-metals.co.uk

tel: 01992 460455
fax: 01992 451207

Midland Lead Manufacturers Ltd
Kiln Way, Woodville, Swadlincote DE11 8ED
email: sales@midlandlead.co.uk
www.midlandlead.co.uk

tel: 01283 224555
fax: 01283 550284

Milbank Floors Ltd
Earls Colne Business Park, Earls Colne,
Colchester, Essex   www.milbank-floors.co.uk

tel: 01787 223931
fax: 01787 220535

Monodraught Ltd
Halifax House, Cressex Business Park,
High Wycombe HP12 3SE
email: info@monodraught.com
www.monodraught.com

tel: 01494 897700
fax: 01494 532465

Naylor Lintels Ltd
Milner Way, Longlands Industrial Estate,
Ossett WF5 9JE   www.naylor.co.uk

tel: 01924 267286
fax: 01924 265672

NCS Colour Centre
71 Ancastle Green, Henley-on Thames RG9 1TS
email: info@ncscolour.co.uk www.ncscolour.co.uk

tel: 01491 411717
fax: 01491 411231

Norbord Ltd
Station Road, Cowie, Stirling FK7 7BQ
www.norbord.com

tel: 01786 812921
fax: 01786 817143

NorDan (UK) Ltd
Nordan House, Green Farm Business Park,
Falcon Close, Quedgeley GL2 4LY
email: windows@nordan.co.uk www.nordan.co.uk

tel: 01452 883131
fax: 01452 883739

Osram Ltd
Neills Road, Bold Industrial Estate,
St. Helens WA9 4XG   www.osram.co.uk

tel: 01744 812221
fax: 01744 831900

Philips Lighting Ltd
The Philips Centre, Guildford Business Park,
Guildford GU2 8XH   www.lighting.philips.com

tel: 01483 293070
fax: 01483 575534

Pilkington Building Products-UK
Prescot Road, St Helens WA10 3TT
www.pilkington.co.uk

tel: 01744 692000
fax: 01744 692880

Premdor
Gemini House, Hargreaves Road,
Groundwell Industrial Estate, Swindon SN25 5AJ
www.premdor.co.uk

tel: 0870 990 7998
fax: 01793 708280

Promat UK Ltd
The Stirling Centre, Eastern Road,   tel: 01344 381300
Bracknell RG12 2TD   www.promat.co.uk   fax: 01344 381301

Range Cylinders Ltd
Tadman Street, Wakefield WF1 5QU   tel: 01924 376026
email: marketing@range-cylinders.co.uk   fax: 01924 385015
www.range-cylinders.co.uk

Rigidal Systems Ltd
Unit 62, Blackpole Trading Estate West,   tel: 01905 750500
Worcester WR3 8ZJ   fax: 01905 750555
email: sales@rigidal.co.uk www.rigidal.co.uk

Ruberoid Building Products, IKO Group
Appley Lane North, Appley Bridge,   tel: 01257 255771
Wigan WN6 9AB   fax: 01257 252986
email: sales@ruberoid.co.uk
www.ruberoid.co.uk

Stowell Concrete Ltd
Arnolds Way, Yatton, Bristol BS49 4QN   tel: 01934 834000
www.stowellconcrete.co.uk   fax: 01934 835474

Saint-Gobain Pipelines MBU
Holwell Works, Asfordby Hill,   tel: 01664 814014
Melton Mowbray LE14 3RE   fax: 01664 812060
www.saint-gobain-pipelines.co.uk

Tarmac Ltd
Millfields Rd, Ettingshall,   tel: 01902 382511
Wolverhampton WV4 6JP   fax: 01902 491674
email: info@tarmac-group.co.uk
www.tarmac.co.uk

Titan Environmental Ltd
Seapatrick Road, Seapatrick, Bambridge,   tel: 028 4062 6260
County Down BT32 4PH   fax: 028 4062 6259
www.titanenv.com

Ubbink (UK) Ltd
Borough Road, Brackley NN13 7TB   tel: 0845 456 3499
email: info@ubbink.co.uk www.ubbink.co.uk   fax: 01280 705332

Velux Company Ltd
Woodside Way, Glenrothes, East Fife KY7 4ND   tel: 01592 772211
email: enquiries@velux.co.uk www.velux.co.uk   fax: 01592 771839

Vent-Axia Ltd
Fleming Way, Crawley RH10 2YX
email: info@vent-axia.com www.vent-axia.com

tel: 01293 526062
fax: 01293 551188

Zehnder Ltd
B15 Armstrong Mall, Southwood Business Park,
Farnborough GU14 0NR
email: sales@zehnder.co.uk www.zehnder.co.uk

tel: 01252 515151
fax: 01252 522528

Bibliography/Sources

Activities and Spaces: Dimensional Data for Housing Design Noble, J. (ed) 1983 The Architectural Press

AJ Handbook of Architectural Ironmongery Underwood, G. and Planck, J. 1977 The Architectural Press

Building Construction McKay, W. B. M. 2005 Donhead Publishing

Building for Energy Efficiency 1997 CIC

The Building Regulations Explained & Illustrated Powell-Smith, V. and Billington, M. J. 1999 Blackwell Science

Building Regulations   Approved Documents 2006 The Stationery Office

Buckingham Nurseries Hedging Catalogue

The Care and Repair of Thatched Roofs Brockett, P. 1986 SPAB

The Culture of Timber McCartney, K. 1994 University of Portsmouth

Dampness in Buildings Oxley, T. A. and Gobert, E. G. 1994 Butterworth-Heinemann

Designing for Accessibility 2004 Centre for Accessible Environments

Easibrief Haverstock, H. 1998 Miller Freeman

Fireplace Design and Construction Baden-Powell, C. 1984 Longman

Tarmac Flat Roofing – A Guide to Good Practice March, F. 1995 Tarmac Building Products Ltd

The Good Wood Guide Counsell, S. 1996 Friends of the Earth

Green Guide to the Architect's Job Book Halliday, S. 2001 RIBA Publishing

The Green Guide to Housing Specification Anderson, J., Howard, N. 2000 BRE Press

The Green Guide to Specification Anderson, J., Shiers, D., Sinclair, M. 2002 Blackwell

A Guide to Planning Appeals The Planning Inspectorate May 2005 planningportal.gov

Guide 'A' Design Data CIBSE Guide 2006 CIBSE

Hillier Designer's Guide to Landscape Plants 1999 Hillier Romsey

Home Security & Safety Good Housekeeping Guide 1995 Ebury Press

Illustrated Dictionary of Building Brett, P. 1997 Butterworth Heinemann

Listing Buildings – The work of English Heritage 1997 English Heritage

The Macmillan Encyclopaedia Isaacs, A. (ed) 1989 Macmillan

Managing Health and Safety in Construction, (Construction Design and Management) Regulations 2007 Health & Safety Executive

Materials for Architects and Builders Lyons, A. R. 2003 Butterworth Heinemann

Mathematical Models Cundy, H. M. and Rollett, A. P. 1997 Tarquin Publications

Metric Handbook Adler, D. 1999 Architectural Press

Party Wall etc. Act 1996: explanatory booklet 1997 Department of Communities & Local Government

The Penguin Dictionary of Building Maclean, J. H. and Scott, J. S. 1995 Penguin Books

Planning: A Guide for Householders Department of Communities & Local Government

Recognising Wood Rot & Insect Damage in Buildings Bravery, A. F. 2003 BRE

RIBA Product Selector 2006 RIBA Enterprises

The Right Hedge for You (leaflet) 1999 Department of Communities & Local Government

Stone in Building Ashurst, J. and Dimes, F. 1984 Stone Federation

Thatch: A Manual for Owners, Surveyors, Architects and Builders West, R. C. 1987 David & Charles

Tomorrow's World McLaren, D., Bullock, S. and Yousuf, N. 1998 Friends of the Earth

Water Conservation in Business DEFRA

Water Supply (Water Fittings) Regulations 1999 DEFRA

What Listing Means – A guide for Owners and Occupiers
English Heritage

The Which? Book of Plumbing and Central Heating
Holloway, D. 2000 Which? Books

Whitaker's Concise Almanack Ward Inna, (ed.) 1996 A & C
Black Publishers Ltd

WRAS Water Regulations Guide Water Regulations
Advisory Scheme (WRAS)

Index